SOCIAL PURPOSE ENTERPRISES

Case Studies for Social Change

Social Purpose Enterprises presents case studies of twelve organizations that operate in a growing niche within the Canadian social economy: market-based entities supported by a nonprofit organization and operated for the benefit of a workforce that lives on the margins of society.

Using a variety of research methods, the contributors examine the work of social purpose enterprises in a range of businesses including food services, child care, furniture, courier services, and microfinance. Combining the expertise of academics and practitioners, each chapter analyses the economic, social, and policy implications of the specific case.

Building on the findings published in *Researching the Social Economy* (2010) and *Businesses with a Difference* (2013), *Social Purpose Enterprises* provides a valuable resource for those involved in the growing push to encourage market-based solutions for those on the social margins.

JACK QUARTER is a professor and co-director of the Social Economy Centre at the Ontario Institute for Studies in Education, University of Toronto.

SHERIDA RYAN is a post-doctoral fellow, co-director of the Social Economy Centre, and faculty member with the Adult Education and Community Development Program at the Ontario Institute for Studies in Education, University of Toronto.

ANDREA CHAN is a doctoral candidate in the Adult Education and Community Development Program at the Ontario Institute for Studies in Education, University of Toronto.

Social Purpose Enterprises

Case Studies for Social Change

EDITED BY JACK QUARTER, SHERIDA RYAN,
AND ANDREA CHAN

UNIVERSITY OF TORONTO PRESS
Toronto Buffalo London

© University of Toronto Press 2014
Toronto Buffalo London
www.utppublishing.com
Printed in the U.S.A.

Reprinted 2016

ISBN: 978-1-4426-4584-4 (cloth)
ISBN: 978-1-4426-1404-8 (paper)

Printed on acid-free, 100% post-consumer recycled paper

Library and Archives Canada Cataloguing in Publication

Social purposes enterprises : case studies for social change/Jack Quarter,
Sherida Ryan, Andrea Chan.

Includes bibliographical references.
ISBN 978-1-4426-4584-4 (bound). – ISBN 978-1-4426-1404-8 (pbk.)

1. Nonprofit organizations – Canada – Case studies. 2. Social entrepreneurship –
Canada – Case studies. 3. Marginality, Social – Employment – Canada –
Case studies. 4. Economics – Canada – Sociological aspects – Case studies.
I. Quarter, Jack, 1941–, editor II. Ryan, Sherida, 1949–, editor III. Chan,
Andrea, 1979-, editor

HD2769.2.C3S633 2014   306.30971   C2014-905228-6

University of Toronto Press acknowledges the financial assistance to its
publishing program of the Canada Council for the Arts and the Ontario Arts
Council, an agency of the Government of Ontario.

Canada Council   Conseil des Arts
for the Arts   du Canada

ONTARIO ARTS COUNCIL
CONSEIL DES ARTS DE L'ONTARIO

an Ontario government agency
un organisme du gouvernement de l'Ontario

University of Toronto Press acknowledges the financial support of the
Government of Canada through the Canada Book Fund for its publishing
activities.

Contents

Preface

This book is based on a large ongoing research project, funded by the Social Sciences and Humanities Research Council of Canada (SSHRC), which studies the impact of social purpose enterprises on the people that they employ – people on the margins of the workforce either with various disabilities or with disadvantages related to recent immigration, race, or limited schooling. Two of the case studies focus on micro-lending programs for people on the social margins, and these might be classified as social businesses. The objective of the research is to understand how social purpose enterprises help to address the needs, both social and economic, of marginalized persons primarily in the Greater Toronto Area (GTA). The study centres on the GTA because it is a large urban complex with high levels of poverty, particularly among racialized minorities from recent immigrant communities.

The GTA had a population of 5.6 million in the 2006 census – about one-sixth of Canada's population – making it one of the largest urban enclaves in North America. The GTA's population is nearly 50 per cent foreign born and increasingly composed of visible minorities (Statistics Canada, 2007). Poverty in the GTA has been carefully documented in a series of reports by the United Way of Greater Toronto and its collaborators: Decade of Decline (2002), Poverty by Postal Code (2004), and Strong Neighbourhoods: A Call to Action (2005) – which was supplemented by the report, Three Cities within Toronto (Hulchanski, 2007) – and the TD Economics Special Report (2007). The reports highlight that the number of poverty neighbourhoods in the GTA has increased from thirty to 120; these neighbourhoods, which are highly concentrated in the inner suburbs, house about 43 percent of poor families. Moreover, two-thirds of the families living in higher-poverty neighbourhoods are recent immigrants (often visible minorities). The gap between rich and poor is growing wider, as shown by the reports. As well, the reports indicate that poverty is becoming racialized. While many forms of service agencies and government programs assist marginalized people in the GTA, another response has been the development of social purpose enterprises and microenterprises.

This book is unique because it compiles twelve case studies on the impact of social purpose enterprises. This research opens the door to a better understanding of these enterprises and the distinct challenges that they encounter.

We are indebted to Jennifer DiDomenico, acquisitions editor, business and economics, of the University of Toronto Press, who has guided us from the beginning of this initiative and who has been unfailing in her support of this work. In addition, we would like to thank Gretchen Albers for her sensitive and high-quality copyediting. We are also thankful to the Social Sciences and Humanities Research Council of Canada for funding the research on which the twelve case studies in this volume are based.

Jack Quarter, Sherida Ryan, Andrea Chan

SOCIAL PURPOSE ENTERPRISES

Case Studies for Social Change

1 Social Purpose Enterprises: A Conceptual Framework

JACK QUARTER, SHERIDA RYAN, AND ANDREA CHAN

The primary purpose of a business is to make money for its owners through selling a product or service to consumers. However, within the last decade, there is a growing trend: a new concept of business that not only attempts to earn revenue from sales but also serves a *social purpose*. This form of business goes by different labels: social business, social enterprise, and social purpose business. The label used in this book is *social purpose enterprise*. We use this label because it combines the salient features of the organizations that are the subject of this book. These organizations have businesslike features because they sell goods and services to consumers – but on a relatively small scale. For this reason, we prefer the term *enterprise* to *business*. Moreover, these organizations differ from conventional businesses in that they are not designed for owners to make a return on an investment. Therefore, we add *social purpose* to *enterprise* to emphasize that the organizations prioritize their social objectives. Earning money through the sale of services and goods is part of their raison d'être, but commerce is subsumed within their social purposes: the betterment of a marginalized social group, which most often is the employees. Betterment includes helping the employees to develop their skills, which in turn enhances their earning capacity and other facets of their being.

This research collection has three objectives: to determine whether social purpose enterprises fulfil their primary mission of helping their employees to function more fully and independently within society; to determine the impact of these enterprises on related stakeholders such as the broader community; and to analyse the challenges that these organizations face in attempting to accomplish their mission. In spite of the growing interest in social purpose enterprises, there is a shortage of research that addresses their impact, especially within Canada.

This chapter discusses the following: the existing research on social purpose enterprises and related organizational forms, meanings of the term "social purpose enterprise" and why it seems most appropriate for the organizations in this book, societal influences on the development of social purpose enterprises, and social purpose enterprises in relation to other business modifications such as corporate social responsibility, social businesses, and social enterprises that earn income for a non-profit organization. This chapter concludes with an outline of the remaining chapters in this book.

Existing Research

The existing impact research in this field uses both the organization and the individual as a unit of analysis. For example, a comprehensive study of social cooperatives in Italy (Carini, Costa, Carpita, & Andreaus, 2012) notes their importance in the delivery of social services, but raises questions about their efficiency, particularly those operating in the south of the country. It is not clear that efficiency is the best criterion for judging the social cooperatives, as most often their employees are people with disabilities and from other marginalized groups. A pan-European evaluation (Spear & Bidet, 2005) focuses more specifically on the effectiveness of social enterprises in combating social exclusion and argues that social enterprises have been helpful overall in achieving workforce integration for marginalized social groups, even though there is variation by country and room for improvement. A similar study about the potential of Korea's social enterprises raises questions about their effectiveness as a form of workforce integration (Kim, 2009). That study points out that the public perceives social enterprises as inefficient, and there is opposition from neighbours when social enterprises attempt to locate in their community. In a review of US research on the use of social enterprises for workforce integration (often referred to under the acronym WISE), Cooney & Williams Shanks (2010) found that there was often tension between the economic and social goals. Social enterprises funded by foundations were under pressure to show results, and, in an effort to do so, favoured more employable people over those who were less so, even though the latter might be more compatible with their mission.

Other studies focus on the individuals involved, which is the primary unit of analysis in this research. A feasibility study with homeless youth in Los Angeles (Ferguson, 2007; Ferguson & Xie, 2008) discovered that a group receiving seven months of vocational and small business training and service referrals experienced significant improvement in several social dimensions relative to a comparable control group with no such training and referrals. However, the study was an assessment of feasibility, not a study of an ongoing social purpose enterprise.

A comprehensive Hong Kong study of sixteen non-governmental organizations (NGOs) and fifty-one WISEs found that the organizations were very successful in workforce integration and in moving their clients from welfare into gainful employment (Ho & Chan, 2010). The study also claimed improvements in building social capital, but suggested that more effort was needed to assess variables such as self-esteem. Research in Sweden on childcare centres (Pestoff, 2000) indicated that the staff experienced an enriched environment with a high degree of decision-making latitude, a measure rarely used in research on social enterprises in spite of its importance to the workplace experience. A British study – of four different forms of social enterprise, broadly defined – focused on social exclusion and concluded that the impact, measured by participant observation, was multidimensional, with success on some forms and failure on others (Teasdale, 2010).

The aforementioned research focusing on the impact on individuals did not target groups with severe disabilities. A study in Singapore (Tan, 2009) looked at the workplace integration of twenty-five people with psychiatric disabilities who had undergone a twenty-month training program at a café. The study discovered a significant improvement on the Work Behaviour Inventory scale; individuals who completed the training program were more likely than those who did not to sustain competitive employment in a forty-four-week follow-up. Similarly, an Alberta study found that persons with psychiatric disabilities had fewer emergency department visits, less ambulatory care, and fewer hospital visits during the period that they were employed at a social enterprise than during pre-employment (Jackson, Kelland, Cosco, McNeil, & Reddon, 2009). The study design did not allow for the cumulative impact of time, but the results were nonetheless promising.

The Alberta study appears to be one of the few Canadian studies involving an empirical investigation on the impact of a social enterprise experience on the individuals involved and, more specifically, on individuals with severe disabilities. Another study looked at the economic impact of a microlending program (Langford, 2010a). There is only a small body of Canadian research on the economic benefits of social enterprises (Elson & Hall, 2010; Langford, 2010b), as well as studies that focus on the policy dimensions (Broad & Saunders, 2008; Curry, Donker, & Krehbiel, 2009; Restakis & Filip, 2008). The research that forms the chapters of this book seeks to fill this gap by providing a multicase study of the impact of social purpose enterprises, primarily on the individuals who work within them, but also on the community and other key stakeholders.

Conceptualizing Social Purpose Enterprises

It is difficult to establish one common denominator among all social purpose enterprises, but suffice it to say that such enterprises are different from conventional businesses. The *social purpose* of social purpose enterprises can vary, but usually includes objectives such as employing people with disabilities (e.g., psychiatric, intellectual, physical) or those on the margins of the workforce (e.g., chronically unemployed youth, recent immigrants, racial minorities with a history of workforce discrimination, homeless people). Some social purpose enterprises are for gainful employment, either full- or part-time; others are for training or workforce integration. Some function without external supports, but most often social enterprises have a parenting or founding organization that assists in various ways – for example, by providing space for the enterprise to operate, management assistance, workforce training, or fundraising.

There is a long tradition of social purpose enterprises. Some well-known and long-standing examples are Salvation Army thrift stores, Goodwill Industries, and even Girl Guide cookie sales. They are businesses designed to make money, but for a social purpose rather than to generate a return for investors. Cooperatives could be viewed as a long-standing form of social purpose business; the first one – the Rochdale Society of Equitable Pioneers – was formed in 1844 in Rochdale, England. The definition of a cooperative by the International Cooperative Alliance (ICA), headquartered in Geneva, Switzerland, stresses that this form of organization is not simply a business, but a business with a social purpose: "A cooperative is an autonomous association of persons united voluntarily to meet their common economic, social, and cultural needs and aspirations through a jointly-owned and democratically-controlled enterprise" (International Cooperative Alliance, 2012).

Cooperatives, with the exception of some social cooperatives, may be viewed as at least one step removed from the social purpose enterprises discussed in this book. Cooperatives, in general, compete effectively in the market with conventional businesses. They are neither subsidized by a parenting organization nor sheltered from the mainstream market through special purchasing arrangements. Non-financial cooperatives in Canada, for example, had sales in 2007 of $30.7 billion (Co-operatives Secretariat, 2011). These organizations vary in scale and in services, but in general they are self-sufficient businesses with a social purpose.

By comparison, the social purpose enterprises discussed in this book are not self-sufficient. They differ from each other, as the case studies that follow show, but in addition to having a social purpose, all of them have extraordinary supports such as those provided by a parenting organization. In addition, consumers may prefer to purchase their services, not necessarily because they offer the best available price or quality, but because they support what the organization stands for. In that regard, social purpose enterprises resemble thrift shops more than cooperatives. Although a thrift shop is a business, it sells donated goods using volunteer labour. It earns money for the parent organization, but only because its cost structure differs from a conventional business. If thrift stores had to purchase their goods at market prices and pay market-based costs for labour, it is unlikely that they would meet their social objectives of making money for the parent organization. The same would be true of the cookie drive of the Girl Guides or the ReStore of Habitat for Humanity.

Table 1.1 situates social purpose enterprises within the spectrum of market-based approaches in general. The figure uses two dimensions: conventional purposes/social purposes and conventional functioning/ supported functioning. The purpose dimension refers to whether the business is intended for conventional purposes such as making money for its owners or enhancing the value of their investment, or for social purposes such as employing people with disabilities or developing a community on the social margins. The functioning dimension refers to whether the organization operates in the market without unusual supports or relies on an extraordinary set of supports. All businesses have some support such as physical infrastructure and a legal framework that is generally the responsibility of government. They may also engage in services through government contracts. Supports of this sort are taken for granted. The supports available to the organizations featured in this book include not only those available to businesses generally,

Table 1.1 Conventional and Social Functioning of Businesses

	Conventional Purpose	Social Purpose
Conventional Functioning	Conventional businesses operating in the market	Farm-marketing cooperatives, credit unions
Supported Functioning	Conventional businesses eligible for aid, e.g., through Atlantic Canada Opportunities Agency	Social purpose enterprises such as the case studies in this book, which have extraordinary supports

but others that, as noted, are extraordinary. For that reason, social purpose enterprises may also be labelled as supported social enterprises. Without the supports, they could not function effectively. There are extraordinary supports available to conventional businesses: for example, small businesses in locations defined by the government as underdeveloped qualify for special financing and technical assistance through programs such as the Atlantic Canada Opportunities Agency. In degree, though, such supports are relatively less important than the support available to social purpose enterprises.

Influences on the Development of Social Purpose Enterprises

By the late 1980s and early 1990s, there emerged a number of public policies aimed at integrating people on the social margins into the mainstream workforce. These policies varied, and included incentives, such as supported employment strategies or wage supplements, for conventional corporations to hire persons on the social margins. These policies were part of a broader humanistic movement that involved strategies for integrating marginalized people into the wider society. In education, the strategy for integrating persons with special needs was referred to as mainstreaming (Schiller, O'Reilly, & Fiore, 2007); in the mental health area, "deinstitutionalization" was the label for the replacement of care in psychiatric hospitals with community settings (Stroman, 2003). Large segregated low-income public housing projects were replaced by smaller social housing developments that were integrated within mixed-income communities (Quarter, Mook, & Armstrong, 2009). These are only a few examples. The intent was to integrate groups on the social margins rather than to segregate them. The replacement of sheltered workshops (segregated settings that employ people with disabilities for subminimum wages) by social purpose enterprises was in part a response to this broader movement.

Another important influence for social purpose enterprises was the neoliberal push for less government intervention and support, and the concurrent emphasis on individualism, self-sufficiency, and entrepreneurship (Thorsen & Lie, 2006). Internationally, the attack on the welfare state was led by Margaret Thatcher in the United Kingdom and Ronald Reagan in the United States. However, the movement was pervasive, affecting government policies in varying degree throughout the world. Governments around the world were pressured to move from deficit spending to balancing their budgets, even if doing so involved sharp reductions in social spending. User fees were introduced or increased for costs associated with universal programs such as health care, and tuition fees for higher education skyrocketed – the rationale being that service users should absorb more of the costs. These changes hurt people on the social margins, who relied most heavily on social spending. In Canada, welfare or social assistance did not keep pace with the cost of living, and expenditures on social programs such as social housing were greatly reduced (Hulchanski, 2005, 2006). Within this context, both individuals and non-profit organizations relying upon government programs have had to turn to the market to earn a greater portion of their revenue.

For organizations and individuals alike, the label "entrepreneur" has taken on a special, almost sacred, meaning, in reference to those attempting to make their own way in the market, if not always by choice. To support entrepreneurs and entrepreneurship, a number of government programs and community and financial industry initiatives have emerged. One such initiative is "microlending," with the participants labelled as "microentrepreneurs."

Social enterprise has varied meanings, but in general refers to an effort to create a business that balances its economic, social, and environmental priorities – what is sometimes called the triple bottom line (Conway, 2001; Roberts & Cohen, 2002). Social enterprises range from businesses that attempt to rise above the usual corporate goals of enhancing investor value and increasing the rate of return to enterprises that are either incorporated as non-profits or are embedded within non-profit parenting organizations. Social enterprise describes not only a form of organization but also a set of practices that transcends all forms of organization, in both the private and public sectors (Whitman, 2010).

Balancing the Social and Economic: Themes and Variations

In this section, we look at four models that aim to strike a balance between economic, social, and environmental priorities:

- business corporations that engage in corporate social responsibility;
- social businesses;
- social enterprises that earn income for a non-profit organization;
- social purpose enterprises that rely on a non-profit organization for ongoing support.

Corporate Social Responsibility

In response to public pressure, some private sector businesses (often referred to as investor-owned businesses) have embraced the philosophy of corporate social responsibility (Carroll, 1991, 1999; Drucker, 1984). CSR, as it is often called, has been interpreted in many different ways throughout its long history; overall, however, it is an effort to make corporate practices adhere to some standard of social responsibility. Although companies have different rationales for incorporating CSR into their culture and activities (Berger, Cunningham, & Drumwright, 2007), the philosophy underlying CSR is that businesses are not simply autonomous entities but are deeply entwined with the broader society. The theoretical roots of this work can be found in Polanyi's (1957) concept of the economy as an "instituted process," in Granovetter's (1985) subsequent elaboration on "embeddedness," and in the more recent concept of "social capital" (Putnam, 1993, 2000). All of these theoreticians make the argument that the economy is not an end unto itself; rather, it is part of the wider society.

There are many different manifestations of CSR, both in faculties of management where it is taught and in business where it is practised. These include corporate social performance (Asmundson & Foerster, 2001; Roman, Hayibor, & Agle, 1999); virtue theory and other theories of business ethics (Arjoon, 2000; Martin, 2002); multiple bottom-line management (Conway, 2001; Fiksel, McDaniel, & Mendenhall, 1999; Roberts & Cohen, 2002; Waddock, 2000); and stakeholder theory (Clarkson, 1995). Although these lines of inquiry are distinct, they all attempt to broaden the framework for evaluating corporate performance, to embed performance within an explicit value framework, and to create methods of accounting for corporate social performance that not only consider the financial or economic bottom line but also the social and environmental bottom line.

A derivative of CSR is the effort to create new methods of accounting, often referred to as social accounting or social and environmental accounting (Mathews, 1997; Mook, Quarter, & Richmond, 2007). Another derivative is the encouragement of socially responsible investment, which usually refers to the inclusion of social and environmental criteria in the assessment of investment impacts (Carmichael, 2005; Hebb, 2001; Quarter, Carmichael, & Ryan, 2008). Large mutual funds have emerged that urge investors to channel their money into corporations designated "best in class" for their higher standards in order to induce other corporations to improve their behaviours. As well, agencies that monitor corporate behaviour (Jantzi, Innovest) now produce reports that can influence investors who value social criteria.

CSR and its related practices have many proponents, but their true impact on corporate practice is less evident. There are some examples of the successful impact of negative sanctions on investment – for instance, the boycott of investment in South Africa under apartheid, though that also involved a concerted effort by governments around the world. There are also examples of firms that are very enthusiastic about their social practices and have converted them into a social marketing strategy, such as Ben & Jerry's and The Body Shop. However, the overall impact of CSR does not appear to be compelling; some might even question whether the difference is even noticeable.

Social Business

There is a subset of business corporations that – through their organizational arrangements and practices – forgo prerogatives normally associated with businesses, such as investor value and maximizing rate of return. Muhammad Yunus (2007), the founder of the Grameen Bank, calls such firms "social businesses." Yunus's conception goes much further than corporate social responsibility, which he readily dismisses, and involves a "self-sustaining company that sells goods and services and that repays its owners for the money they reinvest, but whose primary purpose is to serve society and improve the lot of the poor" (2007, p. 82). Yunus cites the Grameen Bank and the "Grameen family of 25 companies" that were founded to serve the poor (primarily in Bangladesh) as examples of social businesses. He also includes the many microenterprises that Grameen has financed and assisted because these aim to alleviate poverty – an important social goal. However, his primary reference point is the partnership between Grameen and the French multinational corporation Danone, referred to as Grameen Danone, which brings enriched yogurt to poor Bangladeshi villages, at cost. The idea underpinning a social business is that the investment is for social benefit, and the expectation is that the investors will receive return of investment – but they will not receive dividends and capital appreciation, as they might in a capitalist investment.

There is a long history of social businesses that predates Yunus and involves efforts by business owners, often acting in isolation, to innovate and find a better way than the usual corporate practices (Quarter, 2000). For example, some owners have taken their investment and placed it into an indivisible trust that is owned by no one. An early example of this is the huge optical firm, Carl Zeiss AG. Its shares in their entirety are held in the Carl Zeiss Stiftung, a benevolent trust that Carl Zeiss's partner, Ernest Abbe, established in 1889 for the benefit of the employees after purchasing all of the company's shares, which were worth millions of Deutschmarks (Oakeshott & Schmid, 1990). Another example is the John Lewis Partnership (2007), one of the largest retailers in the United Kingdom. Also owned by a trust, it was set up initially in 1929 (and finalized in 1950) by the founder's son, Spedan Lewis, who believed that he was creating "perhaps the only alternative to communism," as he stated on the cover of his 1954 book, *Fairer Shares*.

Ernest Bader, the founder of the British firm Scott Bader, which manufactures and supplies composites and specialty polymer worldwide, pushed the model further. He created a movement of businesses without shares, named the Industrial Common Ownership Movement (ICOM) (Blum, 1968; Hoe, 1978; Quarter, 2000). Bader, a Quaker, was part of a small group of Christian Socialist business owners who met in Northampton in the 1950s to discuss how they could create an alternative to the capitalist model. Like Lewis, Bader gave the company's shares to a trust, in this case a charitable trust limited by guarantee called the Scott Bader Commonwealth. The movement that Bader founded, ICOM, merged with Co-operatives UK in 2001, and its members today are mostly small worker cooperatives.

Newman's Own (2012), a business started in 1982 by actor Paul Newman and his friend A.E. Hotchner, takes a different approach. The business donates all of the firm's after-tax profits – an impressive $330 million over the last thirty years – to education and charitable causes in the United States and internationally, thus forgoing one of the primary prerogatives of capitalist ownership: the right to profit. Newman and Hotchner's memoir of their work is aptly titled *Shameless Exploitation in Pursuit of the Common Good*. Following Newman's death in 2008, the Newman's Own Foundation was created to signal the company's continued commitment to its founders' mission.

In addition to these cases, there are new classes of businesses emerging that have the characteristics of social businesses, but are labelled differently. These include benefit corporations, which are organizations that must meet social and environmental standards determined by their state legislations (Benefit Corp., 2012). This concept is being used in Canada as well.

These examples differ, but they relinquish some of the rights normally associated with businesses: a strong rate of return for investors and capital accumulation that is the property of the owners. They are businesses, but with an important difference.

Social Enterprises That Earn Income for a Non-profit Organization

In response to political pressures for more earned revenue, non-profit organizations have established income-earning businesses that support the organizations' social objectives. Some well-known examples have been given above: the ReStore chains that generate income to support the house-building services of Habitat for Humanity and the thrift shops pioneered by the Salvation Army that are now widespread among charitable organizations. These models differ from those of typical businesses in that their goods are donated and their workforce is predominantly made up of volunteers or unpaid labour.

There are, however, businesses established by non-profit organizations that pay their workers, purchase supplies and products, and generate income for the sponsoring non-profit organization. One example is Travel Cuts (Voyages Campus in French), a business that was set up to help students obtain travel discounts; until 2009 it was owned by nonprofit organizations: the Canadian Federation of Students and the Canadian Student Horizons Group. Another example is the University of Toronto Press (UTP), Canada's largest university press. As a not-for-profit corporation, UTP operates a group of divisions as businesses, such as the University of Toronto Bookstore, that help to subsidize its scholarly books (Quarter et al., 2009).

Businesses owned by Aboriginal communities are akin to the revenue-generating businesses established by non-profits. In brief, these are businesses owned by band councils, tribal councils, or development corporations that are intended to generate profits and assist the community with its services and other development (Anderson, 2002). Many of these businesses received their start-up funds from land claim settlements in Aboriginal communities. They represent a form of entrepreneurship on the part of peoples attempting to overcome historic forms of oppression; hence, they are similar to a social enterprise that generates revenue for a non-profit.

In the United States, the use of businesses to subsidize a non-profit's services has been pushed forward by a new corporate form: the low-profit limited liability company, or L3C (Minnigh, 2009). The L3C, similar to the community interest company in the United Kingdom, is used primarily by grant-giving foundations as a means of increasing their revenue. It is expected that the corporation created to generate revenue will be compatible with the foundation's social objectives and therefore called "program related." Nine US states and two Indian nations have legislation enabling the creation of L3Cs, and an effort is being made to introduce federal legislation (Americans for Community Development, 2011). About six hundred L3Cs have incorporated (Mook, Whitman, Quarter, & Armstrong, forthcoming).

Social Purpose Enterprises Relying on a Non-profit Organization for Ongoing Support

Social purpose enterprises, as noted, are an offshoot of the broader category of social enterprises. In Canada, where the term is not defined by legislation, the diversity of organizations that either are labelled or self-identify as social enterprises makes the field difficult to research (Dart, Clow, & Armstrong, 2010). We have labelled the organizations that rely on a non-profit organization for ongoing support as "social purpose enterprises" in order to differentiate them. As noted, these organizations market services – but they do so for social purposes, such as developing their employees and the surrounding communities. They have some features of a business, but they are unique because their social purpose is primary and they require ongoing support from a non-profit parenting organization. Some are training organizations. Others are employers, offering various arrangements that include full-time, part-time, and transitional positions. Social enterprises require ongoing support because their workforce usually consists of people on the social margins who have extraordinary needs. This might include people with psychiatric disabilities or intellectual disabilities, homeless youth and women, youth with limited formal schooling and training, recent immigrants who have yet to find employment, and urban Aboriginal peoples.

Other forms of social purpose enterprises offer relatively permanent employment for groups at risk. The jobs may be part-time. This is often the case with the organizations that employ people with psychiatric disabilities – for example, those organizations associated with the Ontario Council of Alternative Businesses (Trainor & Tremblay, 1992). These include the Raging Spoon, a café and catering business; Abel Enterprises, which engages in woodworking and cabinetmaking; and Crazy Cooks, a catering business. The participants, many of whom call themselves *consumer-survivors* (a commentary on having survived the treatments of the psychiatric system), may have limits on how much they can work, partly because of chronic health conditions and partly for administrative reasons, since their disability pension might be reduced in relation to their earnings. The pension also carries a subsidy for medications that are often very expensive and would otherwise be unaffordable. Therefore, this type of social purpose enterprise differs from those designed to train people because these participants are more likely to be part-time. Social purpose enterprises meant to generate employment also target other groups experiencing special challenges in the workforce: for example, persons with developmental disabilities such as Down's syndrome.

In Italy and other parts of western Europe, persons with disabilities participate in an organizational form known as the "social cooperative" (Borzaga, Depedri, & Tortia, 2010; Defourny, 2001). The social cooperative is a non-profit organization that is similar to what we refer to as a social purpose enterprise. There are different types of social cooperatives. The type B social cooperative is assisted by the state on the condition that at least 30 per cent of their employees are otherwise unemployed or unemployable people who benefit from national insurance contribution exemptions. The intent of cooperatives is to help their members integrate into the labour force (Gonzales, 2010). They rely on volunteers, who are often family of the members, and they have different membership classes such as consumers of the service, volunteers, community leaders, and employees. This model, or variations of it, has spread to Sweden, the United Kingdom, Belgium, France, Poland, and to a lesser extent to Canada.

The social cooperative in Europe is referred to as a form of social enterprise by the EMES European Research Network. Its definition is: "Social enterprises are not-for-profit private organizations providing goods or services directly related to their explicit aim to benefit the community. They rely on a collective dynamics involving various types of stakeholders in their governing bodies, they place a high value on their autonomy and they bear economic risks linked to their activity" (Defourny & Nyssens, 2008, p. 5).

Many aspects of this definition apply to the concept of social purpose enterprises put forward in this chapter. The organizations typically operate as non-profits, but they do not always incorporate independently. They instead may be a unit of a parenting organization. The EMES definition emphasizes the benefit to the community. Social purpose enterprises seek to benefit their communities in different ways, but often they stress the development of the individuals they employ or train. The EMES definition mentions multiple stakeholders; social purpose enterprises have multiple stakeholders mainly because they typically have a parenting organization that gives ongoing support and their employees often receive benefits from government programs. The EMES refers to "economic risks." For social purpose enterprises, these risks are borne mainly by the parenting organization and any external funders such as government programs, the United Way, and other foundations.

The Canadian organization, Enterprising Nonprofits, defines social enterprise in a way that captures many of the elements of social purpose enterprises: "Social enterprises are businesses operated by non-profits with the dual purpose of generating income by selling a product or service in the marketplace and creating a social, environmental or cultural value" (Enterprising Non-profits, 2012). The ENP definition indicates that social enterprises are dependent on a parenting organization and emphasizes the multiple benefits of these organizations. Like the EMES definition, however, it makes no mention of the participants in these organizations. In addition, referring to them as "businesses" projects an image that may not accurately reflect the many supports that social purpose enterprises require.

Our definition builds on these, but focuses on the participants within these organizations because social purpose enterprises are typically set up for marginalized social groups who most often have not successfully been employed with conventional businesses:

A social purpose enterprise – a subgroup of the classification social enterprise – is a market-based entity founded and supported by a non-profit organization for the purposes of the economic and social benefit of persons on the social margins who are employed in or trained through the enterprise. A social purpose enterprise generates revenue from the sale of services, and most often it and the supporting organization benefit from the contributions of government programs, individual donors, volunteers, foundations, and supportive clientele. A social purpose enterprise is intended to yield a return to society from this investment because its employees are being prepared to function more fully and independently.

Book Outline and Objectives

The Case Studies

The twelve case studies are distinct and were selected with the following intentions:

(a) With the exception of one in southeastern Ontario, all the organizations worked either in total or in part in the Greater Toronto Area, but with different groups: persons with developmental and intellectual disabilities, persons with psychiatric disabilities, homeless women, recent immigrants, social housing residents, and participants in microcredit programs, including one targeted to Aboriginal entrepreneurs.

b) An effort was made to include enterprises that provided various services or products – from restaurants and catering enterprises to those offering housing, childcare, and even pottery.

c) The cases were social purpose enterprises, including two microcredit programs for marginalized groups.

d) A variety of different participation circumstances were included: training organizations and organizations whose targeted participants could become either full-time or part-time employees.

e) The organizations that were the subject of the case study ranged in age from recently established to thirty years in operation.

The twelve case studies are divided into four sections, according to what populations the social purpose enterprises targeted: groups marginalized by stigma; women on the social margins; urban poor and immigrants; and youth. These groups partially overlap. People in all of the categories may experience stigma: some of the women experienced social and economic exclusion because of their race, health, and citizenship status; some of the immigrants as well as the youth lacked work experience that could bridge into more permanent employment.

The collection is multidisciplinary, and the cases are examined through different theoretical frameworks that employ a variety of methods. When we were planning the research that led to this collection, we considered whether to have each team use a uniform methodology or to allow for diversity. A major consideration in making this decision was that context is a primary determinant of method, and the context differed for each of the case studies. Our community partners differed in terms of industry (food, childcare, furniture, courier services, et cetera); in terms of population focus (developmentally disabled, new immigrants, First Nations, et cetera); and in terms of longevity of the organization. Ultimately, we chose methodological diversity because the cases raised different issues, and we felt that a uniform methodology would limit not only what we could learn but also what would be relevant to our community partners.

Another consideration was that this research was funded by a SSHRC community/university research grant, and the expectation is that the community partner organizations will have an important voice in the research, including in the choice of methods. The partners were different organizations with different needs; inevitably, they made different choices.

In brief, the research methods used in the cases that follow were predominantly qualitative and relied heavily on interviews with key participants. This was the preferred methodology, in part because it worked best with the people employed by the social purpose enterprises that were studied – who were often people with disabilities and otherwise on the social margins. It allowed for the necessary rapport building between researchers and research participants. One of the case studies, Miziwe Biik (Chapter 4), which centred on a microloan program for Aboriginal entrepreneurs, used the Medicine Wheel as a mechanism for interpreting the data. Groupe Convex (Chapter 5), which involved a social return on investment, used qualitative methods and document analysis. Two other case studies – Academy of Computer & Employment Skills (Chapter 8) and The Learning Enrichment Foundation (Chapter 9) – used quantitative methods. Notably, both of these cases involved the study of relatively less vulnerable participants who could respond with greater facility to a survey.

Although the decision to choose methodological variety rather than uniformity inevitably affects the generalizability of the results, this collection represents a rich and nuanced view of social purpose enterprises. The book ends with a concluding chapter that synthesizes the findings of the case studies and suggests directions for future research.

REFERENCES

Americans for Community Development. (2011). Laws. Retrieved from http://
www.americansforcommunitydevelopment.org/legislation.html
Anderson, R.B. (2002). *Aboriginal entrepreneurship and business development.*
Toronto, ON: Captus Press.
Arjoon, S. (2000). Virtue theory as a dynamic theory of business. *Journal of
Business Ethics, 28*(2), 159–178. http://dx.doi.org/10.1023/A:1006339112331
Asmundson, P., & Foerster, S. (2001). Socially responsible investing: Better for
your soul or your bottom line. *Canadian Investment Review, 4*(4), 1–12.
Corp, B. (2012). *What is a benefit corp?* Retrieved from http://benefitcorp.net/
Berger, I.E., Cunningham, P., & Drumwright, M.E. (2007). Mainstreaming
corporate social responsibility: Developing markets for virtue. *California
Management Review, 49*(4), 132–157. http://dx.doi.org/10.2307/41166409
Blum, F. (1968). *Work and community: The Scott Bader Commonwealth and the
search for a new social order.* London, United Kingdom: Routledge and Kegan
Paul.
Borzaga, C. Depedri, S., & Tortia, E. (2010). *The growth of organizational variety
in market economies: The case of social enterprises* (Euricse Working Papers
N.003). Italy: Fondazione Euricse.
Broad, G., & Saunders, M. (2008). *Social enterprises and the Ontario Disability
Support Program: Policy perspective on employing persons with disabilities.*
Retrieved from http://usaskstudies.coop/socialeconomy/files/LLL_
Final_Reports/Report_CL5_02_NO.pdf
Carini, C., Costa, E., Carpita, M., & Andreaus, M. (2012). *The Italian social co-
operatives in 2008: A portrait using descriptive and principal component analysis*
(Euricse Working Paper, N.035 | 12). Italy: Fondazione Euricse.
Carmichael, I. (2005). *Pension power.* Toronto, ON: University of Toronto Press.
Carroll, A.B. (1991). The pyramid of corporate social responsibility: Toward
the moral management of organizational stakeholders. *Business Horizons,
34*(4), 39–48. http://dx.doi.org/10.1016/0007-6813(91)90005-G
Carroll, A.B. (1999). Corporate social responsibility. *Business & Society, 38*(3),
268–295. http://dx.doi.org/10.1177/000765039903800303
Clarkson, M. (1995). A stakeholder framework for analyzing and evaluating
corporate social performance. *Academy of Management Review, 20*(1), 92–117.
Conway, P. (2001). *How the triple bottom line can firm up the development and
measurement for reporting on desired outcomes.* Paper presented at the Public
Sector Performance, Wellington, New Zealand.
Cooney, K., & Williams Shanks, T.R. (2010). New approaches to old problems:
Market-based strategies for poverty alleviation. *Social Service Review, 84*(1),
29–55. http://dx.doi.org/10.1086/652680

Co-operatives Secretariat (2011). *Co-operatives in Canada (2007)*. Retrieved from https://www.ic.gc.ca/eic/site/693.nsf/vwapj/coops_in_canada_2007. pdf/$file/coops_in_canada_2007.pdf

Curry, J., Donker, H., & Krehbiel, R. (2009). Development corporations in Aboriginal communities: The Canadian experience. *Journal of Developmental Entrepreneurship, 14*(1), 1–19. http://dx.doi.org/10.1142/S1084946709001119

Dart, R., Clow, E., & Armstrong, A. (2010). Meaningful difficulties in the mapping of social enterprises. *Social Enterprise Journal, 6*(3), 186–193. http://dx.doi.org/10.1108/17508611011088797

Defourny, J. (2001). Introduction: From third sector to social enterprise. In C. Borzaga & J. Defourny (Eds.), *The emergence of social enterprise* (pp. 1–28). London, United Kingdom: Routledge.

Defourny, J., & Nyssens, M. 2008. Social enterprise in Europe: Recent trends and developments. *Social Enterprise Journal, 4*(3). Retrieved from http://ec.europa.eu/internal_market/social_business/docs/conference/defourny_en.pdf

Drucker, P. (1984). The new meaning of corporate social responsibility. *California Management Review, 26*(2), 53–63. http://dx.doi.org/10.2307/41165066

Elson, P., & Hall, P. (2010). *Strength, size, scope: A survey of social enterprises in Alberta and British Columbia.* Retrieved from http://www.enterprisingnon-profits.ca/sites/www.enterprisingnonprofits.ca/files/uploads/TA_C16_-_AB-BC_Social_Enterprises__Final__1__0.pdf

Enterprising Non-profits (2012). *What is a social enterprise?* Retrieved from http://www.enterprisingnonprofits.ca/

Ferguson, K.M. (2007). Implementing a social enterprise intervention with homeless, street-living youths in Los Angeles. *Social Work, 52*(2), 103–112. http://dx.doi.org/10.1093/sw/52.2.103

Ferguson, K.M., & Xie, B. (2008). Feasibility study of the social enterprise intervention with homeless youth. *Research on Social Work Practice, 18*(1), 5–19. http://dx.doi.org/10.1177/1049731507303535

Fiksel, J., McDaniel, J., & Mendenhall, C. (1999). *Measuring progress towards sustainability: Principles, process and best practices.* Retrieved from http://www.eco-nomics.com/images/Sustainability%20Measurement%20GIN.pdf

Gonzales, V. (2010). Italian social cooperatives and the development of civic capacity: A case of cooperative renewal? *Affinities, 4*(1), 225–251.

Granovetter, M. (1985). Economic action and social structure: The problem of embeddedness. *American Journal of Sociology, 91*(3), 481–510. http://dx.doi.org/10.1086/228311

Hebb, T. (2001). The challenge of labor's capital strategy. In A. Fung, T. Hebb, & J. Rogers (Eds.), *Working capital: The power of labor's pensions* (pp. 1–12). Ithaca, NY: Cornell University Press.

Ho, A., & Chan, K. (2010). The social impact of work-integration social enterprise in Hong Kong. *International Social Work, 53*(1), 33–45. http://dx.doi .org/10.1177/0020872809348950

Hoe, S. (1978). *The man who gave his company away: A biography of Ernest Bader, founder of the Scott Bader Commonwealth.* London, United Kingdom: Heinemann.

Hulchanski, D. (2005). *Rethinking Canada's housing affordability challenge* (Discussion Paper). Centre for Urban and Community Studies, University of Toronto. Retrieved from http://www.urbancentre.utoronto.ca/pdfs/ elibrary/Hulchanski-Housing-Affd-pap.pdf

Hulchanski, D. (2006). What factors shape Canada's housing policy? The intergovernmental role in Canada's housing system. In R. Young & C. Luprecht (Eds.), *Canada: The state of the federation 2004* (pp. 221–251). Montreal, QC: Queen's-McGill University Press.

International Co-operative Alliance (2012). *Co-operative identity, values and principles.* Retrieved from http://ica.coop/en/whats-co-op/co-operative-identity-values-principles

Jackson, Y., Kelland, J., Cosco, T., McNeil, D., & Reddon, J. (2009). Nonvocational outcomes of vocational rehabilitation: Reduction in health services utilization. *Work, 33*(4), 381–387.

John Lewis Partnership (2007). John Lewis Partnership. Retrieved from http:// www.johnlewispartnership.co.uk/about/our-history.html

Kim, Y. (2009). Can social enterprise stand for persons with disabilities? The case of South Korean social enterprises, 2007–2008. *Journal of Asian Public Policy, 2*(3), 293–308. http://dx.doi.org/10.1080/17516230903204760

Langford, A. (2010a). *Evaluating the social impact of the OCLF/Alterna Community Micro Loan Program.* Retrieved from http://carleton.ca/3ci/ wp-content/uploads/3CI-Evaluation-of-the-OCLF-Micro-loans-program-September-30-2010.pdf

Langford, A. (2010b). *SPEN Toronto – Social purpose enterprise in the GTA: 2010 Survey: preliminary findings, comparisons and analysis.* Retrieved from http:// carleton.ca/3ci/wp-content/uploads/SPEN-Final-Report-2.pdf

Martin, R. (2002). The virtue matrix. *Harvard Business Review, 8*(3), 69–75.

Mathews, M.R. (1997). Twenty-five years of social and environmental accounting research: Is there a silver jubilee to celebrate? *Accounting, Auditing & Accountability Journal, 10*(4), 481–531. http://dx.doi.org/10.1108/ EUM0000000004417

Minnigh, E. C. (2009). Low-profit limited liability companies: An unlikely marriage of for-profit entities and private foundations. *Tax Management Estates, Gifts and Trusts Journal*, 1–9.

Mook, L., Whitman, J., Quarter, J., & Armstrong, A. (forthcoming). *United States social economy*. Toronto, ON: University of Toronto Press.

Newman's Own (2012). *Our story*. Retrieved from http://www.newmansown.com/our-stories/

Oakeshott, R., & Schmid, F. (1990). *The Carl Zeiss Stiftung: Its first hundred years of impersonal ownership*. London, United Kingdom: Job Ownership.

Pestoff, V. (2000). Enriching Swedish women's work environment: The case of social enterprises in day care. *Economic and Industrial Democracy*, 21(1), 39–70. http://dx.doi.org/10.1177/0143831X00211003

Polanyi, K. (1957). The economy as instituted process. In K. Polanyi, C. Arensberg, & H. Pearson (Eds.), *Trade and market in the early empire* (pp. 243–270). New York, NY: Free Press.

Putnam, R. (1993). *Making democracy work: Civic traditions in modern Italy*. Princeton, NJ: Princeton University Press.

Putnam, R. (2000). *Bowling alone: The collapse and revival of American community*. New York, NY: Simon and Schuster. http://dx.doi.org/10.1145/358916.361990

Quarter, J. (2000). *Beyond the bottom line: Socially innovative business owners*. Westport, CT: Greenwood/Quorum.

Quarter, J., Carmichael, I., & Ryan, S. (2008). Socially responsible investment of pensions: Issues and debates. In J. Quarter, I. Carmichael, & S. Ryan (Eds.), *Pensions at work: Socially responsible investment of union-based pension funds* (pp. 3–41). Toronto, ON: University of Toronto Press.

Quarter, J., Mook, L., & Armstrong, A. (2009). *Understanding the social economy: A Canadian perspective*. Toronto, ON: University of Toronto Press.

Restakis, J., & Filip, O. (2008). *Enabling policy for health and social co-ops in BC*. Retrieved from http://auspace.athabascau.ca:8080/dspace/bitstream/2149/1960/1/BALTA%20A2%20-%20Enabling%20Health%20Co-ops%20Report%20-%20Final.pdf

Roberts, B., & Cohen, M. (2002). Enhancing sustainable development by triple value adding to the core business of government. *Economic Development Quarterly*, 16(2), 127–137. http://dx.doi.org/10.1177/0891242402016002003

Roman, R., Hayibor, S., & Agle, B.R. (1999). The relationship between social and financial performance. *Business & Society*, 38(1), 109–125. http://dx.doi.org/10.1177/000765039903800105

Schiller, E., O'Reilly, F., & Fiore, T. (2007). *Marking the progress of IDEA implementation. Office of Special Education Programs*. Retrieved from http://nclid.unco.edu/Resources/IDEA_Progress.pdf

Spear, R., & Bidet, E. (2005). Social enterprise for work integration in 12 European countries: A descriptive analysis. *Annals of Public and Cooperative Economics, 76*(2), 195–231. http://dx.doi.org/10.1111/j.1370-4788.2005.00276.x

Statistics Canada. (2007). *Census of Population, 2006: Toronto (Code3520), Ontario, 2006 Community Profiles*, Catalogue no. 92–591-XWE [Table]. Retrieved from http://www12.statcan.ca/census-recensement/2006/dp-pd/prof/92-591/index.cfm?Lang=E

Stroman, D. (2003). *The disability rights movement: From deinstitutionalization to self-determination*. Lanham, MD: University Press of America.

Tan, B.L. (2009). Hybrid transitional-supported employment using social enterprise: A retrospective study. *Psychiatric Rehabilitation Journal, 33*(1), 53–55. http://dx.doi.org/10.2975/33.1.2009.53.55

Teasdale, S. (2010). How can social enterprise address disadvantage? Evidence from an inner city community. *Journal of Nonprofit & Public Sector Marketing, 22*(2), 89–107. http://dx.doi.org/10.1080/10495141003601278

Thorsen, D., & Lie, A. (2006). What is neoliberalism? Department of Political Science. Norway: University of Oslo. Retrieved from http://folk.uio.no/daget/What%20is%20Neo-Liberalism%20FINAL.pdf

Trainor, J., & Tremblay, J. (1992). Consumer-survivor businesses in Ontario challenging the rehabilitation model. *Canadian Journal of Community Mental Health, 11*(2), 65–72.

Waddock, S. (2000). The multiple bottom lines of corporate citizenship: Social investing, reputation, and responsibility audits. *Business and Society Review, 105*(3), 323–345. http://dx.doi.org/10.1111/0045-3609.00085

Whitman, J.R. (2010). *The social entrepreneurship model: Past, present, and future.* Unpublished manuscript.

Yunus, M. (2007). *Creating a world without poverty: Social businesses and the future of capitalism*. New York, NY: Public Affairs.

SECTION A

Marginalized by Stigma

This part of the book contains four case studies: Common Ground Co-operative (Chapter 2), A-Way Express Courier (Chapter 3), Miziwe Biik Aboriginal Employment and Training (Chapter 4), and Groupe Convex (Chapter 5).

Common Ground Co-operative is an umbrella organization for five business partnerships of people with developmental disabilities (a catering firm called Lemon & Allspice Cookery, three Coffee Shed outlets, and a cleaning firm).

A-Way Express Courier is an enterprise that employs seventy people with psychiatric disabilities, often part time as a supplement to their disability pensions.

Miziwe Biik Aboriginal Employment and Training has a small micro-credit program for Aboriginal peoples wanting to become self-employed.

Groupe Convex is the hub for numerous social purpose enterprises in southeastern Ontario (in the community of Prescott-Russell) that serve people with intellectual disabilities.

These organizations differ, but they all employ socially marginalized people. The participation of stigmatized groups in the economy represents a departure from more traditional arrangements such as the sheltered workshop. The heyday of sheltered workshops in Canada was during the 1970s and into the 1980s. By the late 1980s, the sheltered workshop was being replaced by alternative policies that sought to integrate people on the social margins into the mainstream workforce.

The same is true of social purpose enterprises for people with psychiatric disabilities, who were inspired by the consumer-survivor movement, and for Aboriginal peoples, who have struggled to integrate into the workforce. The four case studies in this section look at the impact of the social purpose enterprises on the participants: whether they have led to improvements in people's lives, and in what ways.

2 Common Ground Co-operative: Supporting Employment Options

FRANCES OWEN, ANNE READHEAD, COURTNEY BISHOP, JENNIFER HOPE, AND JEANNETTE CAMPBELL

With contributions from Gillian MacKinnon and Daniel Angrignon, Brock University

A hundred years ago, the lives of persons with developmental disabilities in Ontario were circumscribed by the fears and misunderstanding of their fellow citizens, who saw them as a threat rather than as neighbours. Definitions of intellectual and developmental disability and the roles of persons with these labels have changed over the intervening decades. The American Association on Intellectual and Developmental Disabilities (AAIDD) currently describes intellectual disability as "characterized by significant limitation both in intellectual functioning ... and in adaptive behaviour, which covers many everyday social and practical skills. This disability originates before the age of 18" (American Association on Intellectual and Developmental Disabilities, 2013). The broader category of developmental disability has been defined by Isaac, Dharma Raja, & Ravanan (2010) as "long-term impairment leading to social and economic disadvantages, denial of rights, and limited opportunities to play an equal part in the life of the community" (Isaac et al., 2010, p. 627). Research on employment has focused on both persons with intellectual and developmental disabilities; however, for the purpose of clarity, the term developmental disabilities will be used in this chapter.[1] Thanks to the persistence of advocates and self-advocates, and with increasing practical commitment to enacted human rights, the days of segregating persons with these labels are waning. Increasingly, citizens who have developmental disabilities, including intellectual disabilities, are contributing to the social and economic life of their communities in ways that would have been unimaginable a century ago.

This chapter discusses the development and contributions of Common Ground Co-operative and its five related social purpose enterprises (see Chapter 1 for a definition of this term), which are operated by business partners who have developmental disabilities. This innovative model of social entrepreneurship will be analysed within the larger historic context of barriers to employment. As well, we will examine its impact on its key stakeholders, especially the business partners themselves.

Human Rights and Employment

Among the many provisions in the United Nations Convention on the Rights of Persons with Disabilities (UNCRPD) (2007), Article 27 focuses specifically on the right to work and employment. It commits signatory nations to ensuring that the presence of identified disabilities will not prevent persons from obtaining employment freely in an inclusive and accessible environment that provides appropriate accommodation, including vocational guidance and training programs. Of particular relevance to this chapter is Article 27, Section 1f, which states that nations will "promote opportunities for self-employment, entrepreneurship, the development of cooperatives and starting one's own business" (UN General Assembly, 2007, p. 16). While this may seem like an obvious statement in the twenty-first century, in the broader context – namely, the long history of violating the human rights of persons with disabilities (Griffiths, Owen, & Watson, 2012; Owen & Griffiths, 2009) – these protections represent a revolutionary commitment to ensuring that rights that have long been taken for granted by the general population are also secured for persons with disabilities.

Persons identified as having developmental disabilities in Canada are among those whose rights are protected by the UNCRPD; nonetheless, they experience high rates of unemployment and unacceptably low income support. Lack of opportunities for employment hinders their ability to break free from poverty and fosters isolation and social exclusion. According to the Canadian Association for Community Living (2013), 75 per cent of Canadians with a developmental disability living outside of their families live in poverty. Statistics Canada reports that the lowest labour force participation rate for persons identified as having a disability is for those who have a developmental disability (32.7 per cent participation) (Statistics Canada, 2006). In addition to low employment rates, Crawford's (2011) analysis of the 2006 Participation and Activity Limitation Survey (PALS) shows that Canadians with developmental disabilities were less likely than persons with other types of identified disability to have completed formal education, and they were less likely to have had job-related training in the previous five years. As long as persons with developmental disabilities continue to be excluded from the labour market, negative stereotypes about their work abilities will persist (Grant, 2008), and they will continue to be stigmatized.

This stigma has deep historic roots. The contributions of persons with developmental disabilities have tended to be valued when labour is scarce, as it was in agrarian economies in Europe during the Middle Ages, or in the factories of the nineteenth-century industrial revolution. Internationally, while conditions have varied somewhat over the centuries, persons with developmental disabilities have been devalued, actively persecuted, and institutionally excluded (Owen, Griffiths, Tarulli, & Murphy, 2009). However, advocacy and self-advocacy movements in the twentieth century began to shift this focus through actively promoting the social inclusion of persons who had been disrespected for so long.

In Canada, during the 1940s and 1950s, parents spurred public action to address the need for community support services for persons with developmental disabilities. For example, the Parents' Council for Retarded Children was formed in Ontario in the late 1940s. By 1951, they had developed classes for the "trainable mentally retarded" and had gained access to some recreation programs for their children. Similar groups formed around the province and later coalesced as the Ontario Association for Retarded Children (Anglin & Braaten, 1978), which subsequently became the Ontario Association for Community Living. The movement then grew across the country. Today, the Canadian Association for Community Living (CACL) – a federation of four hundred local associations and thirteen provincial and territorial associations that counts 40,000 individual members – is affiliated with Inclusion International, which promotes human rights and community inclusion around the world (Canadian Association for Community Living, 2014.). Sheltered workshops were the start of organized community employment supports for persons with developmental disabilities; the movement now focuses on the achievement of true employment equality (Canadian Association for Community Living Position Statement on Employment, 2010).

The Nature of Employment

For adults, regardless of whether or not they have a disability, employment and community engagement are essential activities that contribute to their quality of life and are an expected part of life (Sandys, 1999). Research indicates that competitive employment environments for persons with developmental disabilities have a more positive impact than segregated work environments, leading to greater self-determination, job and general life satisfaction, autonomy, and also a higher income (Stancliffe, 2001). However, for many years, persons with developmental disabilities were viewed in the context of a deficit model that emphasized disability, and attempted to modify individuals' abilities in order to promote their adaptation to a "normal" standard. This focus did little to reduce the barriers to inclusion of persons with a disability (Galambos, 1999; Parkinson, 2006). As the movement towards social inclusion, deinstitutionalization, and awareness of human rights has increased, human services have moved away from advocating that adults with developmental disabilities work in segregated placement settings such as institutional jobs or sheltered workshops and instead have advocated community jobs and regular competitive employment (Baker, 2007; Canadian Association for Community Living Position Statement on Employment, 2010; Lemon & Lemon, 2003). However, in spite of this change in thinking, the majority of persons with developmental disabilities continue to be engaged within sheltered workshops and volunteer positions, or are offered non-challenging employment consisting of limited hours, token wages, and continued social abjection (Grant, 2008; Hall, 2004, 2005, 2010).

Many people with developmental disabilities rely on government income support. In Ontario, this is distributed monthly by the Ontario Disability Support Program (ODSP) and includes benefits coverage for persons with a formally diagnosed disability (Ontario Ministry of Community and Social Services, 2012). ODSP also offers an employment support program to assist people in obtaining a job or developing their skills. A portion of employment earnings over a specified level can be deducted from the person's ODSP income support (Ontario Ministry of Community and Social Services, 2013), even if the work is part-time. Many persons with developmental disabilities cannot secure full-time work, or the nature of their disability makes it difficult for them to maintain full-time hours – there are many barriers to entering the world of competitive work.

Barriers to Employment Equality and Emerging Alternatives

The obstacles faced by persons with developmental disabilities who seek work outside of sheltered settings tend to reflect social, educational, and pragmatic concerns. The results of Crawford's (2011) analysis of the 2006 PALS data indicate that barriers to employment for persons with developmental disabilities in Canada include lack of support for employment from family and friends; competing responsibilities such as family commitments; lack of adaptation of the job to meet their needs; concern about social isolation on the job; history of discrimination; inadequate training; inadequate accessible transportation; and lack of job availability. The PALS data illuminated the experiences of people who had been employed in the previous five years. Crawford hypothesized that those who had not been employed may have feared losing government income and disability supports. Crawford's analysis suggests that lack of social support and accommodation are among the key factors that limit opportunities for employment for persons with developmental disabilities. The broader social perception of workers who have developmental disabilities was examined by Burge, Ouellette-Kuntz, and Lysaght (2007), who emphasize that employment supervisors and co-workers need to be trained in order to become part of the necessary supports for workers who have disabilities. They also pointed out the need to ensure an appropriate match of skills, interests, and personal characteristics of the worker with the demands of the job.

Because of these impediments to competitive employment for persons with developmental disabilities, a variety of employment and activity options have emerged. While sheltered workshops are still available despite increasing pressure to move away from that model (Rogan & Rinne, 2011), an alternative is supported employment, which is "real work in an integrated setting with on-going support provided by a knowledgeable service provider with expertise in finding employment for people with developmental disabilities" (Community Living British Columbia, 2009, p. 18). Other options that, while not necessarily remunerated, can be productive and rewarding include volunteer activities (Trembath, Balandin, Stancliffe, & Togher, 2010) and involvement in the creative arts (Hall & Wilton, 2011). An emerging alternative besides inclusion in traditional competitive employment and these other options is supported entrepreneurship.

Entrepreneurship among persons with various forms of disability, including persons with developmental disabilities, is on the rise around the world (Van Niekerk, Lorenzo, & Mdlokolo, 2006; Swanson, n.d.; Canadian Association for Community Living and People First of Canada, 2012; Foundation for People with Learning Disabilities, n.d.; Lemon & Lemon, 2003; Sutherland & Beachy, 2004). Cooperatives also open the door to the employment market and offer those with developmental disabilities the opportunity "to live interdependently and to participate as partners in their own businesses" (Lemon & Lemon, 2003, p. 414). The remainder of this chapter will focus on one particularly innovative model of social entrepreneurship for persons with developmental disabilities.

Common Ground Co-operative: Inclusion and Belonging

An example of enacting the spirit as well as the letter of Article 27 of the UNCRPD is Common Ground Co-operative and the five associated social purpose enterprises it supports, which are structured as business partnerships for persons who have developmental disabilities. Common Ground Co-operative is a non-profit charity that employs administrative staff and job coaches who support the catering and wholesale bakery business, Lemon & Allspice Cookery, the three coffee shop locations known as Coffee Sheds, and the toy sanitization business, CleanABLE. Currently, Common Ground Co-operative supports approximately sixty business partners and apprentices, all of whom are eighteen years of age or older and are identified as having a developmental disability. The partners and trainees currently total forty-one women (thirty-seven partners and four Foundation students) and twenty-three men (twenty partners and three Foundation students) aged eighteen to sixty years who have diverse ethnic backgrounds. While it has an active membership, Common Ground Co-operative is dependent on grants, fundraising initiatives, and core funding from the Ministry of Community and Social Services. As described in Chapter 1, social purpose enterprises rely on supports, and that is the case for the five social purpose enterprises that depend on Common Ground Co-operative for job-skills training and the business supports that sustain them.

Common Ground Co-operative and Its Associated Social Purpose Enterprises

A Brief History

As founder Carolyn Lemon states, it all started with "a little cookie business" (Lemon, 2011, p. 1). Her daughter Cathy, along with some friends, began selling coffee and donuts at Community Living in Toronto. She and her friends were interested in starting their own business, so Cathy's parents, Jim and Carolyn Lemon, and five other families obtained an Individualized Quality of Life grant that gave the financial support necessary for Cathy, two colleagues, and a job coach to start a bakery – Lemon & Allspice Cookery – in July 1998.

Initially, Carolyn Lemon looked after most of the business operations. The business grew with donations of money, goods, and services, and the first three Lemon & Allspice business partners were also "beginning to thrive as they gained confidence and recognition" (Lemon, 2011, p. 7). By the time the Cookery celebrated its first anniversary in 1999, it was clear that the business needed to be supported and that the workers needed to play an active role as business partners. A cooperative, separate from Lemon & Allspice Cookery, was established. It could raise money and hire job coaches who would work with the Cookery on a contractual basis. Common Ground Co-operative was incorporated in 2000 and with the help of an adviser, the business partners developed a formal partnership agreement that defined how partners could join the business or be removed from it, and specified their rights as to matters such as decision making and vacation time (Lemon, 2011).

Common Ground Co-operative's first major grant came from the Ontario Employment Supports Program (part of the Ontario Disability Supports Program) in the fall of 2000. This allowed the organization in 2001 to hire a full-time coordinator, who took over many of the administrative responsibilities that had been handled by the founder in addition to providing organizational leadership for future development. The grant also allowed Common Ground Co-operative to pay for professional accounting services and to hire another job coach to help start a new retail coffee shop at Surrey Place Centre, an organization that serves persons with developmental disabilities and autism (Lemon, 2011). Six new partners joined the new Surrey Place Coffee Shed in 2001 (Common Ground Co-operative Inc., 2010). The second Coffee Shed was started with nine partners at New College, University of Toronto, in 2003 (Common Ground Co-operative Inc., 2010).

During this time, Common Ground Co-operative continued to apply for grants; however, the organization's financial foundation was tenuous. Charitable status was achieved in 2006 (Common Ground Co-operative Inc., 2010), allowing for more diversified fundraising. In the same year, Common Ground Co-operative was accepted for permanent core funding through the Ontario Ministry of Community and Social Services (Lemon, 2011).

With continued growth came the need to find systematic ways to recruit and train new partners. An apprenticeship program, now called the Foundation Program, was developed in 2003 (Lemon, 2011). The ten-month Foundation Program provides job training and apprenticeship opportunities for those who are interested in becoming partners in the businesses associated with Common Ground Co-operative, with the final four months being devoted to a co-op placement at one of the businesses. This culminates in the business partners voting on whether or not the trainee will be permitted to continue as a paid apprentice in that location for three months, if the trainee chooses to do so. Follow-ing a successful apprenticeship, the partners vote again to determine whether to offer the apprentice full partnership status (Common Ground Co-operative Inc., 2010). Partners can also vote colleagues out of the enterprises if their behaviour is considered to be inappropriate.

With the recruitment and training process in place, the organization was equipped to add new ventures. In 2004, the third Coffee Shed start-ed with five partners at Jewish Vocational Services. All three Coffee Shed businesses use the products produced by Lemon & Allspice Cookery (Common Ground Co-operative Inc., 2010). By 2005, funding was available to start a fourth Coffee Shed with five partners and a new job coach. However, this business was closed in 2006 following the loss of the job coach (Lemon, 2011).

In 2010, the opportunity arose for business diversification with the ini-tiation of CleanABLE, a toy sanitation service located at Surrey Place Centre. The partners in this business work in the evening without job coach support cleaning toys used in the agency's therapy programs, day-care, and waiting room (Common Ground Co-operative Inc., 2010). In addition to the Cookery, the three Coffee Sheds, and CleanABLE, various other business projects have been started by business partners. The part-ners at the Surrey Place location have a vermiculture composting busi-ness that reduces waste and produces compost that the partners sell for use in gardens or on indoor plants (Lemon, 2011). Partners at the New College Coffee Shed sold donated used books in the summer of 2007.

Since the inception of the Foundation Program, training for partners and prospective partners has grown to include a partnership with George Brown College, offering financial literacy education, and a part-nership with Frontier College, offering literacy education and other programs – nutrition and fitness, money and math skills, resume writ-ing, and workshops on topics such as self-awareness, public speaking, abuse awareness and prevention, and safe social networking. In addi-tion, the partners are encouraged and supported to design and develop programs geared towards specific interests, such as an art program initiated by a partner that is peer led (Common Ground Co-operative Inc., 2010).

Common Ground Co-operative's Vision and Mission

The "societal aim at CGC is to bring together talent and expertise found in existing institutions, agencies, businesses and other community groups to support the creation and maintenance of business enterprises for people with developmental disabilities. We view this model as an integral component of community economic development" (Common Ground Co-operative Inc., 2010). As an administrative support service for the five social purpose enterprises operated by the business partners, the cooperative is not itself a social purpose enterprise, and it does not make decisions for the business partners. Its core values and those of its associated enterprises are "co-operation, empowerment, entrepreneurship, inclusion, independence, initiative, integrity, respect and teamwork" (Common Ground Co-operative Inc. 2010).

Current Structure of Common Ground Co-operative

Common Ground Co-operative has a ten-member board of directors. One is elected to represent the business partners and two are family members of partners. The staff includes an executive director, a finance manager, a training coordinator, six full-time job coaches, and one part-time job coach, as well as volunteers and placement students. The location of job coaches is described in Table 2.1.

The board of directors has a number of standing committees, including the Joint Advisory Committee (JAC), which was established in 2007 to address administrative issues in the businesses like the partnership agreement. The JAC consists of two staff and two board of directors representatives, along with business partner representatives from each of the associated enterprises, who are elected by their fellow partners.

Remuneration of Business Partners

Each month, partners, as a group, are paid 33 per cent of the revenue from their businesses before the cost of goods is deducted. Most partners are recipients of the Ontario Disability Support Program, which

Table 2.1 Enterprises Associated with Common Ground Co-operative

Business	Partners	Job Coaches	Activities
Lemon & Allspice Cookery	17	3 full-time	Bakery and catering Farmer's market booth in summer
Coffee Shed: Surrey Place Centre	17	1 full-time	Coffee kiosk and off-site catering with delivery
Coffee Shed: JVS	12	1 full-time	Coffee kiosk and catering
Coffee Shed: New College, U of T	14	1 full-time	Coffee kiosk and off-site catering with delivery
CleanABLE: two locations, Surrey Place Centre	8	0	Toy sanitation

limits the amount that they can earn before deductions are made. Partners are allowed to earn a maximum of $200 per month over their support payment without encroaching on their ODSP (Ontario Ministry of Community and Social Services, 2013). Increases above that amount lead to ODSP deductions. While partner earnings vary considerably because of differences in the businesses' income and because of variation in hours worked (for reasons such as hours available at a work site and the partners' interests), in 2012 the average yearly earnings for partners in the Coffee Sheds and Lemon & Allspice Cookery was $757.

The associated businesses pay a 5 per cent fee to Common Ground Co-operative for administrative expenses, and the remaining revenue is used to pay the operating expenses of the businesses.

Research Methodology

The focus of the research was to assess the effectiveness of this innovative social entrepreneurship model as an employment option for persons with developmental disabilities and to understand the impact of the cooperative on the business partners. In 2011–12, the research team undertook interviews with thirteen partners,[2] five Common Ground Co-operative staff members, six Ministry of Community and Social Services staff and Common Ground Co-operative board of directors members, as well as a focus group consisting of seven Common Ground Co-operative staff members. Ministry and board interview data were analysed together because there was a small number of participants in each group, and we wanted to maintain participant anonymity. In addition, daily customers of the three Coffee Sheds were surveyed between 3 April and 30 April 2012, with sixty-nine responses received. Eleven Lemon & Allspice Cookery customers were surveyed about their perception of the services, with four responses received. Finally, eight Common Ground Co-operative staff members (four responses) and nine family members of business partners (three responses) were surveyed about their perception of the enterprises' impact on the partners. This impact survey was based on the asset matrix used in the case study of The Learning Enrichment Foundation in Toronto (see Chapter 9, Chan et al., 2014). Aspects of the organization described in this chapter include its social and economic impacts, barriers to employment in competitive businesses for persons with developmental disabilities, and how the model could be replicated.

Results

The business partners described their work in terms of job status, income, job tasks, decision-making authority, business success, their feeling of being valued, and social connections among partners and between partners and staff. Given the limitations on the salaries that partners can make because of ODSP and the practical limitations associated with variable revenues from the businesses, the issue of how partners classified their activities was explored as well as the nature of the business itself. The responses reflect that the partners unequivocally identify the enterprise as work – because they are paid. While "the partners described their level of income as being fair for the job they were doing and indicated that they were satisfied with the amount, they also expressed a desire to make a higher income but felt limited by the ODSP restrictions: 'So yeah, it's not a matter of the company doesn't want to give more money. It's just if they give more plus you get ODSP' (Partner 3)" (Readhead, 2012, p. 47). Participants acknowledged that their income did not compare to competitive employment sector wages: "It is as fair as the Coffee Shed is concerned, but it doesn't measure up to the real world" (Partner 2).

The partners' experience was also described in terms of training but – unlike other programs for persons with disabilities that are geared to moving people into other jobs – partnership in these social purpose enterprises can be an end in itself: "They are developing skills, but they are owning a business in some ways" (Ministry/Board 6). Partners may remain in the businesses, move on to another form of employment, or, as in the case of one partner, combine their business partnership with other employment. The partners perceived their job activities as important to maintaining a successful business and all partner participants described their work with a sense of confidence and pride.

A staff participant contrasted the safety and support provided by a business like Lemon & Allspice with the experience of some partners who have worked in the competitive sector, where "somebody in your department might be very nice to you and treat you like everybody else, but that security guard is calling you names, calling you a [offensive label for persons with a developmental disability], and a lot of customers will say things about you and a lot of people have been spit on" (Staff 1). In contrast, the Common Ground Co-operative businesses offer an environment in which partners dare to dream about new possibilities as their confidence and self-esteem increase: "Now they feel better and better about themselves and they think, oh, maybe I could tackle that thing that I want to do" (Staff 1).

The partners described their experience in community jobs prior to working at the enterprises supported by Common Ground and spoke of difficulties that they had encountered in keeping some of these jobs. One partner described having a problem in a community job and saying to the manager, "is there something else I can do besides that [job position] ... and she said to be honest with you we have nothing here for you to do and if you can't handle what you're doing the best bet ... I think it's better if you leave" (Partner 3). Partners compared the environment of their social purpose enterprises with the demanding nature of previous supervisors. "I like the Coffee Shed better [than my past employment where] there's too many people trying to be the boss and try[ing to] tell you to do that over. Here [the Coffee Shed] is peaceful, quiet like nobody try – well they still tell you what to do but not as much as over there" (Partner 4). Another described the stressful pressure to multitask with little support that the participant had encountered in a competitive job. In contrast, this participant described knowing that people are available to help and answer questions, and that it is possible to take time to learn. As a result, this partner is no longer anxious about making mistakes: "This place here has helped me to gain confidence in myself" (Partner 10).

In supporting the businesses, the administration of Common Ground Co-operative makes decisions on the basis of social as well as economic factors. Whenever possible, materials are sourced from other social purpose enterprises; economic planning takes into consideration the impact on people, and not just on the bottom line. While the business income is only a supplement to ODSP, participation in the social purpose enterprises does offer autonomy and self-determination. Staff members balance promoting autonomy among the partners with meeting their duty of supporting partners' needs. At times, supporting partners' needs in the businesses requires staff intervention and support of the partners' problem-solving skills appropriate to the nature of the concern at hand. Staff also may limit partners' autonomy to ensure that health and safety standards are maintained in the businesses. This reflects the dual foci of these social purpose enterprises: to remain financially viable while providing social support.

Impacts of Common Ground Co-operative and Its Related Businesses

Several key themes became evident in examining the businesses' impacts: the personal and work skill development of partners, the empowering nature of partnership, the development of extended social networks, and the increased community awareness that persons with developmental disabilities are contributing citizens. It was clear from all the participants in this study that Common Ground Co-operative and the businesses it supports are seen as furthering the interests of partners while providing quality business services.

The majority of respondents to the Coffee Shed customer survey indicated their satisfaction with the quality of the businesses. In comparing the Coffee Shed to other coffee shops, 47 per cent rated the Coffee Sheds as being better, and 42 per cent rated them as being the same. 46 per cent had visited their Coffee Shed location more than ten times in the previous month, which suggests that the Coffee Sheds have quite a loyal following. In a similar survey of Lemon & Allspice Cookery's catering customers, all respondents described the Cookery as the same or better than other caterers. Three of the four respondents identified the products as being good, three reported friendly service, and all respondents identified the service as being efficient and reliable.

Partners' Work Skills

Participants from all groups described the range of work-related skills that partners gain as a result of their involvement in the Foundation Program and the business enterprises. Included were descriptions of learning customer service skills, being on time for work, dressing appropriately, and attending to tasks. The importance of a sense of ownership and the related autonomy were also identified. The partners described specific job duties and routines that were vital to the operation of their social purpose enterprise. These included specific tasks such as putting out the sign to advertise that their Coffee Shed was open for business, getting keys to open the Coffee Shed, putting cash in the register, washing their hands and the counters, checking expiry dates on food items, making coffee, setting up the counters with food items, and performing the banking at the end of the day (Readhead, 2012). In the Cookery, the partners described their tasks of baking, taking orders, and making deliveries. "It means taking responsibility seriously" (Partner 12).

Some partners highlighted the importance of their work routine: "You have to wake up early to come to work and you have to be ready to work when you're here" (Partner 6). They spoke of making friends and of their improved well-being. They valued the consistency of a steady job and harmony in their working environment. Related to partners' job satisfaction was the value they described in learning new skills, building social networks, and having an enhanced self-image. Partners described job challenges as being typical for the line of work. They also reported having an improved quality of life that was related to their job: "This job is better because it's our own business" (Partner 8) (Readhead, 2012).

In the Common Ground Co-operative staff survey, respondents were asked to rate the changes that they typically observe in partners at the start of the first week in the Foundation Program, at the end of the first week of co-op placement in one of the businesses, and after six months as a partner in one of the businesses. Respondents were asked to describe the impact of Common Ground and the businesses it supports on the partners using a five-point Likert-type scale (1–no change, 2–small change, 3–medium change, 4–large change, 5–goal attainment). Figure 2.1 illustrates the positive impact of the Common Ground experience in twenty areas. Among the four surveys returned, some questions were left unanswered. The averages reported in Figure 2.1 are based on items for which there were at least three or four responses. Of the twenty-five questions, the following categories received fewer than three responses so averages could not be generated: health, relationship with neighbours, relationship with family support, relationship with friends, and trusting relationships. Respondents who did

Figure 2.1 Average Progress towards Goal Attainment

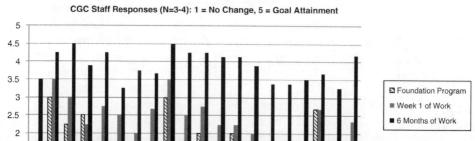

not answer these questions indicated that they did not know or could not answer. The results from this small survey echo the impacts described by the interviewees and the focus group.

Staff survey respondents also commented about the growth they have witnessed in partners. As one staff member explained, "When you are a productive, working member of society receiving a pay check in-hand, but also developing relationships with customers and co-workers, you've created social impact" (Staff Survey 1). This survey respondent emphasized that customers recommend the Common Ground Co-operative-supported businesses because of the quality of their products. The social mandate related to employment of persons with disabilities is seen by customers as an added bonus, not as a detriment. The presence of the business partners in an agency where parents bring their children who have developmental disabilities has also been a source of encouragement: "At Surrey Place Centre, many mothers and fathers take their … children in for treatment, sessions, therapy, assessments, etc. They are worried what their children will be able to achieve in their lives. One mother once expressed that after buying a product from the Coffee Shed located very near to the entrance of the building, she felt a great sense of comfort from witnessing the Partners hard at work" (Staff Survey 1).

Similar surveys were sent to families, asking them to identify the areas in which they have seen growth in their family member who is a business partner. Positive impact was reported for most of the identified areas (see Table 2.2).

Family respondents described how the partners had developed the following: "Long-lasting friendship; learning on the job and in special courses; confidence; speaking and being heard; opinions valued; decision making; listening; caring and being cared about; taking initiative" (Family 1). The development of teamwork skills – the need to "work for the good of the team" (Family 3) – was noted as having had a positive social impact on the partners.

Partnership and Empowerment

The importance of ownership and inclusion in the broader community were discussed by all groups of interview participants. "The partners' remarks suggested their feelings of positive self-esteem and empowerment related to their job: 'Being my own boss is actually pretty good ... I don't know, maybe because [of] just certain decisions we can make'" (Partner 3) (Readhead, 2012, p. 48). This was echoed by a family member who described the businesses as inculcating a feeling of "ownership, the knowledge that the business is theirs; what they do with it matters to them and to their customers" (Family 1).

The partners described learning job duties and other related skills. "I've learned how to count the money from cash ... and what we do is count the money and we subtract 50 dollars and we put the money in a pouch and some of us take it to the bank" (Partner 5). The partners reported learning about transportation, teamwork, work ethic, and they described how these vital skills helped them to gain independence: I take the TTC ... I took the TTC awareness program" (Partner 1) (Readhead, 2012). They also spoke about how they gained interpersonal skills and professionalism through their work experience. Some of these skills were routine, daily occurrences: "I learned how to talk to customers and how to count the money and how to make coffee" (Partner 4) (Readhead, 2012). Partners described teaching new partners job responsibilities, work rules, and professionalism that they had to learn when they joined the partnership. These descriptions involved

Table 2.2 Family Identification of Positive Impact on Partners

Area of Impact on Partners	Families (N = 3) Identifying Positive Impact on Partners	Don't Know (DK)
Income	3	
Motivation	3	
Confidence	3	
Ability to speak about concerns	3	
Ability to work collaboratively	3	
Use of the internet	1	1
Banking	2	1
Purchasing supplies/groceries	3	1
Using transportation	3	
Work skills related to business	2	
Skill working with other people	3	
Decision-making skills	3	
Product knowledge	2	
Customer service skills	3	
Future employability	2	
Ordering skills	2	
Leadership skills	3	
Happy	3	
Healthy	3	
Work networks	2	
Relationship with neighbours	2	
Leisure skills	3	
Relationship with family support	3	
Relationship with friends	3	
Trusting relationships	2	

the mechanics of the job and focused on the specific tasks to be mastered: "We train them to do the coffee, how to do the cart run, how to do the floats, things like that" (Partner 3) (Readhead, 2012). The concept of teamwork appeared to be a core competency for the partnerships and for business success: "I think the people who join a business like this, they have to be willing to work together, because otherwise it's not going to work out" (Partner 2). The assistance that partners gave to new apprentices starting out in the social enterprise included introducing them to existing partners, job coaches, and other auxiliary people in the business environment. The partners also discussed the importance of sharing advice about work ethic, learning from existing partners, the need for teamwork, and the necessity of observing the dress code and other work rules. "Imparting work behaviour norms to new partners included the advice: 'Bring your lunch, wear your Coffee Shed shirt ... be on time' (Partner 5); and 'Prove to me that you really want to be here' (Partner 4)" (Readhead, 2012, p. 55).

Partners found it essential to have the opportunity to learn new tasks without undue pressure: "The good thing about this place was I could take my time, that I can actually learn at my own pace" (Partner 7). "The partners described job duties that they had learned to carry out independently, as well as tasks for which they received support" (Readhead, 2012, p. 50). It was reported that job coaches would appoint a head partner to supervise the business area while they were off site. Partners took pride in being appointed "head partner" and running the business: "just a good feeling if you're independent" (Partner 8).

The partners consistently emphasized the importance of a positive work ethic to being effective and maintaining a successful business. "An effective partner gained recognition by being a hard worker and being responsible or dependable: '[M]y coach has at times selected me to help her out and not others because she knows I'll do the work ... just sit around ... that's not the idea of work' (Partner 2)" (Readhead, 2012, p. 60). To them, work ethic meant following the work rules and respecting the group dynamics of the partnership: "And we got to work as a team" (Partner 3) (Readhead, 2012).

Developing Relationships and Social Networks

As mentioned earlier, partners develop more than work opportunities in their association with the social purpose enterprises. The partners described their relationships with customers, with job coaches, and with each other as partners and as friends. Social networking was identified as an important part of the partnerships, with partners forming friendships and experiencing emotional support among themselves and between themselves and their job coaches.

Customers represented a source of business revenue but were also seen as supportive: "Our customers are [people who work in the building] and they understand where you are coming from and they don't rush you, like they don't say oh hurry up I need my order" (Partner 3). The relationship between partners and job coaches involves a level of support that may not be typical in other job settings: "We go the extra mile because you have a very personal relationship" (Staff 2). This includes listening and advising on issues that extend beyond the workplace but for which the person requires support. Another Common Ground Co-operative staff member confirmed the importance of the social support provided by coworkers and coaches, explaining that "for some of these people it's the only contact they have with people" (Staff 1).

A staff participant, who stated that Common Ground Co-operative is known for a sense of community among the partners, described how people who graduate from the Foundation Program and become apprentices are introduced to more than just the job; they are also invited by the partners to join in their social activities. This participant described how partners' lives are about more than work: "They aren't motivated by money, they're involved in tons of other things" (Staff 2). As new apprentices become engaged in the larger social life of the partner community, they may find themselves too busy to take some work shifts: "They're saying, 'oh, I can't work this day or this day because I'm doing this and this,' so we see their whole life change, not just work, we see their whole life change and it's pretty cool" (Staff 2). Another staff member suggested that some partners get to know one another through work while others knew each other before coming to the businesses, because persons with disabilities are often grouped together in social activities.

Community Awareness

In addition to having a positive impact on partners and contributing to the success of the businesses as part of the social enterprise network, Common Ground Co-operative and the businesses it supports are increasing community awareness of persons with developmental disabilities as contributing fellow citizens. Staff and board members promote the value of breaking down barriers to inclusion of persons with developmental disabilities, as was expressed by one staff member: "People begin to see disabilities differently. Sometimes they are surprised, sometimes shocked; sometimes it's like a discovery of something new for them. It's because we are ruining their stereotypes" (Staff Survey 4).

Common Ground Co-operative staff emphasized the fact that these enterprises are businesses that must compete in a demanding market and offer services of consistently high quality. Everything from the quality of the cookies to the flavour of the coffee in the Coffee Sheds must be up to usual professional standards, not held to a different standard because the business partners happen to have a disability. A staff participant described the surprise of visitors to the kitchen when they realized that the operation is being run by persons who have developmental disabilities, suggesting that "the more people see what individuals with disabilities can do, the more we become more mainstream" (Staff 1).

This increased awareness is fostered by the considerable media interest in Common Ground Co-operative and its related social purpose enterprises – for example, the CBC coverage of the vermicompost enterprise. This coverage increased awareness and resulted in invitations from agencies and the school board for presentations about the greening of businesses (Staff 2). Articles have been written in *Toronto Life*, *Inside Toronto*, *Bloom Magazine*, and the *Toronto Star*. Videos on Common Ground and its related social purpose enterprises have appeared on TV Ontario, Global TV, and Co-op TV. There have been newsletters, blogs, and website features developed to increase public awareness of how social purpose enterprises owned and operated by persons with developmental disabilities contribute to community life.

Reproducing the Common Ground Model

The demand for the services of CGC continues to grow, putting pressure on the organization to make some difficult decisions. If more partners are added to the existing businesses, the amount that each partner can earn will be reduced. Given the partners' already meagre earnings, this is an unappealing option. A second option is to create a new enterprise in a new market – but there are no additional funds for an increased number of support staff. The third option that CGC has considered is to refuse to increase the number of partners it supports beyond an optimal number that would be determined. New spaces would become available only through attrition. This option would jeopardize the funding for the Foundation Program that prepares new partners. This leaves another alternative that the organization has been pursuing: replicating the CGC model in other parts of Canada. Investigation into the other three options continues.

A Ministry/board participant indicated that Common Ground Co-operative is looking at replicating its model – rather than simply growing larger – because increasing the size of the current network could jeopardize its established sense of community (Ministry/Board 4). As a family member explained, "the businesses must be kept relatively small. Replication will allow for many more small business partnerships, but there must be strong community support for this to happen" (Family 1). For groups that may be considering taking on the challenge of creating a supportive and authentic business network like Common

Ground Co-operative, participants made several recommendations. These recommendations reflect the belief that a new network is unlikely to take root without a commitment to sustaining the spirit of the model and to giving it life in a locally meaningful way.

A key theme for replication was the need for "passion and desire, and people with similar interests and ... goals" (Staff Focus Group). Staff emphasized the importance of grass-roots support, as well as "financial support, administrative support, ministry support, Board support, families, partners and community" (Staff Focus Group). They also described the complex mix of skills needed to support the businesses: technical professional skills to produce quality products in a competitive market and human services skills to provide the extra measure of support needed by the business partners. Staff must be prepared to address emergency situations in the partners' lives, especially when other community support alternatives are not in place. Staff members described their jobs as changing constantly. They have to be focused on the success of the businesses, but they also have to be crisis workers, teachers, and advocates; these multiple roles make it challenging to determine the boundaries in their relationship with partners.

From a governance perspective, Ministry/board participants discussed the importance of board members being involved, knowing the partners personally, and understanding the democratic nature of social cooperatives. Community organizing skills are required to bring together the groups necessary to support such a diverse enterprise, since it does not fit an existing model. The range of skills involved necessitates a network of committee members, as well as contacts with people who understand community living, real estate, marketing, fundraising, job coaching, legislation, quality assurance, and also how to cultivate organizational partnerships and how to find money to support a shared vision. Strong and dedicated staff leadership is vital in order to accomplish the day-to-day operation of the organization. Beyond vision, there must be the drive and the will to work through the challenges that organizing groups will face. For Common Ground Co-operative, the driving force was the burning desire to realize the dream of meaningful employment. And achieving that goal takes time.

Conclusion

Common Ground Co-operative and its associated social purpose enterprises are a safe space (Hall, 2010) in which persons who have developmental disabilities can gain work skills, develop a social network, and find their voice. The partners still rely on ODSP support, but they are able to augment their income – albeit not to the extent that would be available in competitive employment. However, as one family survey respondent noted, "perhaps this is the beginning of paying [persons with disabilities] for quality work done rather than just ODSP" (Family 3). For some, the business partnership may become a long-term workplace; for others, it is a place to develop skills that will equip them to find other jobs, some of which they may have thought were unattainable before the training and experience they gained as partners. The partners of the Coffee Sheds and Lemon & Allspice Cookery saw themselves as valued citizens; they described how they obtained networking skills, which could be interpreted as social capital (Condeluci, 2002), and they expressed that being their own bosses gave them a feeling of prestige. As a family survey respondent concluded, "Their work gives them a sense of value and place in society" (Family 2).

NOTES

1 The term developmental disabilities is used in this chapter for the purpose of clarity and to be congruent with the identification used by Common Ground Co-operative. However, some literature reviewed in this chapter used intellectual disabilities specifically, while other material referred to developmental disabilities.
2 Fifteen interviews were conducted with partners. Two partners were unable to answer informed consent comprehension questions, so their data were not included in the analysis.

REFERENCES

American Association on Intellectual and Developmental Disabilities. (2013). Frequently asked questions on intellectual disability. Retrieved from http://aaidd.org/intellectual-disability/definition/faqs-on-intellectual-disability#.U2g7ucavtHg

Anglin, B., & Braaten, J. (1978). *Twenty-five years of growing together: A history of the Ontario Association for the Mentally Retarded*. Toronto, ON: Canadian Association for the Mentally Retarded.

Baker, P.A. (2007). Individual and service factor affecting deinstitutionalization and community use of people with Intellectual Disabilities. *Journal of*

Applied Research in Intellectual Disabilities, 20(2), 105–109. http://dx.doi.org/ 10.1111/j.1468-3148.2006.00313.x

Burge, P., Ouellette-Kuntz, H., & Lysaght, R. (2007). Public views on employment of people with intellectual disabilities. *Journal of Vocational Rehabilitation, 26,* 29–37.

Canadian Association for Community Living. (2014). History. Retrieved from http://www.cacl.ca/about -us/history

Canadian Association for Community Living. (2013). Assuring income security and equality for Canadians with intellectual disabilities and their families. Retrieved from http://www.cacl.ca/sites/default/files/CACL%20 Brief%20-%20Finance%20Committee%20-%20Income%20Equality%20 in%20Canada%20-%20April%202013%20%282%29.pdf

Canadian Association for Community Living Position Statement on Employment. (2010). Retrieved from http://www.cacl.ca/sites/default/ files/uploads/docs/CACL%20Policy%20Position%20Employment.pdf

Canadian Association for Community Living and People First of Canada (2012). *Ready, willing, and able: People with intellectual disabilities creating an inclusive labour force.* Retrieved from http://www.cacl.ca/sites/default/ files/Employment%20Success%20Stories%20-%20Digital.pdf

Community Living British Columbia (2009). Defining a path to inclusive employment. Retrieved from http://www.communitylivingbc.ca/what_we_ do/documents/EmploymentDiscussionPaper.pdf

Chan, A., Hoogendam, R., Frampton, P., Holeton, A., Pohl-Weary, E., Ryan, S., & Quarter, J. (2014). Well-being of childcare workers at The Learning Enrichment Foundation, a Toronto community economic development organization. In J. Quarter, S. Ryan, & A. Chan (Eds.), *Social purpose enterprises: Case studies for social change* . Toronto, ON: University of Toronto Press.

Common Ground Co-operative Inc. (2010). Retrieved from www .commongroundco-op.ca

Condeluci, A. (2002). *Cultural Shifting.* St. Augustine, FL: Training Resource Network, Inc.

Crawford, C. (2011). *The employment of people with intellectual disabilities in Canada: A statistical profile.* Toronto, ON: Institute for Research and Development on Inclusion and Society (IRIS). Retrieved from http:// irisinstitute.files.wordpress.com/2012/01/intellectual-disability-and- employment_iris_cr.pdf

Foundation for People with Learning Disabilities. (n.d.). *In business: Quick guide to self-employment.* Retrieved from learningdisabilities.org.uk/ content/assets/pdf/publications/quick-guide-to-self-employment .pdf?view=Standard

Galambos, D. (1999). Individual approaches to support. In I. Brown & M. Percy (Eds.), *Developmental disabilities in Ontario* (pp. 43-58). Toronto, ON: Front Porch Publishing.

Grant, J. (2008). Paid work: A valued social role that is empowering more people with an intellectual disability and providing employers with dedicated employees. *Journal of Intellectual & Developmental Disability, 33*(1), 95–97. http://dx.doi.org/10.1080/13668250701646355

Griffiths, D., Owen, F., & Watson, S. (Eds.). (2012). *The human rights agenda for persons with intellectual disabilities.* Kingston, NY: NADD.

Hall, E. (2004). Social geographies of learning disability: Narratives of exclusion and inclusion. *Area, 36*(3), 298–306. http://dx.doi.org/10.1111/j.0004-0894.2004.00227.x

Hall, E. (2005). The entangled geographies of social exclusion/inclusion for people with learning disabilities. *Health & Place, 11*(2), 107–115. http://dx.doi.org/10.1016/j.healthplace.2004.10.007

Hall, E. (2010). Spaces of social inclusion and belonging for people with intellectual disabilities. *Journal of Intellectual Disability Research, 54,* 48–57. http://dx.doi.org/10.1111/j.1365-2788.2009.01237.x

Hall, E., & Wilton, R. (2011). Alternative spaces of "work" and inclusion for disabled people. *Disability & Society, 26*(7), 867–880. http://dx.doi.org/10.1080/09687599.2011.618742

Isaac, R., Dharma Raja, B.W., & Ravanan, M.P. (2010). Integrating people with disabilities: Their right – our responsibility. *Disability & Society, 25*(5), 627–630. http://dx.doi.org/10.1080/09687599.2010.489314

Lemon, C. (2011). *Minding our own business.* Toronto, ON: Carolyn Lemon.

Lemon, C., & Lemon, J. (2003). Community-based cooperative ventures for adults with intellectual disabilities. *The Canadian Geographer, 47*(4), 414–428. http://dx.doi.org/10.1111/j.0008-3658.2003.00033.x

Ontario Ministry of Community and Social Services. (2012). Income support: What is it. Retrieved from http://www.mcss.gov.on.ca/en/mcss/programs/social/odsp/income_support/what.aspx

Ontario Ministry of Community and Social Services. (2013). Treatment of income: When you work and earn money. Retrieved from http://www.mcss.gov.on.ca/en/mcss/programs/social/odsp/income_support/odsp_workearn.aspx

Owen, F., & Griffiths, D. (Eds.). (2009). *Challenges to the human rights of people with intellectual disabilities.* London, United Kingdom: Jessica Kingsley Publishers.

Owen, F., Griffiths, D., Tarulli., D., & Murphy, J. (2009). Historical and theoretical foundations of the rights of persons with intellectual disabilities: Setting the stage. In F. Owen & D. Griffiths (Eds.), *Challenges to the human rights of people with intellectual disabilities* (pp. 23–42). London, United Kingdom: Jessica Kingsley Publishers.

Parkinson, G. (2006). Counsellors' attitudes towards Disability Equality Training (DET). *British Journal of Guidance & Counselling, 34*(1), 93–105. http://dx.doi.org/10.1080/03069880500483182

Readhead, A. (2012). Social economy and developmental disabilities: An employment option that promotes a form of authentic work and fosters social inclusion (Master's thesis). Centre for Applied Disability Studies, Brock University, St. Catharines, ON, Canada. Retrieved from http://hdl.handle.net/

Rogan, P., & Rinne, S. (2011). National call for organizational change from sheltered to integrated employment. *Intellectual and Developmental Disabilities, 49*(4), 248–260. http://dx.doi.org/10.1352/1934-9556-49.4.248

Sandys, J. (1999). Work and employment for people with developmental disabilities in Ontario. In I. Brown & M. Percy (Eds.), *Developmental disabilities in Ontario* (pp. 139–156). Toronto: Front Porch Publishing.

Stancliffe, R.J. (2001). Living with support in the community: Predictors of choice and self-determination. *Mental Retardation and Developmental Disabilities Research Reviews, 7*(2), 91–98. http://dx.doi.org/10.1002/mrdd.1013

Statistics Canada (2006). *Participation and activity limitation survey of 2006: Labour force experience of people with disabilities in Canada.* Retrieved from www.statcan.g.ca/pub/89-628-x/89-628-x2008007-eng.htm

Sutherland, K., & Beachy, T. (2004). *Innovative co-ops in the social services sector: A research study to benefit people with developmental disabilities and mental illness.* Vancouver, BC: United Community Services Co-operative.

Swanson, L. (n.d.) *Entrepreneurs with disabilities work for themselves in their home-based businesses.* Retrieved from http://abilities.ca/business-not-as-usual/

Trembath, D., Balandin, S., Stancliffe, R.J., & Togher, L. (2010). Employment and volunteering for adults with intellectual disability. *Journal of Policy and Practice in Intellectual Disabilities, 7*(4), 235–238. http://dx.doi.org/10.1111/j.1741-1130.2010.00271.x

UN General Assembly, Convention on the rights of persons with disabilities: resolution/adopted by the General Assembly, 24 January 2007, A/RES/61/106. Retrieved from http://www.refworld.org/docid/45f973632.html

Van Niekerk, L., Lorenzo, T., & Mdlokolo, P. (2006). Understanding partnerships in developing disabled entrepreneurs through participatory action research. *Disability and Rehabilitation, 28*(5), 323–331. http://dx.doi.org/10.1080/09638280500166425

3 When the Business Is People: The Impact of A-Way Express Courier

KUNLE AKINGBOLA

Introduction

This chapter examines the economic and social impact of A-Way Express (A-Way), a social purpose enterprise that operates a courier business and employs people with psychiatric disabilities. It draws on the concepts of human and social capital to offer insight into how the mission and operation of the organization impact the employees who are "consumer-survivors" of the psychiatric system in Ontario. Specifically, the chapter addresses two related questions: What are the knowledge, skills, and abilities that employees acquire through their work at A-Way? What are the social and economic benefits that are accrued by the employees? The concept of human capital is a particularly relevant framework for analysing the economic and social impact of A-Way because of its focus on the acquisition of knowledge, skills, and abilities that benefit not only the organization but also the employees. As a social purpose enterprise that operates in a predominantly commercial business sector, any analysis of A-Way would be incomplete without a discussion of the competitive environment and the strategy of the organization.

Consistent with Chapter 1, this chapter defines a social purpose enterprise as a market-based entity founded and supported by a non-profit organization for the purposes of economically and socially benefiting persons on the social margins who are employed in or trained through the enterprise. Organizations such as A-Way Express that are established with the mission to employ people with psychiatric disabilities are a subset of the social purpose enterprise taxonomy. Their mission is derived from the challenges that people with psychiatric disabilities experience in the labour market.

This chapter proceeds as follows: after a brief discussion of the context of social purpose enterprises for people with psychiatric disabilities, the concepts of human and social capital and their relevance to A-Way are reviewed. The next section presents an overview of A-Way including its revenue, organizational structure, competitive environment, and strategy. This is followed by the findings on the economic and social and human capital outcomes for the employees of the organization. Finally, the findings are discussed.

Social Purpose Enterprises for People with Psychiatric Disabilities

Social purpose enterprises for people with psychiatric disabilities in Ontario can be traced in part to the efforts of On Our Own, a self-help/mutual aid organization formed in Toronto in 1977 (Burstow & Weitz, 1988; Church, 1997). Church (1997) noted that advocacy work of ex-psychiatric patients and escalating hospital costs prompted the deinstitutionalization of psychiatric care. However, the psychiatric survivors found that they were shut out of the labour market, education, training, and housing in the community. They were basically excluded from actively participating in the economy, which fostered unemployment and entrenched their marginalization (Church, 1997). The negative situation became a source of significant challenge for psychiatric survivors.

In response to this negative experience, On Our Own established a business called the Mad Market, a non-profit goods store managed by members of the organization (Burstow & Weitz, 1988; Church, 1997; Nelson, Ochocka, Griffin, & Lord, 1998). Starting in 1980, On Our Own also published a quarterly magazine, *Phoenix Rising* (Church & Reville, 1988). The basic proposition for the establishment of Mad Market was to facilitate a psychiatric survivor/consumer-run business that employed its members. In addition to the advocacy and initiatives of psychiatric survivors, an important early influence was the release of the Graham Report in 1988 (Czukar, 2008). Among other measures, the report recommended a plan for developing and implementing a comprehensive community mental health system. The implementation process that followed the report also contributed to the launching of the Consumer-Survivor Development Initiative (CSI) by the Ontario government and the funding of over forty CSIs (O'Hagan, McKee, & Priest, 2009). These grass-roots initiatives in the 1980s, coupled with government support, marked the unofficial starting point of social purpose enterprises operated by people with psychiatric disabilities.

Social purpose enterprises for people with psychiatric disabilities are an important part of the broader social purpose enterprise segment of the economy that has grown significantly (Lysaght & Krupa, 2011). Although some of the psychiatric survivor-run organizations established in the 1980s and 1990s, such as ABEL Enterprises and FreshStart Cleaning and Maintenance Company, continue to operate today, many have been integrated into mainstream organizations that are not run by psychiatric survivors (O'Hagan et al., 2009). Social purpose enterprises operated by consumer-survivors represent over 60 per cent of the enterprises for people with disabilities surveyed in 2010, with the majority of these organizations located in Ontario (Lysaght & Krupa, 2011). However, O'Hagan et al. (2009) reported that social purpose enterprises run by people with psychiatric disabilities have not received an increase in funding from the provincial mental health budget since 1991. They also noted that these organizations are relatively new and lack performance measures – problems that are similar in other jurisdictions (Brown, Shepherd, Wituk, & Meissen, 2007; Campbell & Leaver, 2003; O'Hagan et al., 2009; Van Tosh & del Vecchio, 2000). The research suggests that social purpose enterprises operated by people with psychiatric disabilities confront persistent challenges that constitute a major threat to their organizational survival.

It is important to acknowledge that the activities of the organizations in this space and the psychiatric survivor movement at large have been shaped by how they promote and contribute to the empowerment of psychiatric consumer-survivors (Campbell & Leaver, 2003; O'Hagan et al., 2009). Empowerment is characterized by "reciprocity between people in the giving and receiving of help, gaining control over one's life and being able to influence your environment" (Campbell & Leaver, 2003, p. 14). Hence, the discussions about these organizations have examined their role and benefits in terms of whether they successfully contribute to empowerment. This research takes a somewhat different approach, focusing on the role of social purpose enterprises in building human and social capital in consumer-survivors.

Human and Social Capital

This section briefly reviews the concepts of human and social capital. It highlights how both human and social capital benefit the individual employee, the organization, and society.

Human Capital

The concept of human capital refers to the knowledge, skills, and abilities embodied in people (Coff, 2002). It is essentially the competencies that people – employees, volunteers, community partners – in organizations possess. The knowledge, skills, and abilities that constitute human capital can be both explicit and tacit (Polanyi, 1966, 1967). Explicit knowledge involves learning that can be codified and is more likely to be focused on transferrable know-how (Hitt, Biermant, Shimizu, & Kochhar, 2001; Liebeskind, 1996). It is the type of knowledge "that can be expressed formally using a system of symbols" (Davenport & Prusak, 1998, p. 112). Explicit knowledge is often acquired through education. Tacit knowledge is learned through experiences or insights gained from situations and interactions. This type of knowledge is more likely to be embedded in codified routines and in relationships between individuals (Liebeskind, 1996; Szulanski, 1996). Tacit knowledge therefore tends to be personal and more difficult to transfer from one individual to the other (Nonaka & Takeuchi, 1995). In short, human capital includes knowledge, skills, and abilities that are acquired through different forms of learning.

People develop human capital through formal learning, non-formal learning, and informal interactions and processes. Formal learning generally refers to the institutional ladder that goes from preschool to graduate studies, while non-formal learning refers to all organized educational programs that take place outside the formal school system and are usually short term and voluntary (Livingstone, 2002; Schugurensky, 2000). These include many training and learning opportunities offered by organizations. Informal learning happens in spaces and places that are not necessarily governed by curricula, experts, and timelines; it is learning that can be intentional, unintentional, or gleaned through socialization (Schugurensky, 2000). However, regardless of the source of the learning that creates the human capital, it is first an individual process. It has been suggested that the source and the application of knowledge is in the minds of knowers (Davenport & Prusak, 1998). Hence, it is safe to say that a potential primary beneficiary of human capital is the employee who possesses the knowledge, skills, and abilities. Employees can leverage their human capital in their current organization, in the open labour market, and in pursuit of social outcomes that are in the best interest of the community. In other words, human capital has significant economic and social importance to the employee. For example, employees can draw on their human capital to negotiate higher wages or to seek employment with a different organization (Coff, 1997). Employees can also use human capital to build social capital through interactions with direct and indirect stakeholders in the organization.

The benefit of human capital to employees is twofold. First, the employees acquire knowledge, skills, and abilities that increase their economic capabilities (Becker, 1983). This economic benefit can take the form of an actual increase in earnings, an increased potential to earn higher wages, or better job security. There are two categories of human capital, specific and general human capital. Specific human capital benefits only the organization that provided the knowledge, skills, and abilities to the employee. General human capital benefits the organization as well as the entire industry and the open labour market. Therefore, the more general human capital that employees acquire, the more choices they will have to increase the economic benefits that stem from their general knowledge and skills.

Second, employees acquire knowledge, skills, and abilities that enhance their social mobility and social networks. Human capital improves employees' prospects of being promoted within their organization (Saks & Haccoun, 2007). Moreover, employees develop and maintain relationships with clients, partners, and colleagues within and outside the service sector in which their organization operates, which further increases the opportunity to acquire more knowledge and skills (Hitt et al., 2001). Often, these relationships extend beyond the context of the specific organization. It is possible for employees to leverage social networks or social capital gained from previous jobs to their benefit long after they have transitioned to another job or career (Hitt et al., 2001). For example, employees who have built considerable networks can draw on their contacts to build a customer base for their new employer or to access other resources that they need to perform in their new job. They may use their existing social network to develop their relationship with contacts in the new environment.

The extensive body of research on human capital has focused on how organizations use the knowledge, skills, and abilities of their employees. Indeed, human capital is critically important for organizations (Barney, 1991; Lepak & Snell, 1999). In a resource-based view of the firm, it is posited that an organization's capacity to acquire, develop, combine, and effectively deploy its physical, human, and organizational resources creates critical value and competitive advantage (Barney, 1991; Wernerfelt, 1984). More importantly, it is suggested that since many of the skills and abilities that make up human capital, such as organiza-tion-specific experience, are socially complex, they are difficult to imi-tate (Barney, 1991; Carpenter, Sanders, & Gregersen, 2001; Coff, 1997). The point here is that human capital gives the organization a true edge in performance. In the everyday life of an organization, human capital is front and centre in the interactions and processes between employees and with their customers. As Davenport and Prusak (1998) noted, "in organizations, knowledge often becomes embedded not only in docu-ments or repositories but also in organizational routines, process, prac-tices, and norms" (p. 5). In this way, individual employees acquire and develop general human capital – that is, knowledge, skills, and abilities that can be used in other organizations as well as in the larger society (Coff, 1997). Basically, employees acquire and develop human capital that not only adds value to their current organization but also is saleable in the general labour market, to the benefit of the individual. These knowledge and skills are also valuable to the wider community.

Social Capital

Human capital also fosters the development of social capital for the employees and the organization. In effect, human capital is inextricably linked to social capital. The concept of social capital originated in the work of Lyda Hanifan, who described it as "those tangible assets [that] count for most in the daily lives of people: namely goodwill, fellow-ship, sympathy, and social intercourse among the individuals and fami-lies who make up a social unit" (Hanifan, 1916). This definition indicates the significance of relationships and interactions among people. While there is no consensus on the definition of social capital, in recent years, an understanding of the importance of relationships and social capital has been rekindled mostly in the work of Robert Putnam. He notes that social capital is the "connections among individuals – social networks and the norms of reciprocity and trustworthiness that arise from them" (Putnam, 2000, p. 19). Putman (2001) further suggested that there are two types of social capital – bonding social capital (which develops be-tween people in the same community, age, ethnic group, social back-ground, et cetera) and bridging (which develops as a result of connecting with people from different and diverse backgrounds).

The concept of social capital allows us to see that relationships and interactions in society have tangible value. Both the employee and the organization can leverage social capital by developing their relationship with their clients (Hitt et al., 2001). Moreover, social capital is unlike human capital in the sense that it is a resource that is available to all and not a property that can be traded (Herreros, 2004). Hence, the ability to build relationships and navigate interactions could have a profound impact for the employee, organization, and society. However, similar to human capital, which "does not only benefit those who participate in its creation, but also has external effects on the wider community" (Herreros, 2004. p. 20), social capital not only benefits the organization that facilitates its acquisition, or the individual who possesses the knowledge, skills, and experience, but also the larger society.

Human and Social Capital and Social Purpose Enterprises

As discussed in Chapter 1, social purpose enterprises are organizations that rely on a parent non-profit organization for ongoing support. As such, the resource base and the interactions between stakeholders in these organizations are distinct (Akingbola, 2012). It is this distinct context of resource idiosyncrasies that sets the stage for the way human capital can benefit both the organization and the individual employees.

Similar to other non-profit organization, there are three distinct sources of resources and capabilities in social purpose enterprises: structural, institutional, and values (Akingbola, 2012). Human capital underlies each of the three sources. In fact, human capital permeates the structural, institutional, and values characteristics of social purpose enterprises because it is central to their missions, to their interactions with stakeholders, and to their business processes. One can argue that social purpose enterprises are, essentially, in the business of human capital. Therefore, it is through the lens of human and social capital that this chapter will examine the impact of A-Way on employees of the organization.

Study

To examine how A-Way benefited employees, this study adopted a qualitative method supplemented with quantitative data to shed light on the state of employee engagement in the organization. For the qualitative method, the study employed key informant interviews (Gilchrest, 1992) to investigate the context and experience of the organization's stakeholders. The stakeholders interviewed were employees, managers, members of the board of directors, customers, community partners, and organizations that compete with A-Way. Twenty-five semistructured interviews (Borg & Gall, 1989) were completed with stakeholders. The interviews followed a narrative approach (Polkinghorne, 1988) in which the participants were asked to explain their background and their involvement in A-Way's activities. In addition to the interview data, A-Way provided extensive secondary data such as financial statements, annual reports, samples of completed time cards, and other relevant documents. Thirty-four employees completed a survey designed to elicit additional information.

Analysis

The qualitative data were read and reviewed extensively and, where necessary, follow-up questions were sent to the research participants. The interviews and documentary data were entered into NVivo, a qualitative data analysis software. First, the entire interview text was combed for descriptive categories, which were then reviewed to highlight themes consistent with the theoretical concepts (Orton, 1997). The data were coded and analysed with the software to further discover themes that were relevant to the research. The focus of the qualitative data analysis was to draw out narratives from the different participants that best illustrate the human and social capital impact of A-Way for the employees and the organization.

Economic, Human, and Social Capital Impact of A-Way

This section presents the findings about the economic, human, and social capital impact of A-Way on employees of the organization. It integrates the findings with the relevant scholarly literature. First, an organizational overview of A-Way is presented.

Overview of A-Way

A-Way was founded in 1987 through the efforts of consumer-survivors of the psychiatric system and two non-profit organizations – Progress House and House Link Housing Agency – to create a supportive workplace in which employees are empowered (Shragge, Church, Fontan, & Lachance, 1999). The goal was to create work opportunities where consumer-survivors as employees would be accountable and independent. The Ontario Ministry of Health made start-up funding available to the organization through a program meant to facilitate training and employment of consumer-survivors (Shragge et al., 1999).

A-Way provides same-day "green" courier services. The organization delivers documents and small packages using either public transit
or on foot. Hence, it is an organization that promotes both social and
environmental values. Deliveries that are outside the service area of the
organization may be offered to a bigger courier company. A-Way has
approximately seventy employees, six of whom could be categorized as
management – including the position of executive director, which is
currently vacant. In addition, currently there are fifty-nine couriers
who are part-time employees and three nonmanagement office staff.
The demographic data show that most of the employees are male and,
on average, are older than forty-five years old. In addition, many of the
employees have some form of higher education.

STRUCTURE
An analysis of the interview and document data suggests that A-Way
has a hybrid structure (McShane & Steen, 2009). In this structure, the
core work processes (mail order and dispatch) are under the human
resources manager's supervision. Other functions, such as administration and accounting, appear to be structured in a traditional way.
To uphold the importance of the social objectives and engagement of
employees as the core stakeholders in the organization, employees
can attend and participate in the monthly meeting of the board of directors. A-Way's organizational culture emphasizes empowerment
and independence of its employees. Each individual takes responsibility for his or her own work and generally requires little supervision. Front line employees constitute half of the fourteen-member
board of directors. The other members of the board are nominated
from the community.

REVENUE
A-Way had an annual revenue of about $0.9 million in 2010, which was
somewhat higher than in the previous two years. As shown in Table 3.1,
nearly four-fifths of the organization's revenue is from the Ontario
Ministry of Health and Long-Term Care, a percentage that remained
relatively stable between 2008 and 2010. Revenue from courier operations and flyer distributions, which can be considered the business ventures of the organization, was also relatively stable, representing about
17.2 per cent of total revenue in 2010. Its high point was 18.8 per cent in
2009. As discussed below, this revenue is important in the analysis of
how A-Way impacts its employees.

Table 3.1 Revenue of A-Way, 2008–2010

Revenue	2010 $	2010 %	2009 $	2009 %	2008 $	2008 %
Ministry of Health & Long-Term Care	705,585.00	79	662,830.00	79	674,874.00	78
Courier operations	151,780.00	17	153,820.00	18	134,965.00	16
Other funding	34,943.00	4	20,279.00	2	42,434.00	5
Flyer distribution	1,819.00	0.2	6,460.00	0.8	8,702.00	1.0
Total	894,127.00	100	843,389.00	100	860,975.00	100

COMPETITIVE ENVIRONMENT

The courier and local messengers industry in Canada has 19,546 active businesses, which generated an annual operating revenue of $8.7 billion and employed 48,000 people in 2008 (Statistics Canada, 2007 to 2008). Included in the industry is a mixed bag of services ranging from bicycle couriers to delivery by air. Courier and local messengers are a highly competitive service that has experienced significant growth in recent years (Globe and Mail, 2008). The growth in the industry could be attributed in part to increasing consumer demand and package shipments, as well as changing technology (Globe and Mail, 2008; Statistics Canada, 2007 to 2008). The Statistics Canada report shows that the industry is segmented into two distinct but complementary business areas. First, there are large courier businesses that offer national and international delivery services and generate significant revenue. In 2008, they constituted 10 per cent of the businesses and 82 per cent of the total revenue (Statistics Canada, 2007 to 2008). Second, there are local messengers such as A-Way that operate within a restricted area; these represent 90 per cent of the firms but account for 18 per cent of the revenue (Statistics Canada, 2007 to 2008). Many of the local messengers are small businesses and include independent self-employed workers. The complementary market segments suggest that the competition in the industry overlaps because the big establishments can leverage their significant economies of scale and brand recognition to sideline the local messengers and threaten their survival. Hence, to be successful, a local messenger must embrace a differentiated strategy and find a unique market niche (Hitt, Ireland, Hoskisson, Sheppard, & Rowe, 2009).

STRATEGY

A-Way's business strategy is characterized primarily by differentiation (Hitt et al., 2009) based on a social purpose enterprise brand within the local City of Toronto messenger market. To drive business, the organization emphasizes its social mission. This might be labelled as social marketing. The evidence suggests that many customers of A-Way – for example, CAG Rubber Stamps – started to use A-Way's service in a spirit of charity. However, the survival of an organization in a competitive business environment cannot be based solely on benevolent patrons. Hence, A-Way's competitive advantage is derived from a combination of quality service, operational flexibility, and social mission. For example, A-Way offers a later pickup time for same-day deliveries. Couriers and local messengers generally have a cut-off time that is between ten o'clock and noon for same-day deliveries. A-Way accepts orders until three o'clock, provided that the delivery can be completed on time.

Moreover, while the courier and local messengers industry in Canada is striving to be more environmentally friendly (Globe and Mail, 2008), A-Way Express Courier is exemplary in this regard because it uses the local public transit system for deliveries. It is this environmentally friendly operation – along with its primary social mission of employing people with psychiatric disabilities and its quality service – that differentiates A-Way from its competitors. Customers appear to recognize this quality service. As one long-time client indicates: "A-Way's service has been consistently reliable, prompt and courteous. It is precisely what we look for in a courier service."

Focusing on customer service has enabled A-Way to retain important clients, including private companies, law firms, health-care organizations, government departments, non-profit organizations, and professional associations.

Economic Impact of A-Way

The economic impact of A-Way can be examined from two intersecting perspectives: direct and indirect. The direct impact includes the commissions, wages, and benefits received by the employees. Since many of the employees participate in the Ontario Disability Support Program (ODSP) – a government program that financially supports people with disabilities who are in need – the A-Way compensation structure is linked to income from the government program. Currently, employees who are couriers and receive ODSP are paid a different rate of commission than those who are not part of ODSP. The commission is based on the cost of the delivery. Table 3.2 shows the compensation and benefits at A-Way. In addition to the compensation structure below, employees are compensated for any additional responsibilities. The commissions below are based on the fee paid by customers.

A-Way's couriers have different hours and shifts, which may affect their wages. The data suggest that the ability of employees to work more shifts is determined in part by their psychiatric condition and their medication needs. Based on a sample of completed time sheets, Table 3.3 illustrates the average biweekly hours and pay of couriers at A-Way.

Based on interview data, couriers receive on average around $750–800 monthly in ODSP benefits, or approximately $10,000–11,000 annually. Following from Table 3.3, a courier on ODSP who works an average of twenty-four hours bimonthly will earn about $2,848 in commission per annum, while a non-ODSP colleague will earn $4,397 in commission per annum. It is important to note that the pay will be higher if the employee works more hours. The courier who is on ODSP will receive about $3,000 less in ODSP payments due to that individual's employment income. This highlights the impact of the ODSP on employees who are part of the government program. Employees are paid for additional roles such as taking minutes at meetings ($15/hour) and attending external meetings and workshops ($10.25/hour). Although the benefits couriers receive are above the employment standard requirement, as evidenced from the data above, the pay from commission for the average courier can fall below the minimum wage. As noted by one courier: "And that's the disadvantage – that we can't seem to work enough hours at a high enough wage to actually become financially self-sufficient" (Employee A).

However, one of the direct economic impacts for ODSP couriers, non-ODSP couriers, and management employees is the opportunity to participate in the labour market. Through A-Way, employees are able to contribute their paid labour to a social purpose enterprise. Non-ODSP and management/administrative employees are paid for their work rather than being shut out of the labour market and the economy (Church, 1997). Employees on ODSP are able to earn income that supplements their government disability pensions. Moreover, since the data suggest that close to 90 per cent of the business revenue of A-Way Express Courier is used to pay for couriers' commission and benefits, the economic impact is dependent on the organization's ability to generate business. The stability of the organization's government grant is another important factor that contributes to the employees' income. As shown in Table 3.1, A-Way's government funding remained

Table 3.2 Compensation and Benefits at A-Way

Employee	Compensation	Benefits*
Courier (with ODSP)	70% Commission**	6% vacation pay, statutory holiday pay, Metropass, weather clothing
Courier (no ODSP)	85% Commission	6% vacation pay, statutory holiday pay, Metropass, weather clothing
Management/ Admin Staff	Wage	4% vacation pay, statutory holiday pay

* There are eligibility requirements for the benefits
**There is a plan to introduce 85% commission for all couriers

Table 3.3 Average A-Way Courier Hours & Pay

Courier	Hours Worked (Two-week period)			Average Pay (bi-monthly)	ODSP Clawback (50%)
	Minimum	Maximum	Average		
ODSP recipient	11.83	52	24	$118.70	$59.35
Non-ODSP recipient	6.88*	63	28.38	$183.22	N/A
COMBINED			25.22	$136.62	

* Minimum workload is supposed to be a 4.5-hour shift.

relatively stable between 2008 and 2010 at just under four-fifths of the organization's total income.

In addition to the direct economic impact on A-Way's employees, there is an indirect economic impact consisting mainly of benefits employees are able to access through their affiliation with A-Way (Long & Ravichander, 2006). For example, eligible employees can participate in a group benefits plan that includes drug and extended health coverage and an addiction program. The group benefits plan has a direct economic impact on employees because the cost of such plans is generally too expensive for individual employees to afford. In addition, other services that benefit employees are available at A-Way; for example, employees receive breakfast one day a week. By offering a supportive work environment that helps to reduce the need for hospital stays and situations that involve the justice system, A-Way could have indirect economic impacts on employees. Although A-Way cannot track employees' hospital stays, many employees have anecdotally reported decreased hospital stays after they started working at A-Way. For example, one employee reported:

Well, my physical health is good. I'm just barely past two years out of the hospital, which is the longest that I've been out since I've been eighteen. And that may be related to working, or it may not, it's really difficult to tell. Because I've worked before, and I've tried many things to stay out of the hospital. The main advantage, to answer your question, I'd say, would be my physical health. (Employee A)

In fact, as an employee and a manager appear to suggest below, both the direct and indirect economic impacts of the organization on employees could be summarized in terms of cost avoidance as a result of a caring workplace environment and resources:

The understanding is that you have to practise self-care. So they don't just talk about it, they give you the tools to do it. (Employee B)

I think just to be gentle and caring and make sure, that the person is looked after, for their mental health, to make sure the job works out for them. We don't want to be dictatorial or draconian with our policies. We want to have a place where a person feels safe and comfortable working, and has a good work environment, and does the job well, but also is content with the way they're treated. (Manager A)

Human Capital Impact of A-Way

Developing the human capital of its employees appears to be a major impact of A-Way. Most employees identified the distinct systems, processes, and activities of the organization as the learning context that enabled them to develop specific knowledge, skills, and capabilities. While there are non-formal learning opportunities such as workshops, most of the knowledge and skills are acquired through informal learning processes. To develop the operational and customer service skills that are required to be a good courier, new couriers at A-Way are paired with a courier trainer in an on-the-job training program for three or more days. The training process involves experiential learning and behavioural modelling (Saks & Haccoun, 2007). Courier trainers are long-time employees who have been identified as effective teachers. According to the executive director:

They go out with the courier, usually the first day, just kind of follow along. The second day they'll practise using the map books and trying to figure out where things are at and learn the basics of the radio, and the third day usually the trainer will follow around the person and just give advice if they need it, but that's totally flexible.

This non-formal learning process is reinforced with continuous informal learning opportunities for the courier to develop customer service and administrative skills as well as personal well-being. The work processes are set up to foster learning by employees who may not have these competencies and who may face challenges due to their psychiatric disability. By offering these opportunities, A-Way is developing the human capital of its employees. From a business standpoint, it is the core resource and a way of gaining competitive advantage (Barney, 1991; Wernerfelt, 1984) in the local messenger delivery market. The interview data with the employees underline why the development of human capital is important to them beyond the benefits that will accrue to the organization:

> It was a rough patch in the beginning while I was learning the ropes on how to answer the phones. Like, I don't want to answer phones, but they did it the way they want to … I mean faxing, copying, blah, blah, blah. But, I'm feeling more confident than I used to. (Employee C)
>
> They make it easy on me to learn things that other people would expect me to know already. I mean, I have to be polite. I have to be capable. I have to deal with money and personal property, and a radio, and peers, get dressed every morning and show up on time, and that kind of thing. (Employee D)
>
> Somehow, they've made us smart, y'know… I've learned a lot of things I never thought I could. I never saw myself working at an office, or as a mailman or on the same level as an ambulance driver, or something like that. (Employee E)

While the point about confidence and personal well-being may seem mundane to the mainstream population, they are critical skills for people with psychiatric disabilities who have been marginalized and desire to participate actively in the labour market (Shragge et al., 1999); or, as one employee pointedly states:

> People with mental health issues didn't learn a lot of social skills because they were at home by themselves for years on end and they have a disease that is still telling them things. (Employee F)

Employees also noted that the knowledge and skills that they acquire at A-Way also prepare them for other jobs within the organization and in other organizations. The research shows that human capital development can create a career path within the organization. For example, most of the administrative staff and managers including the executive director joined A-Way as couriers and rose through the ranks, a point emphasized by one of the managers:

> Oh yes in countless occasions we've been a stepping stone for [people] … to get back into the workforce, it's definitely a job for people that are isolated or haven't worked in a while to get out and work and move onto better jobs and also within A-Way there is lots of room to move up. For example, I started as a courier and I moved up to the Business and Projects Manager after going through several other positions. So, definitely it's a stepping stone to get out there and to get a good career going. (Manager B)

Since many of the employees have never worked or have not been able to work for a long period of time, the knowledge, skills, and experience that they gain at A-Way are the marketable competencies that they can offer to other employers. For some employees, the knowledge, skills, and experience offer hope of not just employment but additional training or formal education that will lead to a new career. A-Way is the harbinger of hope that previously seemed improbable:

> Yeah, it depends on where I work. And I'm thinking of going to beauty school because they use a lot more natural products so that would tend to have less fumes and that might work better for me. I have to ask around. So, yeah, I do have goals to move on from here and I'm not sure they will be successful and I'm really glad this place exists because at least if that were not to work out I could come back here. (Employee G)

Similarly, "Employee H," who continues to work part-time with the organization, was able to transition to other employment mainly because of the experience provided by A-Way:

> I'm a peer support specialist in a mainstream mental health provider, right now. And, and so, a lot of the learning I've learned here in the history of the movement has given me a lot of tools to understand what's going on

in that environment. And certainly mental health policy, but also how those policies (work) … Y'know, how those connections are made and how to do things a little differently. (Employee H)

The development of human capital at A-Way is evidenced in the extensive insight provided by the employees, managers, and other stakeholders. The knowledge, skills, and capabilities that are essential for the competitive advantage of the organization are also critical for the employees' quality of life – and in many cases, their careers. In addition to administrative and customer service skills, employees gain critical personal wellness skills, increased self-esteem, and better knowledge of the psychiatric system. These have significant impact on the well-being of the employees and their ability to function as active members of society. Indeed, the expectation of the performance system at A-Way was identified as a tool that has helped employees to develop personal accountability and basically function without supervision.

Social Capital Impact of A-Way

Many of the employees indicated that A-Way is a primary source of their social capital through which they build social networks, both professional and personal. Consistent with McKee & Associates (2006) and Shragge et al. (1999), the findings indicated that A-Way provides a "natural network of peers and friendships" (McKee & Associates, 2006, p. 3). Employees noted that the friendships and experiences they share with colleagues not only enhance their personal and professional network but also lead to peer support and education. The employee interviews stress how their A-Way networks have helped them not only to develop supportive relationships – through which they mutually support and learn from each other – but also to overcome some of the trauma of psychiatric disability:

I've kind of got friends here and we get together and do social things from time to time. When somebody asks me what I'm doing this weekend I don't just have one person, my boyfriend, to turn to. I can say, "Well, I'm actually going skating with my friends from A-Way. We're going to do whatever." I just did that on Friday. Or, "We're gonna go see a movie together" or "There's a party coming up at Christmas." The Christmas before I came to work was really bleak. I didn't have any friends because how could I meet anyone because of the inevitable question of "What do you do for a living?" Who are you as a person, which is what they are really asking you. I was nothing, no one [laughs], sitting in the house, painting pictures that no one will see, staring out of the dark windows. Snow fills up in the basement window. I don't know how I got through it. (Employee I)

And isn't this neat, we get to meet more people and get to know more things and learn more about ourselves. And learn how to be more caring and empathetic and patient. And maybe learn that if we get a chronic illness or have an accident or have a trauma in our lives that – hey, we can still work and contribute and we're still going to be wonderful people. And we can still be kind and loving and we'll create a better world. (Employee J)

The findings suggest that A-Way is important to generating social capital because it is connected to a number of social networks. These links help the employees to connect with people who are not part of A-Way. The organization itself is an important player in the social policy and educational network of the psychiatric system. Through A-Way, employees gain access to education and contacts that are required to be active members of society, as expressed by "Employee K": "You are now in a community, part of the larger community. And you learn to network. Like, they have all kinds of things up there. From programs, peer support, sometimes they have outings. It's more about being a member of society."

A-Way employees interpret their work not only as delivering parcels but also as a form of public good. From this perspective, their work is about making a difference in society by enabling the customers to achieve their goals and to connect people to each other:

When I think about all the things that are in those packages, it makes me feel good inside. I can remember picking up packages for Make-A-Wish Foundation and taking them to people who could then fulfill the wish. I can remember taking a letter to Gordon Lightfoot from a child from a school downtown … at the Harbourfront. (Employee L)

In summarizing this section of the findings, the evidence from our research indicates that in addition to providing some economic benefits, A-Way develops both human and social capital for its employees who are consumer-survivors of the psychiatric system. The systems and processes that the organization adopts to develop human capital directly impact the knowledge, skills, and behaviour of the employees. This same human capital drives the competitiveness of A-Way as a social purpose enterprise. Moreover, the findings also suggest that social capital is a by-product of the systems and processes of the organization. As employees acquire knowledge and skills in administration, customer service, and personal well-being, they have opportunities to develop social capital through the social and professional networks they can access through their work at A-Way. The findings suggest that the human and social capital can and has provided opportunities for employees to gain employment in mainstream organizations and pursue careers that were previously unlikely.

Discussion and Conclusion

Similar to the other social purpose enterprises in this book, A-Way Express Courier plays a pivotal role in the lives of employees who are consumer-survivors of the psychiatric system. However, as explained in Chapter 1, very little is known about the impact of this type of social purpose enterprise that is focused on marginalized population. As a result, two key questions were examined in this chapter: 1) What are the knowledge, skills, and abilities that employees acquire through their work at A-Way?; and 2) What are the social and financial benefits that are accrued by the employees through their work at A-Way?

In general, the findings indicate that employees acquire diverse knowledge and skills such as customer service and administrative skills, knowledge of personal wellness, and basic financial and interpersonal skills. The findings extend our understanding of A-Way as a social purpose enterprise. Notwithstanding its limited economic impact, A-Way represents a supportive work environment for the employees. For a marginalized group of people who face major challenges in the mainstream labour market (McKee & Associates, 2006; Shragge et al., 1999), this impact is significant. More specifically, the findings reveal that A-Way has a significant impact in terms of the human and social capital that employees derive from the organization. The development of human and social capital is an important return on investment for employees. There is some correspondence between what is good for the organization and what is good for the employees. As a social purpose enterprise, A-Way uses its human capital to build relationships and social networks to support the mission and access or acquire resources such as funding. For example, the organization is a member of Social

Purpose Enterprise Network Toronto (SPEN), an umbrella organization established to "provide business development and peer support through collaborative action, networking and skills development" (Langford, 2010, p. 5). This network ultimately benefits the employees because it grants them access to sector-wide advocacy and the opportunity to develop human and social capital and support. Very importantly, these findings demonstrate that A-Way Express is fundamentally an organization driven by a social mission. The organization is a product of its normative institutional context and this is reflected in the impact it has on employees.

In conclusion, despite the important impact that A-Way has on its employees, the organization must contend with inadequate recognition and support. In addition, the findings in this chapter – which appear to suggest that some employees experience reduced hospital stays – is consistent with evidence from previous research that indicates that organizations such as A-Way reduce hospital stays and contribute to cost saving for the health care system (Church, 1997; Shragge et al., 1999). A-Way relies heavily on government funding to sustain itself. This research suggests that there are many positive benefits to A-Way that result from this public investment. There may be potential for A-Way to increase its revenue from its courier service, but this has to be balanced with the couriers' needs – which are the organization's social mission – and the highly competitive business environment in which A-Way operates.

ACKNOWLEDGMENT

Thanks to Tammy Rogers for her assistance and dedication to this project. I also thank Joyce Brown and Terry Krupa for their contribution.

REFERENCES

Barney, J.B. (1991). Firm resources and sustained competitive advantage. *Journal of Management, 17*(1), 99-120.

Becker, G.S. (1983). *Human capital: A theoretical and empirical analysis with special reference to education.* Chicago, IL: University of Chicago Press.

Borg, W.R., & Gall, M.D. (1989). *Educational research.* New York, NY: Longman.

Brown, L.D., Shepherd, M.D., Wituk, S.A., & Meissen, G. (2007). Goal achievement and the accountability of consumer-run organizations. *Journal of Behavioral Health Services & Research, 34*(1), 73–82. http://dx.doi.org/10.1007/s11414-006-9046-y

Burstow, B., & Weitz, D. (Eds.). (1988). *Shrink resistant: The struggle against psychiatry in Canada.* Vancouver, BC: New Star Books.

Campbell, J., & Leaver, J. (2003). *Emerging new practices in organized peer support.* Alexandria, VA: National Technical Assistance Center for State Mental Health Planning and National Association of State Mental Health Program Directors.

Carpenter, M.A., Sanders, W.G., & Gregersen, H.B. (2001). Bundling human capital with organizational context: The impact of international assignment experience on multination firm performance and CEO pay. *Academy of Management Journal, 44*(3), 493–511. http://dx.doi.org/10.2307/3069366

Church, K. (1997). *Using the economy to develop the community: Psychiatric survivors in Ontario.* Ottawa, ON: Caledon Institute of Social Policy.

Church, K., & Reville, D. (1988). *User involvement in mental health services in Canada: A work in progress.* International Conference on User Involvement in Mental Health Services, Sussex, England, September 26–28.

Coff, R.W. (1997). Human assets and management dilemmas: Coping with hazards on the road to resource-based theory. *Academy of Management Review, 22,* 374–402.

Coff, R.W. (2002). Human capital, shared expertise, and the likelihood of impasse on corporate acquisitions. *Journal of Management, 28*(1), 107–128. http://dx.doi.org/10.1177/014920630202800107

Czukar, G. (2008). *Unfinished business, mental health policy in Ontario since 1983. Honouring the past, shaping the future. 25 years of progress in mental health advocacy and rights protection.* Toronto, ON: Queen's Printer for Ontario.

Davenport, T.H., & Prusak, L. (1998). *Working knowledge.* Cambridge, MA: Harvard Business School Press.

Gilchrest, V.J. (1992). Key informant interviews. In B.F. Crabtree & W.L. Miller (Eds.), *Doing qualitative research* (pp. 71-85). London, United Kingdom: Sage.

Globe and Mail (2008, February 25). A special information supplement for the Canadian courier & logistics association. *Globe and Mail,* p. CCLA 3.

Hanifan, L.J. (1916). The rural school community center. *Annals of the American Academy of Political and Social Science, 67*(1), 130–138. http://dx.doi.org/10.1177/000271621606700118

Herreros, F. (2004). *The problem of forming social capital: Why trust?* New York, NY: Palgrave Macmillan. http://dx.doi.org/10.1057/9781403978806

Hitt, M.A., Biermant, L., Shimizu, K., & Kochhar, R. (2001). Direct and moderating effects of human capital on strategy and performance in professional service firms: A resource-based perspective. *Academy of Management Journal, 44*(1), 13–28. http://dx.doi.org/10.2307/3069334

Hitt, M.A., Ireland, R.D., Hoskisson, R.E., Sheppard, J.P., & Rowe, W.G. (2009). *Strategic management: Competitiveness and globalization: Concepts* (3rd Canadian ed.). Toronto, ON: Nelson Education Ltd.

Langford, A. (2010). *SPEN Toronto – Social purpose enterprise in the GTA 2010 survey: Preliminary findings, comparisons and analysis.* Toronto, ON: Carleton Centre for Community Innovation/SPEN Toronto.

Lepak, D.P., & Snell, S.A. (1999). The human resource architecture: Toward a theory of human capital allocation and development. *Academy of Management Review, 24,* 31–48.

Liebeskind, J.P. (1996). Knowledge, strategy and the theory of the firm. *Strategic Management Journal, 17* (Special Issue), 93–107.

Livingstone, D.W. (2002). Working and learning in the information age: A profile of Canadians. CPRN Discussion Paper. Ottawa, ON: Canadian Policy Research Network.

Long, R.J., & Ravichander, H.S. (2006). *Strategic compensation: A simulation* (3th ed.). Scarborough, ON: Nelson Education Ltd.

Lysaght, R., & Krupa, T. (2011, March). *Social business: Advancing the viability of a model for economic and occupational justice for people with disabilities.*

McKee, H., & Associates. (2006). *Consumer-survivor initiatives: Impact outcomes & effectiveness.* Toronto, ON: Canadian Mental Health Association, Ontario; Centre for Addiction and Mental Health; Ontario Federation of Community Mental Health and Addiction Programs; Ontario Peer Development Initiative.

McShane, S.L., & Steen, S.L. (2009). *Canadian organizational behaviour* (7th ed.). Toronto, ON: McGraw Hill.

Nelson, G., Ochocka, J., Griffin, K., & Lord, J. (1998). "Nothing about me, without me": Participatory action research with self-help/mutual aid organizations for psychiatric Consumer-survivors. *American Journal of Community Psychology, 26*(6), 881–912. http://dx.doi.org/10.1023/A:1022298129812

Nonaka, I., & Takeuchi, H. (1995). *The knowledge-creating company: How Japanese companies create the dynamics of innovation.* New York, NY: Oxford University Press.

O'Hagan, M., McKee, H., & Priest, R. (2009). *Consumer survivor initiatives in Ontario: Building for an equitable future.* Toronto, ON: Ontario Federation of Community Mental Health & Addiction Programs.

Orton, J.D. (1997). From inductive to iterative grounded theory: Zipping the gap between process theory and process data. *Scandinavian Journal of Management, 13*(4), 419–438. http://dx.doi.org/10.1016/

S0956-5221(97)00027-4

Polanyi, M. (1966). *Personal knowledge: Toward a post-critical philosophy*. Chicago, IL: University of Chicago Press.

Polanyi, M. (1967). *The tacit dimension*. Garden City, NY: Anchor Publishing.

Polkinghorne, D.E. (1988). *Narrative knowing and the human sciences*. Albany, NY: State University of New York Press.

Putnam, R. (2000). *Bowling alone: The collapse and revival of American community*. New York, NY: Simon & Schuster. http://dx.doi.org/10.1145/358916.361990

Putnam, R. (2001). Measurement and consequences. *Isuma*, 2(1), 41–51.

Saks, A.M., & Haccoun, R.R. (2007). *Managing performance through training & development* (4th ed.). Toronto, ON: Thomson Nelson Learning.

Schugurensky, D. (2000). The forms of informal learning: towards a conceptualization of the field. NALL Working Paper, 19.

Shragge, E., Church, K., Fontan, J., & Lachance, É. (1999). *Alternative/Training businesses: New practice, new directions. Human Resources Development Canada*. Social Development Partnerships.

Statistics Canada (2007–2008). *Surface and marine transport results of the survey of the couriers and local messengers industry*. (No. 50–002-X). Ottawa, ON: Author.

Szulanski, G. (1996). Exploring internal stickiness: Impediments to the transfer of best practice within the firm. *Strategic Management Journal*, 17 (Special Issue), 27–43.

Van Tosh, L., & del Vecchio, P. (2000). *Consumer-operated self-help programs: A technical report*. Rockville, MD: Center for Mental Health Services.

Wernerfelt, B. (1984). A resource-based view of the firm. *Strategic Management Journal*, 5(2), 171–180. http://dx.doi.org/10.1002/smj.4250050207

4 Miziwe Biik Case Study: Microloans in the Urban Aboriginal Community

MARY FOSTER, IDA BERGER, KENN ROSS,
AND KRISTINE NEGLIA

Background on the Organization

In 1991, the Aboriginal community in the Greater Toronto Area (GTA) established Miziwe Biik Aboriginal Employment and Training Centre as a non-profit organization to address the community's unique training and employment needs. Fifteen staff members offer employment programs, services, and resources (including counselling, community project training, skills development, work placement, and access to computers, Internet, and fax machines) that attract approximately one thousand client visits per month. In 2004, the Miziwe Biik Development Corporation was added to facilitate the economic advancement of the Aboriginal community within the GTA, and in 2007, the Aboriginal Business Resource Centre (ABRC) was established to provide entrepreneurs with access to business training, skills development, and microloans. The seventy-five clients who access the services of the ABRC service each year are referred through Miziwe Biik's general employment and training programs, the small business course offered by Aboriginal Business Canada, and other Aboriginal organizations in the GTA.

The microloan program began with a modest pool of $60,000 from Miziwe Biik and the RBC Foundation to support Aboriginal entrepreneurs through offering loans between $1,000 and $5,000 at 2 per cent above prime rate, with a repayment plan of twelve equal monthly instalments. Designed to be a sustainable program that generates income through interest, the microloan program is the first of its kind to specifically target the unmet financial needs of urban Aboriginal entrepreneurs. To date, the microloan program has loaned $43,500 to nine

Aboriginal entrepreneurs in various industries: arts and crafts, food services, health and wellness, and consulting services. In total, $25,035 (including interest) has been repaid, representing a financial success rate of about 50 per cent. Of the nine borrowers, four were able to earn a living wage, become self-sufficient, and pay back their entire loans, although two borrowers in this group missed at least one payment. The purpose of this case study is to examine the features and impact of a microloan program that targets the urban Aboriginal community.

Microfinance in Canada

Microfinance programs are primarily associated with developing countries where a high proportion of citizens have difficulty meeting basic needs for shelter, food, education, and health care (Richardson, 2009; Rubach, Bradely, & Brown, 2010). However, few are aware that the first *caisse populaire*, founded by Alphonse and Dormène Desjardins in Lévis, Quebec, entered the field of microfinance in 1900 through providing credit services to those who could not access traditional bank loans (Coyle & Wehrell & MacDonald 2006; Reynolds & Novak, 2011). The need for financial services outside mainstream traditional institutions has not abated. Indeed, a survey by the Financial Consumer Agency of Canada (2005) reveals that 4 per cent of Canadians have been unable to set up a bank account, mostly because of a poor credit track record.

In response to the need for financial inclusion of marginalized populations and the negative features of payday loan services, organizations and institutions developed microcredit programs. Calmeadow, for instance, was founded in 1983 with the goal of supporting small entrepreneurs in the developing world, but in addition, it tested the peer-lending model in North America. Between 1987 and 1999, through its Metrofund initiative, it dispersed more than $4.6 million in loans to Canadian entrepreneurs (Frankiewicz, 2001). Under the umbrella of the National Aboriginal Capital Corporation Association (NACCA), a number of programs were established to service the needs of Aboriginal people in Canada. Calmeadow launched the Native Self-Employment Program in three Aboriginal communities in Ontario in 1987, followed by the First Peoples' Fund in 1990. Unfortunately, in 2000 Calmeadow concluded that a stand-alone microloan program was not viable in the current Canadian context, and its portfolio was sold to the credit unions Vancity and Alterna Savings (Coyle & Wehrell & MacDonald 2006; Reynolds & Novak, 2011). Specifically, external factors – such as the size and sophistication of the microenterprise market, the availability of other options, regulatory limitations, the complexity of business in Canada, and high transaction costs – joined forces to impede the development and sustainability of a robust and enduring microfinance model (Coyle, Wehrell & MacDonald, 2006). However, the need for microfinancing, especially in some specific communities, did not disappear.

A recent study identified twenty-eight microcredit programs across Canada (Aliu, Cosentino, & Panasyuk, 2009). Of these programs, fifteen operate on a bank-guarantee model, nine on peer lending, and five on an escalating scaled-loan system. The targeted borrowers for all programs are individuals, with twelve specifically focusing on new businesses and twelve on existing businesses. Twenty out of twenty-eight require entrepreneurs to present a viable business plan before the loan is given; five provide upfront training and eight ongoing mentoring or technical assistance. In the peer-lending model, the borrower's relationship with other members of the group is used to exert influence to repay the loan on time, thus ensuring a low default rate (Dua, Subbiah, & Visano, 2007). However, this model has not been as successful in Canada as it has been in developing countries, in part because of the availability of a social safety net, the creation of a poverty trap (where because of joint liability all are obligated to repay a bad loan), and the more transient nature of social relationships in urban communities (Visano, 2008). On the other hand, one of the benefits of microcredit programs is that they are often bundled with enhancements to human capital: they offer business training and other skill development services (Visano, 2008).

The Aboriginal Entrepreneurial Community in Canada

Over one million Canadians, or about 3.8 per cent of the total population, identify themselves as Aboriginal. The Aboriginal population is younger than the general population – with a median age of twenty-seven years old as opposed to forty years old – and it is growing at a faster rate. The Aboriginal population is less educated: 50 per cent have finished postsecondary school as opposed to 67 per cent of the general population, and Aboriginal people face higher levels of poverty and unemployment (8 per cent of adults are unemployed as opposed to 5.4 per cent of adults in the general population, according to Statistics Canada, 2009). The Aboriginal population is also becoming increasingly urbanized. The GTA experienced a 31 per cent increase in its

Aboriginal population since 2001, making it the fourth-largest Aboriginal community in Canada (Environics Institute, 2010; Statistics Canada, 2009). While some attribute this growth to migration from reserves, a closer look indicates higher fertility rates, more reliable data collection, and, most importantly, ethnic mobility. The latter occurs when children of mixed heritage choose to identify as Aboriginal, and when persons change their ethnic affiliation over time. Most of the ethnic transfers to Aboriginal have occurred in urban areas. This growth in Aboriginal identification has been credited to a renewal of ethnic pride coupled with amendments to the Indian Act, which make it easier to acquire or to reacquire Indian status (Guimond, Robitaille, & Senecal, 2009).

The Aboriginal community has experienced both social and economic marginalization that can be traced to the first European arrivals to Canada, who simply claimed the land for themselves (La Prairie, 1994; Jaccoud & Brassard, 2003; Monchalin, 2010). Further, the psychological and social dislocation associated with residential schools resulted in a loss of connection to family, social supports, and traditional culture and values for those who attended these schools and for subsequent generations (Monchalin, 2010). Researchers have documented specific impacts that include deficits in life skills and parenting; lowered self-esteem, self-confidence, and respect; and higher rates of physical, emotional, sexual, and substance abuse (Chansonneuve, 2005; Jacobs & Williams, 2008; Wesley-Esquimaux & Smolewski, 2004).

Importantly, those connected or newly reconnected to traditional cultural norms also face issues of marginalization and misunderstanding. Historically, survival for Aboriginal people required harmonious interpersonal relationships; therefore, it is part of Aboriginal culture to reduce conflict by not dealing with it directly. Brant (1990) identified eight defining principles of Aboriginal culture. These include noninterference, where trying to influence the behaviour and attitudes of others is viewed as undesirable; noncompetitiveness, where intragroup rivalry is discouraged; emotional restraint, where the expression of both negative and positive emotions is suppressed; sharing, where everyone in the community partakes in prosperity and success; having a flexible concept of time; limiting verbal praise or rewards; valuing manners and ceremony; and teaching through modelling. As Brant (1990) notes, some of these norms and values are different from mainstream norms and may be misinterpreted by mainstream society. For example, noninterference can be seen as permissiveness; noncompetitiveness may be viewed as a lack of initiative and ambition; sharing contradicts the mainstream emphasis on individual success; and limited external approval may result in a reluctance to try something new as Aboriginal people always are expected to exhibit competence.

At a communal level, successful businesses mean more than just profit for individual owners: success translates into resources to help close the socio-economic gap between Aboriginal and non-Aboriginal populations (CCAB, 2005; Sisco & Stewart, 2009). According to the Canadian Council for Aboriginal Business (CCAB), Aboriginal entrepreneurs strive to improve the socio-economic conditions within their families and communities by employing other Aboriginal people. It is estimated that Aboriginal businesses have created approximately 61,500 full-time jobs and 13,500 part-time jobs for Aboriginal people in Canada, as well as 20,500 full-time and 4,500 part-time jobs for non-Aboriginal people (AANDC, 2008). About 37 per cent of Aboriginal business owners report having at least one employee (CCAB, 2011). Despite these promising trends, access to capital remains a major obstacle for Aboriginal entrepreneurs, particularly in urban settings in Canada. This problem is similar to that found among disadvantaged groups in less developed countries.

While there are advantages enjoyed by Aboriginal entrepreneurs (such as property or income tax exemptions on reserves and Aboriginal procurement strategies within federal departments), these are not perceived to negate the unique challenges that exist for this community, particularly in urban settings (Sisco & Stewart, 2009). In addition to subtle and overt forms of racism, stereotyping, and band-governance issues, Aboriginal business developers must overcome limited or no access to capital, inability to use property or land on reserve as collateral, remoteness, prohibitive legislation, lack of materials, and inadequate business skills (Caldwell & Hunt, 1998; Sisco & Stewart, 2009). A 1998 study explored the characteristics of Aboriginal businesses in Canada and found that the majority (63 per cent) use less than $25,000 as start-up capital (Caldwell & Hunt, 1998). Of the 63 per cent who needed start-up capital, approximately one-half needed less than $5,000. The study found that Aboriginal entrepreneurs are more likely to use equity rather than debt for starting their businesses (61 per cent), and that 45 per cent of Aboriginal businesses are free of debt. Of the groups that make up the Aboriginal community, the Métis population has the highest number of self-employed people, at 49.3 per cent. First Nations follow with 45 per cent, while only 1.9 per cent of the Inuit community report being self-employed (CCAB, 2011). In terms of sectors,

18 per cent of Aboriginal entrepreneurs operate in construction, 13 per cent in agriculture, forestry, fishing, hunting, mining, and oil and gas, and 28 per cent in the knowledge-based sectors including professional, technical, scientific, education, health, and social services. Thus, the microcredit program established by Miziwe Biik operates within the framework of both economic constraints and a culture with values and norms that may not be consistent with the mainstream.

Method

Research Design

This is one of twelve case studies undertaken as part of a CURA project on social purpose enterprises among marginalized groups. The case study was conducted as a collaborative partnership between Miziwe Biik (MB), an Aboriginal employment and training organization in Toronto, and the Ted Rogers School of Management at Ryerson University (TRSM). The research design was qualitative and included content analysis of existing reports and records, seven in-depth interviews with clients and staff of Miziwe Biik, one in-depth interview with management at Aboriginal Business Canada (ABC), one in-depth interview with the loan committee of the microcredit program, three in-depth interviews with leading members of the GTA Aboriginal community, and a focus group with participants in the self-employment training program. In total, twelve in-depth interviews and one focus group discussion were completed. We identify the sources of verbatim quotations in the results section by respondent number.

Cultural Context

Although much research has been conducted on Aboriginal communities in Canada, few studies have incorporated Aboriginal methodologies, analysis, or interpretation (Crowshoe, 2005). In order to make this research more meaningful, the team used research techniques and instruments that respected the practices, histories, and experiences of the Aboriginal community. First, we structured the project as a partnership between the Aboriginal community, as represented by Miziwe Biik, and the university (Kenny, 2004). Next, we consulted Cat Kriger, an Aboriginal Elder, seeking insight into traditional teachings, practices, and Aboriginal ways of looking at the world. His guidance, as well as recent scholarship, led us to the concept of the Medicine Wheel as a foundational Aboriginal frame of reference and structure. The Medicine Wheel is a vessel that holds many traditional teachings, both ancient and contemporary; it is a lens through which life experiences are understood and represents the fundamental teachings that guide daily life. While the presentation of the Medicine Wheel can differ among Aboriginal cultures and between Elders, its general structure evokes the cyclical nature of the world – for example, the cycles of day and night, the seasons, and life. It is also a reminder of the interconnectedness of all things, natural and constructed, such as the land, the people, and the four parts of the self – mental, emotional, physical, and spiritual (Loiselle & McKenzie, 2006).

The challenge for the project team was to integrate the powerful teachings of the Medicine Wheel, illustrated in Figure 4.1, with the data gathering and the analytical strategy for the study. The natural cycle of the Medicine Wheel and the Four Directions provided a cultural framework for interpreting the results. By incorporating the teachings shared by the Elder, we can explore the microloan process in a manner that is culturally familiar and relevant to the research participants.

Like the Medicine Wheel, the CURA cultural framework begins in the east. As the east represents, among many things, new life and new beginnings, the research explores the loan application process and the motivation behind it. The southern quadrant of the framework examines the resources available through Miziwe Biik and other service providers that are needed and used by microloan clients. In keeping with the holistic nature of the cultural framework, the resources explored move beyond financial and business matters to address the emotional, physical, and spiritual aspects of the client. In the western quadrant, we study how the microloan clients carry out their work, as well as the challenges that they face and the impact of the microloan on the individual, the family, and the Aboriginal community in Toronto. The final quadrant of the framework, the north, reflects and reassesses the microloan experience and discusses its future direction. This framework underlines the importance of the interconnectedness of the spiritual and material worlds in the Aboriginal world view and the concept of balance among the four elements of self (Loiselle & McKenzie, 2006).

Because we integrated the cultural framework into the research design and used an Aboriginal interviewer, the team believes respondents

Figure 4.1 Medicine Wheel

have been more candid about their attitudes, beliefs, and experiences associated with the microloan program and being part of the Aboriginal community in Canada. Furthermore, the partnership with an Aboriginal institution and the Aboriginal interviewer/interpreter supported our desire to understand the data in culturally relevant terms.

Results

The Eastern Door

The beginning of our understanding and the starting point on the Medicine Wheel is at the Eastern Door – the location of the rising sun, where new life and new beginnings emerge. In the context of the microloan, this includes the factors that motivate respondents to seek a loan, the reasons for seeking a microloan from Miziwe Biik, the uncertainties encountered in making the decision, the entry points and opportunities for getting a loan, and the loan approval process itself.

While the Eastern Door is the location of new beginnings for Aboriginal entrepreneurs, regulatory structures can limit entry points for urban Aboriginal microloan seekers, as the mainstream lending system in Canada is very formal and regulated. In response to the special needs of the Aboriginal community for access to capital, the federal government agency, Aboriginal Business Canada (ABC), and others have set up capital corporations to serve the community. However, as R1 notes, these "were set up in the eighties," before the significant increase in the Aboriginal population in Toronto. So the capital available to Toronto entrepreneurs from these organizations is not proportionate to the population.

The mainstream banking system also may not be accessible to many Aboriginal entrepreneurs because they cannot satisfy the fundamental financial expectations of the institutions. Mainstream lending institutions consider it part of their due diligence to ensure that a satisfactory business plan is in place, that the loan can be secured with other assets, and that the payback is worth the lending effort (transaction costs) because their primary goals are institutional profitability and sustainability. R5, for instance, applied for a loan through Miziwe Biik (MB) because she "needed a chunk of money to secure funding through ABC [Aboriginal Business Canada] and I couldn't go through the bank because I had previously claimed bankruptcy." Furthermore, the cost of transactions for small loans is an issue for potential microlenders, as noted by R2: "There's a lady who makes jewellery, she might make ten thousand in sales; she's more work than the guy looking for a hundred thousand commercial machine." Thus, there is a reluctance to make loans to microbusinesses because relative to the loan size, the transaction costs are greater.

By contrast, MB does not follow the traditional lending practices of the broader banking system; it does not measure the success of the microloan program solely in terms of its ability to be profitable or self-sustaining. Forging social connections and building community are also key goals of the MB microloan program. As R1 explains: "We don't secure it [the loan] with chattel; we don't do a credit check because we know in the Aboriginal community that credit issues are big factors." For this reason, the door to starting a business was opened through Miziwe Biik for R5, who recognized: "I had the worst credit in the world, really bad. So I had to go to Money Mart to get a credit card because sometimes I had to make a purchase online. And somehow I have built up my credit to A1." Like the Eastern Door, Miziwe Biik offers an entry point for Aboriginal entrepreneurs. Although MB only has a 50 per cent repayment record, "we have made a positive difference. I know that half the people have launched businesses that they likely would not have done so if it had not been for us" (R1).

While the goals of Miziwe Biik go beyond profit – and for that reason, it is willing to provide unsecured loans – there are debates within the

Aboriginal community about how far to push this philosophy. R2 states that "business has simple rules, whether you are Chinese, Japanese, red, or white you have to follow certain standards." He further argues: "In terms of Miziwe Biik, they are just casting too wide of a net. Not everyone should be in business. It's not an option for everybody" (R2). In contrast, R1 says: "I think what I have learned even from my employment training days is that it doesn't matter what skills or talents a person has, if they're healthy physically, mentally and emotionally, spiritually, if they are in a good place, they can do anything" (R1). R1 also suggests that the MB program combines economic development with empowerment. "It's much more about building up the community's confidence" (R1).

The scepticism within the Aboriginal community towards mainstream institutions hinders those seeking funding from these institutions or organizations, and thus may block entry points into the business world. As noted earlier, this mistrust is rooted in the colonial and assimilationist policies governing the everyday lives of Aboriginal people in Canada. As one very successful Aboriginal entrepreneur reports:

> I am now paying Industry Canada back the $10,000 they granted to me [without using it], because I just refuse to follow their parameters [they required $4,000 in insurance]. Their program is very inflexible and they have been very condescending to me. Many Elders tell me not to take money from the government and now I have learned my lesson. I would never encourage other people to take grants from the government because of this experience. (R3)

Perhaps this cynicism towards mainstream lenders is a reason why the latest CCAB report (2011) on the Aboriginal business community found that the majority of entrepreneurs (55 per cent) rely mostly on personal savings rather than on business loans or bank credit (17 per cent), government programs (17 per cent), or loans from Aboriginal lending institutions (15 per cent), for both start-up and ongoing financing of their businesses.

Miziwe Biik employs a more collaborative approach to its application process than mainstream lenders, thus increasing accessibility for Aboriginal entrepreneurs. Miziwe Biik is concerned not just about facilitating a successful application, but also about increasing the knowledge and capacity of loan applicants.

It's not cut and dried for us ... to level the playing field to make sure our community members had not only equal access to dollar resources, but to the experience and to the expertise the committee provides. It's not just an application put through a computer and scored and then declined or passed ... if we have questions we go back to the client ... one because we feel the application needs to be strengthened and the other part is to do a little bit of education ... to teach those entrepreneurs what other people are looking at. (R10)

The Miziwe Biik approval process is modelled after that of the Canadian Youth Business Foundation (CYBF). As R1 indicates: "we've recreated their process in miniature ... we conduct the initial interview ... based very much on the CYBF questions and score out of about 39 ... We are looking at ... does this person's idea make sense? Do they seem like the sort of person who can pull it off or are they doing anything already to realize their dream?" Nevertheless, MB is cautious about making loans: "MB didn't just want to have a pool of capital available for anyone to apply for it ... I think it would be irresponsible to just give money away, if we didn't think it [the business idea] would work" (R10). This is in line with a central value of many Aboriginal communities: not setting up their children (or adults) for failure.

Miziwe Biik makes loans to individual applicants rather than to groups. "Peer-lending programs just don't work in the community, not for our community anyway" (R1). This may be because many Aboriginal people do not identify with their culture. In less developed countries, where the peer-lending model is the most common feature of a microcredit program, the strong social ties of the community provide a powerful mechanism for ensuring repayment (Kibria, Lee, & Owen, 2003; Portes & Sensenbrenner, 1993). A recent Environics Institute survey (2010) found that 40 per cent of Aboriginal people living in Toronto feel that they belong to a mostly non-Aboriginal community, 27 per cent to a mostly Aboriginal community, and 29 per cent equally to Aboriginal and non-Aboriginal communities. Our respondents echo this feeling of being disconnected from their culture: "I was never born on the reserve ... we didn't know our culture" (R4).

However, another perspective is that the norms, values, and culture of the Aboriginal community are the reason peer lending does not work. As Brant (1990) explains, noninterference is a very strong behavioural norm of North American Aboriginal communities. This norm promotes positive interpersonal relationships by viewing any attempt to persuade or influence another person's thoughts or behaviour as very undesirable. Thus, a peer-lending model for an Aboriginal micro-lending program directly contradicts the norms and values of the community.

The repayment options are one of the features that underline MB's focus on outcomes other than profit: "It's a fixed rate ... we don't want to complicate it ... people know what the payments are going to be every month and for how long; we make a few hundred dollars per loan, but we aren't in it really for the money" (R1). "We do look at ... how does this business fit in the Aboriginal community ... is it going to enhance the life primarily of the entrepreneur, but will it [also] contribute to the overall life of the Aboriginal community in terms of economic development?" (R1).

Similar to other microcredit programs in Canada, the MB program emphasizes skills development and training. "We have a small business certificate course and you have to, in order to apply for the loan, either have taken our small business certificate course or have some sort of equivalent experience ... It is really a boot camp on getting your business up and running and understanding what goes into it ... and there is also one-on-one coaching" (R1).

In keeping with the Medicine Wheel theme of balance and interconnectedness, although the loan application focuses on business needs, the applicants have to balance the start-up requirements of their businesses with the other financial pressures in their lives. While some use the loan money solely for business-oriented activities ("The money was used to register the business, to place my first order for ingredients, bottles, [and] everything to get started" [R12]), others use it to relieve financial hardship in other parts of their lives ("I was in a breakup with my spouse and he had left our home and left me in arrears of rent ... so that is where I had to put the loan money" [R8]).

Balance in life includes more than just being able to keep up with financial obligations, according to loan holders, and therefore personal issues can be barriers to business start-ups. "Emotionally, I wasn't ready [to go into my own business]. I had a lot of family crises happening that didn't leave me emotionally strong to be able to venture out on my own, to be able to do the footwork that was needed" (R8).

Thus, it appears that through the Eastern Door, Miziwe Biik is able to support urban Aboriginal entrepreneurs in their new beginnings by understanding their particular needs and challenges, by focusing on outcomes that are communal and developmental, and by mutually re-inforcing attitudes and beginning processes.

The Southern Door

In the southern quadrant, the Medicine Wheel framework focuses on the resources required and challenges faced during the early growth phase of any endeavour. The framework considers the resources other than the loan itself that are necessary to achieve success. Some of these resources were available to the microloan recipients, while others were identified as missing, which resulted in hardship.

Many loan recipients identified being able to access additional financial support within Miziwe Biik's network as an important resource. As R10 explains,

> Miziwe Biik partners with ABC ... We direct individuals to ABC because there are grant dollars available to them. We also work with them to build an application to approach a bank or financial institution ... If they wanted to go outside the GTA [to build a business or expand this business], we would link them up with other resources like Wabateque, Nishnawbe Aski Development Fund, Tecumseh ... other organizations that do similar work.

In addition, Miziwe Biik "also has the Toronto Aboriginal Business Association, so there is a networking piece for business people in the city, to give them a chance to come out and meet face-to-face with each other, share some ideas, maybe see some synergies" (R10).

In terms of their challenges, respondents describe having experienced a lack of trust, lack of confidence, and fear. Aboriginal borrowers do not necessarily feel that they are part of the mainstream. As R8 explains: "I wanted an Aboriginal agency to help me with my business plan ... and I didn't have a good experience with the mainstream planning business side of it." Some of this lack of trust is rooted in history. "Aboriginal people have many barriers to starting businesses. Some are the same barriers that other entrepreneurs face. Some are legal preclusions only Aboriginal people face due to the Indian Act" (R2). R10 reiterates the same issue. "We've not been well served by institutions and there is a reluctance ... to have to do it. As a result, I think people do shy away from approaching some of the big financial institutions or leveraging ABC or getting involved in [AANDC] because there is a lack of trust."

Respondents also acknowledge that a lack of knowledge or business skills can limit success. "The problem is when you start a business, few people appreciate how much work is involved" (R7). Recognizing the challenge is intertwined with fearing the future. As R13 points out: "A lot of women have difficulties following through ... scared they can't complete it or scared what's to come after they complete it." R6 expresses it in terms of achieving goals: "fear of standing out ... fear of success."

Other challenges have to do with how money is viewed. R6 explains: "They don't know how to handle money; they don't know how to save a little for themselves because they weren't trained ... they are not taught how to handle money ... Sometimes people come with fantastic business ideas and they're embarrassed or they refuse to make money from this great idea." R2 suggests that this view of money might originate from living on a reserve. "For all intents and purposes ... you go to the central bureau to get your 'whatever,' and then you go away with it."

R1 sees the situation more positively and suggests that "Aboriginal people are just trying to get themselves recalibrated and back into the game." This separateness from the mainstream culture, regardless of the complexity of causes, makes the Aboriginal borrower quite different from the typical borrower in the less developed countries where microloan programs are more prevalent. In those locations, borrowers are more collective in outlook and more homogeneous with respect to language, ethnicity, and social class (Haque & Harbin, 2009). The borrowers in developed countries tend to be individualistic and ethnically and socially diverse (Kibria et al., 2003), but this does not describe the Aboriginal borrower in Canada. Aboriginal Canadians represent an ethnic group that does not share the norms and values of the mainstream, yet must conform to the mainstream culture in order to access capital from Canadian lending institutions. This leads to tension and stress among Aboriginal borrowers, and MB responds to that by attempting to balance respect for the culture with fiscal accountability.

In contrast, there are Aboriginal lending institutions that do not have the same optimistic expectations of their community members. "You get the unfortunate impression from some of those people that when they come, we are giving them money to live on. We are not giving them money to live on; we are giving them money to develop their business, and if their business doesn't go, we ask for the money back. They don't seem to understand that part of it" (R2). Several respondents talk about the Indian Act and residential schools as factors that have affected how Aboriginal people feel about themselves, their culture, and their abilities. "I was never born on the reserve. However, it has affected us terribly; we didn't know our culture. Many things are really hidden ... it is very important to know your culture and understand who you are and where you come from" (R4). In contrast, some feel that the Indian Act and the residential schools disaster "have nothing to do with business ... that is a crutch now" (R2).

Consistent with the holistic and progressive nature of the Medicine Wheel, the importance of integrating broader cultural elements into the microlending experience is mentioned often by loan holders. Aboriginal borrowers continue to run up against mainstream business practices that are different from their own experiences and are searching for appropriate routes to success. They recognize that to be successful "we have to branch out ... You've got to go beyond your own community to be successful" (R10). However, as R8 points out, it is a learning process: "We have a system here where there are no receipts ... Here is your money and that's it ... The mainstream wants to see a portfolio. They want you to sit before a committee before they actually accept your wares. [In] the Native community, most of the time you just phone somebody up and they put your name on a list, and you are set up ... You pay your money when you get there ... so it is a lot different ... to go mainstream."

In other words, the participants seem to be looking for culturally familiar and appropriate ways of approaching and dealing with the growth challenges of their enterprises and their life journeys through the southern quadrant. "I would like Aboriginal people to be training Aboriginal people about how to run a business. It makes things more real. When a white woman comes to tell us about her business and how she does it full-time, I just think she has a husband behind her who is working full-time and giving her health benefits. It's not my reality" (R3). "We never did anything traditional like use a sharing circle or doing a smudge or doing a visioning quest. Something like that would have been nice" (R3).

The Western Door

The Western Door reflects the overall work, the results of the work, and the holistic impact of the loan on the individual, the family, the community, and society. For the most part, Aboriginal borrowers are starting a business to meet basic needs. As R13 states: "They are not in it to get rich or to go buy a mansion or buy big fancy cars. They are just in it to feed their families and to survive."

Despite these modest goals, several respondents speak of much broader and deeper consequences. R3 points out the positive impact the experience has had for him individually. "Having my own business helped me overcome the intergenerational effects of the residential school system, the '60s scoop, and the foster care system. It allowed me to create a bond with my young son, so that he will grow strong and be proud of his identity as a Native person." Others also indicate that this has been instrumental for cultural identity. "I have been doing a lot of powwows, which I had never really gone to or known anything [about] prior to this ... I grew up in a small white town. I didn't know much about Aboriginal culture ... other than [that] my mom was Native. I have gotten more in touch with the Native community because of that, because of the business and because of Miziwe.Biik and because of the powwows" (R12). Several mention that when they are successful business owners "the community benefits because I can be a role model for some people" (R3), and their family receives benefits that include "inspiration ... my family is really proud" (R4). On a more practical level, Aboriginal business owners are creating jobs for the community. R3 "had several Aboriginal subcontractors, including a homeless person ... I regularly donate a portion of my business income to a charity that improves the lives of First Nations children."

Not all of the impacts have been positive, however – some respondents have been unable to make their loan payments. "The payback of the loan has not been happening. I had to decide if my son gets the money or Miziwe Biik gets the money" (R8). Like this client, several respondents mention personal as opposed to business challenges that negatively – sometimes ruinously – affected their businesses. Family health issues and marriage break-ups often siphoned off the funds that were needed to support the business itself. Other times, poor or questionable business decisions precluded business success. For one client, trusting the wrong supplier led to business failure, even though the business idea itself was viable. "I have been able to make the first few loan payments ... [but] I have defaulted on it ... In the first four months, I think I had close to fifty stores carrying my product ... then I ran into problems with the co-packer messing up the product" (R12).

A holistic Western Door perspective recognizes that success and positive impact might entail more than "the loan being paid off" (R10). As R10 explains, "To me, success is watching that small business grow, being able to hire staff ... being able to take the business from micro-business to the next plateau ... job creation and profit ... [and] giv[ing] back in the form of creating employment." Those borrowers who successfully paid back their loans clearly gained and contributed more than the simple success of their businesses. Even some of those who defaulted may have learned valuable business lessons or contributed to their communities in the money and effort that they did expend. Entrepreneurship research suggests that many ultimately successful entrepreneurs experience several "failures" before hitting on a successful formula. The lessons learned by the defaulters and their community may yet bear fruit in subsequent activities. The important result of looking at the impact of the Western Door is to keep in mind both the holistic results that are possible and the longer-term perspective that this framework adopts.

The Northern Door

Pushing our perspective even more broadly into the northern quadrant presents the opportunity to reflect on and reassess the value and challenges of the MB program. In terms of the loan process, some see microlending as going beyond helping an individual. As R1 expresses: "Aboriginal goals in terms of profit are different than what we see in other communities. It is about benefiting the commonwealth of Aboriginal people in that community." "It's the ripple that resonates throughout the community, and we want to see positive energy run through the community" (R10). In other words, seeing the loan program in more holistic and broader terms reflects the greater community-building aspects of the program. In a very real sense, there is the feeling that the program builds community, particularly community capacity – or that it has the potential to do so. It leverages and integrates aspects of the GTA's developed economic system, with a rich and nuanced understanding of the Aboriginal community's developing economic nature. As such, it provides a bridge to the mainstream for the Aboriginal entrepreneurial community.

At the same time, reflecting on more practical aspects of the process, we heard (and can see) ways to strengthen and enhance these impacts. In particular, respondents pointed to ways in which MB could be even more community focused. For example, entrepreneurs would like to see more support from the broader Aboriginal community and its institutions. "They could have hired me to do training for the business course since I am living proof that businesses can work, but I've never been asked to come and do this ... Often we work in silos in the Aboriginal community, and we don't come together often enough to learn from one another and to figure out how our work and aspirations link together" (R3). "There's no central meeting place for Aboriginal business in Toronto" (R3). Likewise, respondents suggested that MB should "hire mentors and role models to work in the agency. We need networking sessions" (R3). "Harder screening. More one on one" (R2). "Mentorship has to be augmented because when I talk to you in private, it's a lot easier than talking to you in a crowd" (R7).

Even successful entrepreneurs have crises of confidence and express fears about maintaining their business success: "Moments of doubt or fear ... even now. I mean I had my phone ringing off the hook today. I had seventeen messages when I checked at lunchtime. I have major companies calling me. But every day I live in fear. Not fear, but you don't know what tomorrow is going to bring ... you know, if this doesn't work, what do I do?" (R4). "When you are selling your stuff ... sometimes you have a good day, and sometimes you have a bad day, and you have to have capital for the bad days" (R8).

Reflecting and reassessing is not limited to loan holders, as Miziwe Biik is also considering its future. Respondents suggest that MB continue on its current path, but expand its efforts, and build more bridges between the urban Aboriginal community and the mainstream economic system. Furthermore, participants state quite explicitly that they need more help with intracommunity bonding. Through one-on-one mentoring and intracommunity role modelling, respondents hope that programs like MB's will develop the kinds of social capital networks that Canadian policy and structures too often preclude.

Discussion and Conclusions

We attempted to push beyond the classic methods of research investigation to examine and understand the MB program using the traditional Aboriginal Medicine Wheel framework. This framework of four directional factors represents a more holistic and culturally appropriate lens through which to view the microloan program. In particular, we see that entry into entrepreneurship for Aboriginal loan seekers is often closed, or at the very least inaccessible, due to mainstream structures, attitudes, and expectations. Through the MB program, this Eastern Door opens the way to Aboriginal entrepreneurship by connecting with and supporting the Aboriginal community, by understanding their particular needs and challenges, by focusing on outcomes that are communal and developmental, and by mutually reinforcing attitudes and beginning processes. This MB program recognizes the importance of integrating elements relevant to a developing and marginalized community (such as lack of good credit, lack of skills, lack of experience, and high transaction costs) within a developed economic system where strong social capital bonds (and communal support networks) do not exist.

Further, the southern quadrant of the Medicine Wheel allows us to better understand the many resources needed to attain success after the initial microloan. These include accessing further infusions of capital, developing business skills such as marketing, human resources, finance, and accounting, and supporting family and community.

As we look to the Western Door's assessment of results and impacts, we are pushed to adopt a more holistic perspective – one that recognizes that success and impact may be more than return on financial investment or a loan being repaid. The outcomes include financial success for some, but also there are broader communal effects: skill development, employment opportunities, communal attitudes, self-confidence, and perhaps a willingness to try again.

Finally, the Medicine Wheel's reassessment at the Northern Door provides useful information regarding what is working and what can be improved in the MB microloan program. Reflection suggests that the MB's role as a bridge into the mainstream economic system is important for the Aboriginal community. For some, the microloan experience awakened a connection to their roots and a pride in their Aboriginal heritage.

These results bring to mind research on bridging and bonding capacities of different ethnic communities in Canada, in particular, Berger, Foster, and Meinhard (2008). The purpose of that study was to investigate the relationship between bridging and bonding kinds of civic engagement and indicators of social and economic success. The researchers found that the more homogeneous an ethnic group's social network (i.e., the more developed the intragroup bonding), the more limited was socio-economic adaptation in terms of acquisition of language skills and access to job opportunities and other types of economic resources. In addition, among the strongly bonded groups, there were lower perceived levels of social well-being, as measured by feelings of satisfaction, comfort, and trust in others. In contrast, ethnic communities with higher levels of bridging to the mainstream, as measured by social connections outside their ethnic community, scored higher both on measures of social and economic success. This same study revealed that the Aboriginal population has the lowest levels of both ethnic bonding and mainstream bridging. This marginalized position, in which there were few intracommunity supports and few intercommunity connections, is also associated with the weakest socio-economic outcomes. While the causes of these communal challenges are many, and are largely known, their remedy is not apparent. However, even limited success – in terms of dollars loaned and repaid or number of borrowers in the MB microloan program – suggests that it may be an interesting and valuable mechanism to consider in this context. The MB microloan program appears to provide both valuable bridges to the mainstream financial community in the GTA and bonding opportunities for the Aboriginal entrepreneurial community.

Thus, as a case study in social enterprise among marginalized groups, we see the MB microloan program as a major success, as it provides social and economic benefits for both the individual entrepreneur and the broader Aboriginal community. On an individual basis, we see increased self-esteem and confidence through the establishment of a credit rating. Respondents report a deeper connection to the Aboriginal community and more pride in their Aboriginal roots, which they are anxious to pass on to the next generation. This program also has led to desperately needed bridging to the mainstream community, at the same time that it supports and develops critical social capital capacity within this marginalized community. Economically, individuals have greater financial independence and stability, and small business course participants have learned useful skills. On a community level, new businesses are established to serve the Aboriginal and the broader community, as well as to create job opportunities for Aboriginal people.

Afterword

The future of the microloan program at Miziwe Biik is in some doubt. In August 2012, the program manager left for another employment opportunity. His leadership, vision, and contribution will be sorely missed by both the organization and the community. The lack of bench strength in the Toronto Aboriginal community is an ongoing challenge. In mid-November 2012, a new manager was finally hired, and he may revive the purpose of the fund. One option for the new manager to consider was previously discussed by the leaders of Miziwe Biik: a partnership with Alterna Savings. This collaboration would give the fund an administrative backbone as well as provide ongoing coaching to clients, thus building capacity in the program and the community.

REFERENCES

Aboriginal Affairs and Northern Development Canada (AANDC). (2008). *Toward a new federal framework for Aboriginal Economic Development.* Ottawa, ON: Government of Canada.

Aliu, L., Cosentino, J., & Panasyuk, B. (2009, September). Highlights of existing microcredit programs. Report to the Black Creek Community Capacity Building Project – Microcredit Working Group, York University.

Berger, I., Foster, M.K., & Meinhard, A.G. (2008). Civic engagement, social cohesion and integration in Canada. International Conference on Economic Development and Competitiveness - Canada and India, S.N.D.T. Women's University Mumbai, India.

Brant, C. (1990). Native ethics and rules of behavior. *Canadian Journal of Psychiatry, 35,* 534–539.

Caldwell, D., & Hunt, P. (1998). *Aboriginal businesses: Characteristics and strategies for growth.* Ottawa, ON: Industry Canada.

Canadian Council for Aboriginal Business (CCAB). (2005). Community and commerce: a survey of Aboriginal economic development corporations. In partnership with Environics Research Group.

Canadian Council for Aboriginal Business (CCAB). (2011). Promise and prosperity: the Aboriginal business survey. In partnership with Environics Research Group.

Chansonneuve, D. (2005). *Reclaiming connections: Understanding residential school trauma among Aboriginal people.* Ottawa, ON: The Aboriginal Healing Foundation.

Coyle, M., Wehrell, R. & MacDonald, J (2006, November). Small is beautiful, big is necessary; Canada's commercial and cooperative answers to the global challenge of microfinance access. Presentation to the Global Microcredit Summit, Halifax, Canada.

Crowshoe, C. (2005). *Sacred ways of life: Traditional knowledge.* Prepared for the First Nations Centre, National Aboriginal Health Organization. Retrieved from http://www.naho.ca/documents/fnc/english/2005_traditional_knowledge_toolkit.pdf

Dua, V., Subbiah, S., & Visano, B.S. (2007, August). Microcredit programs: Key characteristics and design considerations. Report to the Black Creek

Community Capacity Building Project – Microcredit Working Group, York University.

Environics Institute. (2010). Urban Aboriginal Peoples Study. Toronto Report.

Financial Consumer Agency of Canada. (2005, March). Public experience with financial services and awareness of the FCAC.

Frankiewicz, C. (2001, April). Calmeadow Metrofund: A Canadian experiment in sustainable microfinance. Unpublished manuscript.

Guimond, E., Robitaille, R., & Senecal, S. (2009). Aboriginal populations in Canadian cities: Why are they growing so fast? *Canadian Issues, 38*(2), 11–18.

Haque, M.A., & Harbin, J.L. (2009). Micro credit: A different approach to traditional banking: Empowering the poor. *Academy of Banking Studies Journal, 8*(1), 1–13.

Jaccoud, M., & Brassard, R. (2003). The marginalization of Aboriginal women in Montreal. In D. Newhouse & E. Peters (Eds.), *Not strangers in these parts: Urban Aboriginal peoples* (pp. 131–145). Canada: Policy Research Initiative.

Jacobs, B., & Williams, A.J. (2008). Legacy of residential schools: Missing and murdered Aboriginal women. In M.B. Castellano, L. Archibald, & M. DeGagne (Eds.), *From truth to reconciliation: Transforming the legacy of residential schools* (pp. 11–40). Ottawa, ON: The Aboriginal Healing Foundation.

Kenny, C. (2004, October). A holistic framework for Aboriginal policy research. Status of Women's Policy Research Fund.

Kibria, N., Lee, S., & Owen, R. (2003). Peer lending groups and success: a case study of Working Capital. *Journal of Developmental Entrepreneurship, 8*(1), 41–58.

La Prairie, C. (1994). *Seen but not heard: Native people in the inner city*. Ottawa, ON: Department of Justice.

Loiselle, M., & McKenzie, L. (2006, May 27). An Aboriginal contribution to social work. Workshop conducted at First North American Conference on Spirituality and Social Work, University of Waterloo, Waterloo, Ontario.

Monchalin, L. (2010). Canadian Aboriginal peoples victimization, offending and its prevention: Gathering the evidence. *Crime Prevention and Community Safety, 12*(2), 119–132. http://dx.doi.org/10.1057/cpcs.2009.23

Portes, A., & Sensenbrenner, J. (1993). Embeddedness and immigration: notes on the social determinants of economic action. *American Journal of Sociology, 98*(6), 1320–1350. http://dx.doi.org/10.1086/230191

Reynolds, C., & Novak, C. (2011, May). Low income entrepreneurs and their access to financing in Canada, especially in the province of Quebec/City of Montreal. Unpublished manuscript.

Richardson, M. (2009). Increasing microlending potential in the United States through a strategic approach to regulatory reform. *Journal of Corporation Law, 34*(3), 923–942.

Rubach, M.J., Bradley, D.B., III, & Brown, J.E. (2010). The determinants of the success of microlending: a comparison of Iraq and the United States. *International Journal of Entrepreneurship, 14*, 59–70.

Sisco, A., & Stewart, N. (2009, December). True to their visions – 10 successful Aboriginal businesses. Conference Board of Canada.

Statistics Canada (2009). 2006 Aboriginal population profile for Toronto. Retrieved from www.statcan.gc.ca/pub/89-638-x/2009001/article/10825-eng.htm

Visano, B.S. (2008). Different and unequal: Payday loans and microcredit in Canada. *Journal of Economic Asymmetries, 5*(1), 109–123.

Wesley-Esquimaux, C.C., & Smolewski, M. (2004). *Historic trauma and Aboriginal healing*. Ottawa, ON: The Aboriginal Healing Foundation.

5 Groupe Convex: Measuring Its Impact[1]

USHNISH SENGUPTA, CAROLINE ARCAND,
AND ANN ARMSTRONG

J'aime mon travail parce que je sens qu'on a besoin de moi, ici.
(I love my job because I feel that I am needed here.)

Jennifer Cyr, Groupe Convex

Groupe Convex (GC) is an innovative non-profit organization under which there is a group of diversified social purpose enterprises that employ people of various abilities from the rural community of Prescott-Russell in eastern Ontario, including people who are at great risk of unemployment. The term "convex" was selected because when individuals look into a convex mirror, they are magnified. The organization similarly aims to magnify their employees' self-esteem by helping them to assume a valued role at work and to develop and maintain significant relationships with other members of their community. The intention of GC is to help the employees to become active and equal members of society.

The purpose of this case study is to apply a social return on investment framework to one of the social purpose enterprises within GC and to try to understand the utility of that approach for an organization like GC. This chapter first describes GC in more detail, then discusses social return on investment (SROI), and finally applies SROI to GC.

Groupe Convex (GC)

GC is a network of eight social enterprises employing over 160 people, 70 per cent of whom face serious obstacles on the job market. Most of GC's targeted employees have an intellectual disability. The employees work at one of the following businesses: a printing shop; a café; an antique refurbishing shop; a woodshop; a three-location transfer site for recyclable materials; a packaging and assembly facility; a service business offering indoor and outdoor maintenance, moving, and painting services; and a farm labour pool that operates vegetable stands in various villages.

GC is located in the Prescott-Russell region of eastern Ontario, which is about sixty kilometres due east of Ottawa. It is an area where French is the primary language. The Prescott-Russell region has a disproportionate number of individuals with intellectual disabilities. While the reasons are unclear, it is a pressing social challenge that GC and others address (EOHU, 2009; Ministère des Services Sociaux et Communautaires, 2009).

GC's focus is on providing good employment for people with intellectual disabilities, who are frequently unable to participate in the workforce. According GC's executive director, Caroline Arcand, and according as well to various reports, it is particularly hard to secure employment in the Prescott-Russell region: the community's unemployment rate is high, and the rural part of the community lacks public transportation (Broad & Saunders, 2008). The unemployment rate in one community, Hawkesbury, is 9.9 per cent,[2] and the unemployment rate for individuals with intellectual disabilities is significantly higher than that of the general population (Smith & Butterworth, 2009).

GC was created by another social organization, Valoris, which is a multiservice agency for children and adults of Prescott-Russell that assists adults with intellectual disabilities. Valoris's leaders came to believe that a social service agency was ill suited to create employment for its clients. Valoris meets its mandate to provide day activities to adults with disabilities by subsidizing each individual who is employed by Groupe Convex (Valoris, 2011).

GC's approach is grounded in and supported by the social role valorization theory developed by Wolf Wolfensberger of Syracuse University (Wolfensberger, 2000). Wolfensberger was a pioneer in recognizing the social value of individuals with disabilities, and he promoted the use of typical and valued social opportunities (i.e., social roles) as a way of putting an end to their social exclusion. His work contributed to the establishment of community services and was invoked in support of deinstitutionalization. Osburn (1998) goes on to note that the major goal of social role valorization is to create or support socially valued roles for people in their society. If someone holds socially valued roles, that person is highly likely to be granted from other people the opportunities for good things in life (Osburn, 1998, paragraph 2).

In a moving tribute, Etmanski (2011) notes that Wolfensberger's approach

> led to a conceptual breakthrough on the importance of challenging cultural stereotypes about people with disabilities if you want to make profound change. Otherwise your change will rest on shaky ground and become merely tactical. That's why we no longer, for the most part, call adults with disabilities, children. If you want people to act like [adults], treat them accordingly. (Etmanski, 2011, paragraph 4)

GC describes itself as follows: "A mission based on true values. A socio-economic engine. Devoted workers. Affirmative enterprises" (Arcand, 2007). GC is a non-profit organization created in 2004 that creates and fosters social purpose enterprises (see Chapter 1). Not only is GC an employer, it is a catalyst for change. It forces the community to see those with intellectual disabilities not as clients or as second-class citizens but as equal and contributing members of the community. GC is committed to generating work of value, which is described by the organization as team-based, fairly compensated work that occurs in a stimulating environment, recognizes good employees, and provides them with responsibilities and rights as well as opportunities for skill development (Groupe Convex, n.d.).

The social purpose enterprises that form GC adhere to the following important principles in their overall operation:

- A number of jobs are created for targeted employees;
- A number of positions are filled by ordinary people who are not targeted by the social mission per se, and there is a positive influence of these average and above-average people on targeted employees;
- Opportunities are provided to develop skills and knowledge;
- Employees are able to contribute to the best of their abilities;
- Work areas are stimulating;
- Working conditions respond to the needs and capacities of each targeted employee;
- Work involves tasks that allow the dignity of risk while being within a safe environment;
- Functions are held that provide opportunities for employees to interact with ordinary people and stakeholders, including customers, other employees, suppliers, walk-in clients, business partners, and so on.

GC has measured its impact on a variety of indicators. For example, in 2010, it concluded that it had positively affected the community on several dimensions ranging from economic capacity to learning (Arcand, 2010). However, GC does not currently monetize its quantifiable social impacts and costs into a SROI metric. GC would like to adopt a method for determining a quantified SROI of its social purpose enterprises. Ideally, the SROI method should provide a bottom-line number that can be published – for example, for every dollar invested to support a social enterprise, the government gets a return on its investment of approximately "X" per cent. The end goal is to use the SROI to determine, for the information of funders and other stakeholders, the impact of every dollar invested into GC. The results of the SROI would enable the organization to grow in terms of its capacity to maintain, support, diversify, and start new enterprises.

Social Return on Investment

While there are many formulations and definitions of social return on investment (SROI), we favour the one developed by Lingane and Olsen (2004). It is clear, and it builds from the better-known metric return on investment. They define SROI as

> a term originating from Return on Investment (ROI), as used by traditional investors. It describes the social impact of a business or non-profit's operations in dollar terms, relative to the investment required to create that impact and exclusive of its financial return to investors. (p. 118)

> *Social* – This term refers to all of the non-investor stakeholders affected by business: individuals, employees, communities, and society. These stakeholders may also be described as those affected by market externalities. (p. 117)

A method for calculating social return on investment in the context of a social purpose enterprise was first developed in 2000 by Roberts Enterprise Development Fund (www.redf.org), a California-based fund that makes long-term grants to social enterprises. The use of SROI has now spread across multiple organizations, and the Foundation Center website on "Tools and Resources for Assessing Social Impact" (http://trasi.foundationcenter.org/) lists over sixty tools. A number of classification schemes that delineate the different ROI methods have been developed (Clark et al., 2004; Mass & Liket, 2011). In selecting a method for performing a SROI analysis, a simplified classification scheme was used that compares related methods along time, vertical, and horizontal dimensions. The time dimension indicates the long-term versus short-term nature of the method. Some methods are useful in shorter-term applications, while other methods are more useful over a longer-term application. The vertical dimension of SROI indicates the completeness of the method. A vertically integrated method is more useful than a method that requires additional supplemental analyses. Vertical integration in the context of SROI methods indicates the level of dependence or independence each method has from other related activities. The horizontal dimension of comparing SROI methods indicates the applicability across different sectors and subsectors of the social economy. A method with a broad range of applications is more useful than a method with a narrow range of applications.

According to the dimensions of analysis presented, the most vertically complete SROI method is the UK SROI method (Nicholls, Lawlor, Neitzert, & Goodspeed, 2009), which includes a stakeholder analysis as well as a theory of change analysis. The UK SROI method includes sufficient time-factor calculations since it is an expansion of the REDF model, which includes these factors. The UK SROI method has been applied to a number of projects. Some examples have been published on the SROI Network's website (www.thesroinetwork.org).

Nicholls suggests the following stages for carrying out an SROI analysis (Nicholls et al., 2009):

1. Establishing scope and identifying key stakeholders;
2. Mapping outcomes;
3. Evidencing outcomes and giving them a value;
4. Establishing impact;
5. Calculating the SROI;
6. Reporting, using, and embedding.

As the guidelines make clear, calculating an accurate and meaningful SROI is not an easy task. Further, it is important to note that there are limitations to the SROI methodology. There will be some benefits that are important to stakeholders but cannot be monetized. Determining SROI remains more an art than a science, and it is important that any caveats are stated in the reporting. (Sample SROI analyses are demonstrated in subsequent sections of this case study.)

One of the dangers of SROI is that people may focus on monetization without following the rest of the process, which is crucial to proving and improving the calculation. There is no external accreditation, and no brand or mark is available. SROI can be relatively time intensive the first time it is deployed by an organization, because an organization might not be able to easily access some information. Some outcomes and impacts (e.g., increased self-esteem or improved family relationships) cannot easily be given a monetary value. The following are some possible outputs of completing an SROI analysis: a stakeholder analysis; a well-defined value chain of inputs and activities; a quantifiable monetary value; a comparative ranking of different projects; and a comparison of risks and rewards for different investment options.

SROI in Practice at Recycle Action

Recycle Action (RA) is one of the social purpose enterprises in the GC portfolio. RA is a recent initiative for GC and is the largest collection site for recyclable materials in the area. GC bid for and won a multi-year contract to handle municipal recycling for five towns. Recyclable materials collected include the Blue Box materials, paper products, plastics, metal products, and electronics. Recyclable material is sorted, processed, packaged, and shipped for additional processing at RA. One indication of the quality of RA's work is that it has been recognized by the Ontario Electronic Waste Recovery program.

RA is used here to demonstrate an SROI process because of the substantial financial investment required to start and operate the business. RA is GC's largest capital investment, which included bank financing. RA required long-term investment in land and building infrastructure through community partners and capital investment for the acquisition and replacement of equipment. Finally, RA is currently the largest employer among GC's businesses.

Recycle Action enhances the portfolio of GC businesses by creating new and different opportunities for employment of individuals with intellectual disabilities. GC is able to further its mission of social role valorization though meaningful work by offering a broad range of opportunities, from conveyor-paced work such as sorting recyclables to more individual-paced work such as recycling books and documents or operating the press and the styrofoam densifier. GC is able to find work that is appropriate for a person's ability, and RA is an integral part of the network of businesses and serves to broaden the portfolio of work opportunities. RA also enables the employment of additional individuals who otherwise would be unemployed. The assumption behind making available the opportunity to work and socialize with different types of coworkers is that it benefits individuals with intellectual disabilities through normalizing their work environments; as well, it increases valorization through allowing for interaction with other coworkers who previously may have had little contact with individuals who have intellectual disabilities.

Scope of Analysis

According to the process outlined by Nicholls et al. (2009), the first step in SROI analysis is a delineation of scope and a stakeholder analysis. Scope can include multiple dimensions such as organizational boundaries, geography, and time horizon.

Organizational Scope

As a subsidiary business of GC, RA benefits from the centralized services provided by GC. These include management accounting services, as well as classroom training for managers and employees. Both the costs and benefits stemming from corporate services provided by GC to RA should be included in SROI calculations.

Geographical Scope

As an environmental service, the benefits of RA's collection and processing of recyclable materials extends beyond the simple geographical boundaries of the collection area. For example, there may be secondary benefits to processors downstream from RA and tertiary environmental benefits. Since environmental benefits are difficult to calculate accurately, the geographical boundaries of analysis are assumed to be limited to the Prescott-Russell region.

Time Horizon

The time horizon is assumed to be ten years. The capital invested in RA is anticipated to lead to a positive return on investment after the first few years. As the operation matures and costs stabilize, there is an expected increase in both financial and social return on investment.

Stakeholder Analysis

RA interacts with the following stakeholders: individuals with intellectual disabilities (employees), Valoris (social service agency), family members of employees, local businesses, the municipal government, the regional government (a combination of eight municipalities), the provincial Ministry of Environment, the provincial Ministry of Community and Social Services, federal government departments such as Human Resources and Skills Development Canada, citizens, and schools.

The Table 5.1 on pages 106–7 summarizes the stakeholder benefits.

Sample SROI Calculation

Table 5.1 presents a complete list of stakeholders with projected qualitative benefits for each of the stakeholders. Selected quantitative benefits for a subset of stakeholders are analysed in this section. The following is a sample SROI calculation for demonstration purposes. Assumptions are made wherever the data are not available, and therefore the numbers used for calculation are examples and not necessarily factual statements.

To determine the social return on investment, the main elements to be considered are the quantifiable investments and returns for the *major* stakeholders. The social return on investment for following stakeholders is presented below:

- Valoris (social service agency)
- Municipality (Hawkesbury)
- Families of individuals with intellectual disabilities
- Individuals with intellectual disabilities

Valoris Social Investment Calculation

As identified in the stakeholder analysis, the social service agency Valoris is one of the major stakeholders of Groupe Convex and Recycle Action. Valoris makes a direct financial investment through subsidizing the wages of targeted GC employees who are also clients of Valoris. Valoris provides a direct financial contribution to GC since it is the most cost-effective solution to achieving its mission for the targeted employees, allowing Valoris to reallocate remaining funds to complementary programs for individual needs that are not met by GC. GC utilizes the

Table 5.1 Stakeholder Benefits

Stakeholder	Stakeholder Benefits
Employees	1. Greater financial independence 2. Higher level of self-confidence 3. Increased social network 4. Development of social skills 5. Development of job skills 6. Public-speaking roles 7. Valorizing social role as employee rather than client 8. Ownership in the success of a business 9. Increased role in environmental stewardship
Valoris	1. Increased quality of life for clients, including reduction of potential harmful situations through employment at GC 2. Ability to meet the mandate of valorizing individuals with intellectual disabilities 3. Ability to provide services in a cost-effective manner, i.e., because GC earns market revenues, contracting out to GC costs less than providing the same services in house
Family members of employees	1. Greater respect for individuals with intellectual disabilities on the part of the community 2. Confidence that family members are treated with respect and given responsibility in the workplace 3. Ability to work rather than needing to stay at home as a concerned parent or caregiver 4. Reduction in family members' health issues due to improvement in overall mental health 5. Pride in family members being recognized publicly, e.g., in newspaper articles on social businesses 6. Greater financial flexibility for parents and family 7. Peace of mind that family members are in a safe and healthy work environment 8. Increased aspirations that family members can evolve and may eventually advance in their careers despite their disabilities
Local Businesses	1. Availability of local recycling facility reduces transportation and waste management costs 2. Increased customer traffic from customers dropping off materials for recycling 3. Higher revenues due to increase in local employment 4. Availability of a trained and experienced labour force 5. Ability to act as suppliers to RA and therefore increase their business
Municipal Government	1. Saves on recycling costs by contracting with GC/RA instead of with an out-of-region facility 2. Creates local jobs that have economic spin-offs 3. Receives funding from the provincial government 4. Receives revenue from taxes and business permits (over $70,000 per year)

Table 5.1 Stakeholder Benefits (*cont.*)

Stakeholder	Stakeholder Benefits
Regional Government (combination of eight municipalities)	1. Increased revenues due to increase in local employment 2. Increased job creation means that individuals and families are able to stay in region 3. High level of prestige through associating with social mission-driven organizations such as GC and taking part in valorizing individuals with intellectual disabilities through employment
Provincial Ministry of Environment	1. Reduces waste management costs for the area 2. Increases compliance with recycling requirements 3. Achieves goals for diversion of waste from landfills
Provincial Ministry of Community and Social Services	1. Invests public funds better and more effectively 2. Saves in costs per client over the long run 3. Potentially reduces health-care costs 4. Reaches its goal of social integration
Federal Government	1. Enhances local competency and diversity of industry 2. Creates jobs, resulting in additional tax revenues 3. Allows for greater mobility of workforce
Citizens	1. Have a place to dispose of their old electronics six days a week 2. Positive business model for children in their community and increased awareness about recycling 3. Regular sponsor for golf tournament, fundraisers for charities, and exhibits in local events
Schools	1. Employer for student job placements and co-op placements 2. $1/tonne recycled put in special fund for educational programs 3. Option for after-school work for students who will not pursue postsecondary school and part-time jobs for students on Saturdays 4. Presentations in schools to increase awareness among youth

subsidies contributed by Valoris across all its enterprises, including RA; however, the following section focuses on the costs and benefits related to RA.

An exercise conducted by GC demonstrated that 60 per cent of GC's managers' time is spent resolving issues with employees with intellectual disabilities. Some examples are repeating and supervising simple tasks; assisting employees with personal care and transportation; communicating with family members and social workers; creating flexible shifts according to employee needs; and evaluating the environment. An equivalent business that does not employ individuals with intellectual disabilities would not typically incur these costs; therefore, it is a social cost for RA that is partially subsidized by a direct financial contribution from Valoris. The direct financial contribution from Valoris to cover RA's social costs was $315,200 for the fiscal year 2012–13.

Valoris also contributes indirect support that can be quantified and monetized. For example, Valoris supports Groupe Convex by employing the executive director, who oversees all enterprises, including RA. Valoris also offers social support services for targeted employees. The annual wages and benefits for the executive director are estimated to be $120,000. GC divides administrative costs evenly over its eight enterprises; therefore, the portion of Valoris social support allocated to Recycle Action is assumed to be $15,000 ($120,000/8).

There are additional Valoris employees, such as social service workers, who support targeted RA employees. As an estimate, four Valoris employees spend 25 per cent of their time supporting targeted employees at all Groupe Convex enterprises, including RA. Assuming the average wages and benefits are $80,000 per Valoris employee, it is estimated that there is a contribution to GC of $80,000 ($80,000 × 4 × 25%). GC divides administrative costs evenly over its eight enterprises; therefore, the portion of Valoris social support allocated to RA is assumed to be $10,000 ($80,000/8).

Valoris also covered some of the start-up funding for RA. These costs are estimated to be $20,000 for RA. Distributed over a ten-year time horizon, we assume the start-up costs amortized on an annual basis are $2,000 per year. In a more refined calculation, a relevant interest rate can be used to determine the value of the initial investment on an annual basis.

The direct investments from Valoris to RA over one year include: $315,200 in wage subsidies for the targeted employees at RA; $15,000 in wages and benefits for GC's executive director; $2,000 in start-up costs per year amortized over ten years. The indirect investments from Valoris to RA over one year include $10,000 in additional social support to targeted employees and $10,000 in transit costs for some employees.

The total direct and indirect investment by Valoris into RA over the course of one year is therefore estimated to be $352,000.

Valoris Benefits Calculation

At an organization level, the main quantifiable benefit for Valoris is the cost savings generated by GC employing individuals with disabilities by operating RA as a non-profit, income-generating enterprise as opposed to a traditional non-profit. If Valoris were to operate a daycare centre or sheltered workshop with full-day services for the same clients, the cost is estimated to be $15,000 per client annually, or $525,000 for the thirty-five clients employed by RA. Therefore, Valoris gains $525,000 in savings from an investment of $352,000, or a 49 per cent return on investment.

Municipality Investment

The municipality pays a direct fee of $58 per tonne to RA. At an estimated 10,000 tonnes per year, the fees paid by the municipality to RA over ten years are $5,800,000 ($58 × 10,000 × 10). Preexisting investment in waste removal transport and equipment are considered to be historical sunk costs and are therefore not included as a calculation of investment costs. In a more refined calculation, the remaining value of the equipment would be amortized over ten years. Advertising and promotion costs paid by the municipality to promote recycling activities are estimated to be $20,000 per year, for a total of $200,000 over ten years.

Municipality Benefits

The municipality gains direct savings by paying $58 per tonne to RA, instead of $60 per tonne to a service provider outside the municipality. With an estimated volume of 10,000 tonnes per year, the saving over ten years is $200,000 ($2 × 10,000 × 10). Another direct benefit is the increase in property taxes – from $35,000 to $60,000 per year – now that RA occupies a formerly vacant building. The total increase in property taxes over ten years is estimated to be $250,000 ($25,000 × 10). Increased revenue from business permits is $200 a year for RA, or $2,000 over ten years.

A secondary savings is in transportation costs as a result of using a more local processing plant rather than one farther away. The reduction on distance travelled is 120 kilometres per round trip. Savings on fuel and maintenance may be calculated at $0.49/km, and transportation is required five days per week for fifty weeks (accounting for holidays). With an estimated ten trips required per day, the savings are $1,470,000 over ten years (120 × 10 × 0.49 × 5 × 50 × 10). Another indirect savings is in waste clean-up and enforcement. With an increase in volume of Blue Box recycling (2 per cent) and electronics (43 per cent), the estimated reduction in clean-up and enforcement costs is $5,000 per year – therefore, a savings of $50,000 over ten years.

A tertiary benefit is property taxes from employees who are able to live in the five municipalities rather than relocating to find work. RA employs one manager, one project coordinator, thirty-five employees who are part of the target population, and nineteen employees who are not part of the target population. We estimate that half of the employees who are not part of the targeted population – or ten employees – would be required to relocate for employment purposes if employment were not available at RA. Out of the estimated ten employees who are able to stay in the five municipalities, we estimate that half, or five employees, are homeowners who pay municipal property taxes. Property taxes are estimated to be $50 per month or $600 per year. The total gain in property taxes over ten years is calculated to be $30,000 ($600 × 5 × 10). A related tertiary benefit is service revenue from employees who are able to live in the five municipalities rather than relocating to find work. Based on the previous calculation, we assume that ten employees would be required to relocate for employment purposes if employment were not available at RA. Municipal services and fees are estimated to amount to an average of $50 per person per year. The total gain in service fees over ten years is calculated to be $5,000 ($50 × 10 × 10).

Therefore, the municipality gains $1,962,000 in savings from an investment of $6,000,000 – or a 33 per cent return on investment. This calculation is specific to the local municipality. If a calculation were to be made at a provincial or federal level, property taxes and service revenues from individuals would not be included, as they would be paid in a different municipality within the province and country.

Local Business Community Investment

The investment required to benefit from RA activities is specific to each business. For example, a local business is able to sell recyclable material to RA when it would normally be waste sent to a landfill site. The benefit calculation is calculated as follows: RA purchases 294 tonnes of cardboard at $60/tonne in a year from a local business. The cost for the local business to send the same quantity of cardboard to a landfill site would be $200/tonne. Therefore, the annual savings of avoiding sending cardboard to the landfill is $58,800 ($200 × 294 tonnes). The annual benefit of selling the cardboard to RA is $17,640 ($60 × 294 tonnes). Therefore, the total annual benefit for the local business from savings and sales is $76,440.

Other benefits to local businesses that could be quantified include savings in reducing travel to a processing plant farther away; savings in waste management costs; increased customer traffic for local business-es near RA; increase in revenues due to greater local employment; reduction in training expenses for the local labour force; and increase in revenues as suppliers of RA.

Family Investment

It is assumed that family members of individuals working at RA incur no additional direct costs. For example, we assume that if an individual with an intellectual disability were part of a sheltered workshop pro-gram, the transportation requirements for the family member would be the same, whether the individual were transported to the sheltered workshop or to RA. We also assume that there are no clawbacks of a family's government financial supports as a result of a targeted indi-vidual's employment at RA.

Family Benefits

The main family benefit is an increase in income through working ad-ditional hours rather than staying at home as a concerned parent or caregiver. RA employs thirty-five individuals who are part of the tar-geted population. We assume that twenty of these targeted employees live at home with family members, and the others live independently. Of the twenty targeted employees who live at home with family mem-bers, we assume that half have family members who are able to find employment if they do not have to stay at home. Ten family members able to find part-time employment (twenty hours a week) at mini-mum wage ($10.25) results in an average gain of $10,250 (12 × 20 × 50) per year.

A secondary family benefit is the reduction in the number of family members' health problems because of improvement in overall mental health. We estimate that there is a reduction of one medical appoint-ment per year. In most cases, the cost of a medical visit is a cost ab-sorbed by the health-care system rather than being a direct cost to the family member. An average cost of a medical visit could be estimated to be $200 per visit. Since the investment per family member is difficult to quantify, no return on investment is calculated.

Individual Investment

Individuals who are part of the target population have to invest additional time and effort through their employment at RA. But we assume that the opportunity cost of employment at RA is minimal – in other words, it is assumed that employees from the target group would not be able to find other paid employment, and therefore there is no loss of employment income. The majority of targeted employees are assumed to be recipients of the Ontario Disability Support Program or ODSP, estimated at $900 per month or $10,800 per year. The average earnings for the majority of employees will exceed the clawback threshold of $200 per month and therefore will result in a loss of government funding for many individuals. For the majority of individuals employed by RA, the increase in income is significantly greater than the loss of government benefits, leading to additional disposable income that they would not have while on government-funded social assistance.

Individual Benefits

The future employability of targeted individuals is a long-term benefit that can be calculated for RA. We assume that one year of full-time employment at RA increases employability. We also assume that 5 per cent of employees with intellectual disabilities will be employable in a different business after one year of being employed with RA. Employment for a targeted individual at a different business will typically be at minimum wage ($10.25 per hour). Employment, on average, will be half time or twenty hours per week for fifty weeks (since the ability of employees to work ranges from two hours per week to forty-eight hours per week). Therefore, a potential increase in annual income per employee from one year of employment at RA is $10,250 (10.25 × 20 × 50). Note that this is an average benefits calculation. For example, some individuals will remain on government assistance and work limited hours to maintain government benefits. Others will be able to work significantly more hours a week, and their regular income will be greater than remaining on government assistance.

The Sustainable Livelihoods Framework (Ferguson, 2003), applied in some of the case studies in this book, represents a useful starting point for further analysing impact at the individual level. It represents a somewhat different approach to understanding the impact of social purpose enterprises.

Environmental Benefits

There are a number of environmental benefits stemming from having a recycling plant in the local community, including recycling increased quantities of materials that might otherwise have been sent to a landfill; reducing land and water pollution caused by illegal or unethical dumping; and reducing carbon emissions through decreased transportation requirements.

The reduction in carbon emissions can be calculated as a demonstration. The previous calculation for the municipality indicated that there was a reduction in distance travelled of 120 km/round trip. Transportation is required five days per week for fifty weeks (accounting for holidays). With an estimated ten trips required per day, the total kilometres that are saved is 3,000,000 over 10 years (120 × 10 × 5 × 50 × 10). The website http://www.eea.europa.eu/data-and-maps/figures/specific-co2-emissions-per-tonne-2 estimates that a range of 60 to 150 grams of carbon dioxide are emitted per metric tonne of freight and per kilometre of transportation. Assuming each truckload is 20 tonnes, and using the lower value in the range of 60 grams of carbon dioxide, the carbon emissions that are avoided total 3,600 tonnes (3,000,000 km × 60g × 20 tonnes/1,000,000 g/tonne). The benefits of reduced carbon dioxide emissions can be monetized using the costs of purchasing equivalent carbon offsets. The pricing for carbon credits is well established; there are a wide variety of providers and projects. The website www.carboncatalog.org estimates a range in cost of $10–$45 per metric tonne of carbon offset for Canada. Using the lowest value, the environmental benefit of reduced transportation over ten years is $36,000 (3,600 × $10).

Discussion and Conclusions

GC provides meaningful employment principally to members of the Prescott-Russell communities who have intellectual disabilities. The work of GC is grounded in the belief that everyone can – and should be – valued for their abilities to contribute to their communities.

The focus of this analysis is on SROI, a complex metric that needs to rest on sensible assumptions and to be assessed by rigorous analysis. What was perhaps the most important in determining the preliminary SROI for RA was the long, detailed, and participative process that the research team followed. Assumptions were specified and data were collected. While SROI is useful in quantifying social impact, it requires that we critically evaluate the many assumptions that are built into the SROI calculation. These are estimates – they are not calculations that can be presented with total certainty.

The results of this research will become a tool to inform funders and contributors. But the results are also very important in demystifying the role of organizations in the social economy, as organizations like GC are often stereotyped as dependent "takers" rather than positive contributors. This analysis of GC and RA illustrates the value of their contributions. In the past five years, the market share of the enterprises within Groupe Convex has increased at a rate of $250,000 annually. Although the majority of companies in the region support this socio-economic initiative, the social purpose enterprises among the GC network compete with other, ordinary businesses. The subsidies that GC receives lead to legitimate questions and criticism. Some critics are not familiar with the reality of GC social enterprises, which employ very limited and vulnerable people. For some clients of these enterprises, the social objectives of Groupe Convex are an incentive to purchase. For them, a purchase or supply from a company under GC becomes a vote for a cause they believe in. But in most cases, clients base their decision to purchase on market considerations such as price and quality.

Further, SROI serves as a tool both to measure social impact and to drive organizational decision making. The process of conducting SROI calculations forces the organization to assess many of the internal and external variables that can have an impact on its effectiveness. As it is nearly a truism that "what gets measured gets done," the process and the outcomes of SROI calculations can alert the organization to the key components of its work and the relative importance of its activities in achieving its mission.

The UK SROI method applied to RA has resulted in the development of a stakeholder analysis; a program logic model; and quantifiable monetary costs and benefits for a subset of stakeholders. The method can be further applied for a comparative ranking of different projects, or a comparison of risks and rewards for different investment options. Further development of the method for RA can include a detailed enumeration and monetization of SROI using individuals with intellectual disabilities as the unit of analysis.

In addition, it has been a valuable process of mutual learning for the research team and GC to engage in this study's thinking and writing processes. The researchers learned about the realities of managing a complex and innovative organization, while GC learned, in more detail, how to apply some tools to measure its impact. We see this case study as a good example of action research, in which both researchers and community leaders work together to generate knowledge in a process of mutual influence.

NOTES

1 We would like to acknowledge the time and effort contributed by the employees, staff, and management of Groupe Convex, Recycle Action, and Valoris, as well as the CURA project team.
2 Final Report, Prescott-Russell Community Development Corporation, Prescott and Russell Economic Development Plan, February 22, 2011.

REFERENCES

Arcand, C. (2007). *Groupe Convex. Our social enterprises*. Prescott-Russell, ON: Groupe Convex.

Arcand, C. (2010). Groupe Convex – A social business network turns a profit – & Much more besides. Unpublished report.

Broad, G., & Saunders, M. (2008). Social enterprises and the Ontario Disability Support Program: A policy perspective on employing persons with disabilities. Victoria, BC: CCEDNet.

Clark, C., Rosenzweig, W., Long, D., & Olsen, S. (2004). *Double bottom line project methods catalog*. New York, NY: The Rockefeller Foundation.

Eastern Ontario Health Unit (EOHU). (2009). *People in need: A descriptive and comparative analysis of the counties of Prescott-Russell*. Ontario, Cornwall: Author.

Etmanski, A. (2011). One of the seven wonders in the world of disability – Wolf Wolfensberger. Retrieved from http://www.aletmanski.com/aletmanski/2011/03/a-nobel-for-truth-telling-wolf-wolfensberger.html

Ferguson, M., & The Canadian Women's Foundation. (2003). Practitioner resource #1: Sustainable Livelihoods backgrounder. Retrieved from http://www.canadianwomen.org/economic-development-resources

Lingane, A., & Olsen, S. (2004). Guidelines for Social Return on Investment. *California Management Review, 46*(3), 116–135. http://dx.doi.org/10.2307/41166224

Mass, K., & Liket, K. (2011). Social impact measurement: Classification of methods. In R. Buritt, S. Schaltegger, M. Bennett, T. Pohjola, & M. Csutora (Eds.), *Eco-Efficiency in Industry and Science: Vol. 27. Environmental management accounting and supply chain management* (pp. 171–202).

Ministère des Services Sociaux et Communautaires. (2009). *Rapport le phénix:Au-delà du handicap, rapport d'étape de 2009 du programme Ontarien de soutien aux personnes handicapées.* Plantagenet, ON: Lalande & Associes.

Osburn, J. (1998). An overview of social role valorization theory. *The International Social Role Valorization Journal/La revue internationale de la Valorisation des roles sociaux,* 3(1), 7–12. Retrieved from http://www .socialrolevalorization.com/articles/overview-of-srv-theory.html

Smith, F.A., & Butterworth, J. (2009). Indicators of labor market success for people with intellectual disabilities. DataNote Series, Data Note XXII. Boston, MA: Institute for Community Inclusion. Retrieved from http:// www.communityinclusion.org/article.php?article_id=277

Nicholls, J., Lawlor, E., Neitzert, E., & Goodspeed, T. (2009). A guide to Social Return on Investment. Cabinet Office, London. Retrieved from http:// www. thesroinetwork.org/publications/cat_view/29-the-sroi-guide-2009

Valoris (2011). Our 2010–11 service statistics. Retrieved from http://www .seapr.ca/en/ valoris/statistics

Wolfensberger, W. (2000). A brief overview of social role valorization. *Mental Retardation,* 38(2), 105–123. http://dx.doi.org/10.1352/0047-6765(2000) 038<0105:ABOOSR>2.0.CO;2

SECTION B

Women on the Social Margins

Four of the case studies in this book – Inspirations Studio (Chapter 6), Alterna Savings (Chapter 7), Academy of Computer & Employment Skills (A.C.E.S.) (Chapter 8), and The Learning Enrichment Foundation (Chapter 9) – analyse social purpose enterprises that focus primarily on women on the social margins.

Inspirations Studio was started in 1994 by **Sistering,** a non-profit agency serving homeless, marginalized, and low-income women in Toronto. The agency assists the women in supplementing their income. These women are semi-autonomous business people who benefit from Inspirations Studio's support.

Alterna Savings – the Community Micro-Finance Program is a primary source of finance for recent immigrants and other low-income individuals who want to start businesses. This case study focuses on the impact of the program on microloan recipients.

Academy of Computer & Employment Skills (A.C.E.S.) is a social purpose enterprise that was established by its parent, the Working Skills Centre, in 2008. Primarily serving immigrant women, A.C.E.S. generates income through offering diplomas for a variety of training courses with the intent of integrating its clientele into the workforce.

The Learning Enrichment Foundation is a community development corporation that has operated in the GTA since 1978. This case study focuses on its eighteen childcare centres – social purpose enterprises that employ low-income women who are predominantly first-generation immigrants and racialized minorities.

The case studies in this section address social purpose enterprises that help women with extreme needs. These are primarily women who are precariously housed and affected by mental health issues (Inspirations) and recent immigrants who are struggling to break into the workforce through a training program (A.C.E.S.), through microentrepreneurship (Alterna Savings), or through lower-wage employment (the childcare centres at The Learning Enrichment Foundation [LEF]). Women at the LEF have comparatively stable employment with benefits – although they make relatively low wages for the city of Toronto. The women in the other enterprises have much less security. In two cases – Inspirations and Alterna – they are engaged in self-employment. In A.C.E.S., they are part of a training program designed to help them access a very tight employment market.

The participants in these enterprises are not exclusively women, and many are recent immigrants, meaning that they could have been included in Section C of this book. Nevertheless, a gendered context is essential for understanding these enterprises.

6 Inspirations Studio at Sistering: A Systems Analysis

AGNES MEINHARD, ANNIE LOK, AND PAULINE O'CONNOR

> The highest form of charity is to help a person find employment or establish themselves in business so as to make it unnecessary for them to become dependent on others.
>
> Maimonides' Mishneh Torah, Laws of Gifts to the Poor, 10:7–14

This chapter presents a case study of a social purpose enterprise, Inspirations Studio at Sistering, that is engaged in this highest form of charity: offering disadvantaged women an opportunity to create and sell their artistic products. Sistering/Inspirations is one of a growing number of social purpose enterprises that apply innovative means to resolve some of society's pressing social, economic, and environmental problems. As more and more non-profit organizations embrace the idea of "social enterprise," much still needs to be understood about these enterprises. This case study uses a systems analytic, value-proposition framework to identify the elements and relationships necessary to create and deliver value to the stakeholders of the organization. This model can be used by professionals and practitioners who are engaging – or are planning to engage – in these types of organizational endeavours.

Brief Description of Inspirations Studio and Sistering

Inspirations Studio is a semi-autonomous unit within Sistering, a drop-in centre that offers practical and emotional support to women through programs that enable them to take greater control over their lives (http://www.sistering.org). It serves low-income women affected by trauma, displacement, and mental health issues. Living in poverty and often homeless, the women using the studio are recipients of social assistance (Ontario Works [OW]) or the Ontario Disability Support Program (ODSP). Inspirations Studio "focuses on building [these] women's capacity to supplement their income and enhance their livelihoods though arts/craft training, production and business development" (http://inspirationsstudio.org/).

Inspirations Studio describes itself as "a micro-business incubator helping low-income women to enhance their earning potential by teaching them how to produce, market, and sell ceramic art" (http://inspirationsstudio.org/). Founded independently in 1994 under the sponsorship of the Ontario Council of Alternative Business, Inspirations was originally located in four hostel and drop-in centres. Later, it became part of the 761 Community Development Corporation, consolidating its operations in a studio at 761 Queen Street West. In 2001, when the 761 Community Development Corporation closed, Inspirations looked for another home and became a semi-autonomous project of Sistering. Since that time, Inspirations has evolved into a professional training and production studio funded by the Toronto Enterprise Fund (TEF), The Co-operators, and the ELJB Foundation, with other supporters such as United Way, Trillium Foundation, the City of Toronto, and Human Resources Development Canada. Sistering administers the funding for Inspirations Studio, and Inspirations staff members are employees of Sistering.

The women who work at the studio are self-employed and operate independent microbusinesses. They are called "members." Although some of the members were referred by Sistering – or their hostels or other social agencies – many found out about Inspirations either serendipitously or by word of mouth. Most found their way to the studio because they were experiencing homelessness and had some interest in the arts that was recognized by their social workers. The studio is a production space that gives members access to potter's wheels and a kiln and provides them with clay and glaze. The objective is that they will make items to sell and use this income to better their lives. Members are charged for their clay based on how much they use. In addition, members pay a consignment fee when staff personnel sell their work. Members also sell their pottery in studio sales and special shows arranged by Inspirations. The women are free to sell their products privately, and these sales are not subject to commission. Three professional potters make up the support staff of the studio. They help the women hone their pottery skills and teach them the fundamentals of pricing, marketing, and selling their products, as well as developing business plans. The revenue garnered from the studio's commission on the sales, plus the fee charged for the clay, helps to pay for almost half of the costs of the art supplies, such as the clay and glazes.

Using Inspirations Studio as a model, Sistering has now added one other social purpose enterprise: Spun Studio, specializing in knit and sewn accessories. On the Path – a sewing, training, and employment program – preceded Inspirations by a few years. The plan is to integrate the social purpose enterprises and employment programs under the On the Path umbrella, and house these and any future enterprises as a cluster of studios in a larger space. This comes at the right time, as Inspirations will soon have to move out of their current studio space.

Study Framework

Figure 6.1 represents the framework used to analyse the data collected during two years of field observation, interviews with key informants and focus groups, and document analysis. The upper half of the figure represents the open systems model of organizations (Katz & Kahn, 1966). This model describes organizations as living systems in constant interaction with their environments, acquiring needed resources from the environment (inputs) and exporting products and/or services to the environment (outputs). The core purpose of an organization is to transform the inputs into something new that is of value to the environment. If the organization's output is not desired or accepted by the environment, then the organization's revenue stream will be compromised, and the organization may not be able to support the cost structure needed to acquire resources and continue operating (the feedback loop). Therefore, it is essential for the organization to monitor the environment and assure that its product or service is valued. The lower part of Figure 6.1 illustrates what an organization needs to pay attention to on both the input and output side in order to create and deliver value for the environment in the form of a product or service.

Normally, in for-profit organizations, revenue is generated on the output side through sales or fees for service, while in non-profit organizations, revenue is generated on the input side by acquiring grants and donations. In social purpose enterprises, revenue is generated both on the input side and the output side as will be illustrated in the discussion below.

Our analysis will focus both on the social values and product values being created by Inspirations Studio: the former is necessary for continued funding on the input side, and the latter is essential for the generation of income on the output side.

Figure 6.1 Study Framework

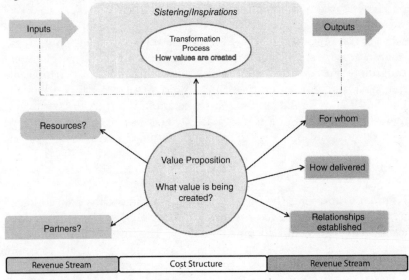

Methodology

This project was carried out with the full cooperation of Sistering management and the participation of staff and members of Inspirations Studio. A case study methodology (Yin, 1989) was used that involved thirty hours of field observations both in the studio and at sales events; five key informant interviews with staff members and Sistering executives; two focus group interviews, which included a total of nine members of Inspirations; analysis of fifteen documents made available to the researchers by Sistering/Inspirations; and an organization profile questionnaire. The data gathered were then analysed for content and grouped according to themes to create a holistic picture of Inspirations Studio as a social purpose enterprise project of Sistering.

Analysis of Data

Although Inspirations Studio is a project of Sistering, the analysis will focus predominantly on Inspirations. Following the framework depicted in Figure 6.1, we begin by discussing the value proposition of

Inspirations – in other words, what value does Inspirations create? We fan out clockwise to look at: a) the output elements – in other words, for whom the values are created, how they are delivered, and the relationships established to assure continued performance; b) the transformation process, or how the values are created; and c) the input elements, or what resources are needed and what partners are engaged to ensure the flow of resources.

What Is Inspirations' Value Proposition?

As a social purpose enterprise, Inspirations has a dual purpose: to create both social and economic value. The social value is to enable women who have experienced homelessness, long-term poverty, and possibly mental health issues to develop artistic and business skills for income generation and enhanced well-being. This is pursued through the creation of economic value, which takes the form of an artistic product attractive to buyers.

Who Are the Beneficiaries of the Values and What Are the Channels of Delivery?

The social values created at Inspirations benefit primarily the women members who use Inspirations Studio; however, the immediate community and society benefit in direct and indirect ways, as well. In our research, societal impact is anecdotal rather than empirically measured. As a form of business, the women at Inspirations have to create high-quality products valued by their clientele: individual customers, shops, corporations, and other non-profit organizations.

VALUE TO THE WOMEN MEMBERS OF INSPIRATIONS

The raison d'etre of Inspirations is helping women to sell their art "so they will be able to earn whatever supplemental income they can before the clawback of ODSP or OW" (Key Informant-1 [KI-1]). Income from the sales of their products makes a significant difference in their lives, enabling them to pay rent, to buy food and clothes, to make their own lives more comfortable, and even to buy presents for family, thus helping them to "feel less outside of what is normal" (KI-4). The women's earnings range from $400/year to more than $6,000/year; this corresponds to up to 20 per cent of their annual income. (Document: Presentation to United Way [Doc:UW]).

However, "the money thing for whatever reason does not seem very dominant for some" (KI-1). There are many who "come here for years but earn very little money – so obviously there are other needs that are being met" (KI-3). It seems that what the women value above the economic benefits is the sense of self-worth, community, family, friendships, and education that they gain from attending the studio. Working at Inspirations helps many of the women to find community and friendship. Our field observations are full of examples of camaraderie and discussions, with many examples of women helping one another out, as well as giving comfort and support.

> People come and talk and socialize which is really nice, knowing that people come to work on clay but also to see their friends. People are all friends here, like a family. They get along really well and it is nice to see. (KI-3)

All of the women in the focus groups indicated that they felt good in the studio and were comfortable around other people. This sense of comfort was evident in the way they interacted during the focus group interviews. In the field notes we recorded that a positive outlook seemed to emanate from the conversation:

> [I am] grateful for Inspirations because there isn't a place of work where it's flexible and you come in only when you're feeling well and you won't get fired. It is a free space to learn to be creative. (FG)

Both in the focus groups and in the staff interviews, there was much evidence of increased confidence and self-esteem as the women became more accomplished in the studio. Several talked about feeling less depressed, more secure, and having peace of mind:

> When I found Inspirations, I started coming out and [to] get out of the shelter to do something. I didn't want to stay in the shelter and be depressed every day. Each time I came here, I thought it was an outlet. (FG)
> All of the tension is taken away and then you begin to understand the essence of microbusiness and the social enterprise idea. (FG)
> I am happy. I have self-worth, not necessarily about money. (FG)

The women in the focus groups all recognized how much they were learning at Inspirations: artistic skills as well as entrepreneurial and business skills such as pricing, marketing, recordkeeping, and the importance of having a quality product.

> Each time I come here, I learn more and … when I realized I could make money … I thought to myself "oh my god, I may be able to do that with my life." (FG)
>
> I also find you have the opportunity to learn business and stuff. You know many of us … have never seen a college certificate. (FG)
>
> Well I learned how to throw a bowl, learned how to make [different types of pottery] … It never ceases to amaze me that there are no limits to creativity. I am always blown away. I am always [thinking], "Wow, never thought of that." (FG)

The women's education is not limited to art and business skills. Inspirations Studio offers other educational programs, either through its staff or by inviting speakers. An example is a workshop in anti-oppression.

The financial, educational, social, and psychological benefits that the women experience are attained through their participation in the work and activities of the studio. At all times, there is at least one staff member present in the studio to provide instruction, maintain a safe environment, and support the women. Their presence enhances the probability of the women not only achieving their production goals but also ensuring that social and psychological benefits are accrued through membership at Inspirations.

Besides receiving training in clay production and business skills, Inspirations offers special programs, seminars, and events for the women. The camaraderie, help, and support available at these functions give the women a feeling of friendship. The staff members are especially eager to promote a friendly atmosphere that supports the women's self-confidence and self-esteem.

VALUE TO COMMUNITY AND SOCIETY

This is perhaps the most difficult outcome to discern, as it requires longitudinal measures as well as some kind of control group comparison. However, some studies in other areas involving the engagement of people with mental health difficulties point to reductions in hospitalizations and even reductions in medications (Meinhard et al., 2007). The active participation of these individuals in the community also helps to create a more tolerant society. Inspirations asserts that the women's participation in the studio and the art shows "reduces use of emergency services and hospitalization, and builds a community of artists" (DOC: UW).

VALUE TO CUSTOMERS

For both Inspirations and the women studio members, it is important to create products of value for their customers. Therefore, they need to understand what the customers want and constantly improve the quality of their products. Without creating product value for the customer, sales will decline, Inspirations will not be able to continue its operations, and the social values discussed above would be harder to attain as they are intricately connected to the creation and sale of the product.

Besides the actual value of the product, there is a secondary value for some customers: the knowledge that they are supporting a worthwhile cause through the purchase of these products. The steady increase both in clientele and women's income as recorded in the year-end reports to the Toronto Enterprise Fund (Doc: TEF2007, 2009, 2010) is an indication that the value of the product is also improving. For example, in the reported years, women's income from sales increased by an average of 10 per cent yearly. This increase is not only the result of better and more varied product lines, but it is also due to better marketing and competitive pricing. However, regardless of the marketing, if the product value had been low because of poor quality, sales would not have increased.

Inspirations' products are delivered through various channels: studio sales, special orders, consignments and direct sales to stores, crafts fairs, and sales at corporate and public venues such as banks, hospitals, and municipal buildings. Some women approach stores directly and sell to them outright or on consignment. The main marketing strategy of Inspirations is to convey the idea that buying gifts from Inspirations is a way to support less fortunate people in the community: "Inspirations Studio – Gifts that Give Back to the Community." Artistic pottery is a very competitive field, with many artists trying to make a living at it, and emphasizing the community aspect creates a niche: "Our customers purchase because they wish to support the women and they like the story that is behind the art work" (Doc:UW).

Members of Inspirations Studio rely heavily on the staff to market their products and to find venues for sales. However, the staff members have not had formal business training, so marketing skills are new to them, too. In order to overcome this limitation, Sistering has hired marketing consultants and has hosted workshops to help increase staff skills. Also, Inspirations Studio has developed a catalogue and other marketing materials. The catalogue presents their products as gift-giving options to honour volunteers or retiring board members and staff, or as conference giveaways and speaker gifts (Doc:UW). More recently, much of the marketing is done through social media.

Both members and staff have mentioned that marketing is one of the problem areas that needs attention:

> I don't think it [our marketing] is very effective. I don't think we are near anywhere where we could be financially. (KI-1)

Over the years, Sistering has hired several marketers but because of the unique situation with the members, this has not been particularly successful.

> If there is somebody who really knew how to market what we are doing we would be excited to be working with that, but right now we always found somebody that has a couple of the characteristics but not somebody that has all of them. (KI-1)

Competitive pricing is crucial to selling a product. Inspirations' members price their own products. It has been a challenge for staff members to get the women to realistically appraise their products. Some women undervalue their products; others overvalue them, and in this way prevent sales from happening:

> They can set their own price, but I will also tell them – well, I cannot sell it for that price and just hand it back to them. Other times … I will just go back and put it on her shelf because I cannot sell it for that. It is not about being unkind to someone, it's just that I cannot sell it for that price. (KI-1)

The creation of long-term relationships contributes to the sustainability of the enterprise. There are two levels on which relationships are being built with respect to sales: at the organizational level, between Sistering/Inspirations and organized client groups, and at the individual level, between the artists and the clients. At the organizational level, Inspirations Studio is building ongoing relationships with other nonprofit organizations, corporations, and community businesses in order to ensure that their products will continue to have a venue. For example, in its 2010 report to a particular funder, Inspirations wrote:

> This fall we were able to capitalize on a United Way visit, to penetrate the banking sector that has been promoting corporate social responsibility policies to their staff and managers. Our intention is to continue this trend and to maintain relations with the two banks. Board room invitational sales are considered a successful venue. In a span of 3–4 hours members can make a total of $2,000. (Doc:TEF2010)

Inspirations Studio has had off-again, on-again success in partnering with organizations in their neighbourhoods, but there are many neighbourhood businesses that are not even aware of this organization. Inspirations has also established relationships with several selling outlets such as local retail outlets looking for tailored, branded products for philanthropy programs; retail outlets selling unique crafts such as public gallery gift shops; craft stores; hospital gift stores; local shoppers to the Queen Street West district; and arts and crafts collectors who appreciate the artistic quality of the Inspirations' products. These bring in steady sales.

On an individual level, some of the artists have long-term relationships with stores that sell their products.

> This lady has a store and she carries them [my pieces]. I showed her my pieces before and she said she would buy them off me, and now she has been buying off me ever since. (FG)

How Are the Values Created?

The core of any organization's operation is to create the product or service that it is offering to its clients (Thompson, 1967). If this core does not operate well, then the quality of the output will be unacceptable to the environment, and the resources flowing to the organization will cease. Without these resources, the organization will eventually cease its operations. In a for-profit organization, the relationship between quality of output and continued operations is clear. If people do not buy the product or service, then the organization will not be able to sustain its operating costs. In non-profit social service organizations, where the recipients of the service are not paying for it, the relationship is less clear. In these organizations, fundraising is not directly related to the organizational output. It often has more to do with fundraising skill or making successful grant applications than with the quality of the service; therefore, incoming resources are not always related to the output of the organization. A situation can arise in which, despite excellent value and organizational outcomes, funding is cut for reasons unrelated to organizational performance. The opposite can also occur: funding can continue even in the face of poor service. In a social purpose enterprise such as Inspirations, resources flow mostly from the input side, from funders and donors; however, some revenue comes from the sale of products. The challenge for Inspirations Studio is to help their members create quality ceramics so that it continues to gain revenue from the sales of its members' products, and also to convince funders and donors of the social value of the enterprise so that they continue their support.

On the surface, Inspirations Studio operates like many other studios that serve a collective group of artists. The members share the space and equipment under certain rules and guidelines; they price and sell their products individually or in shared retail space attached to the studio. These collectives are organized around the single goal of offering space and equipment to allow individual artists to create and produce pottery and clay sculptures. At Inspirations Studio, however, the overriding goal is to help women on government-support programs such as OW or ODSP to enhance their incomes through sales of their artistic products, and through these sales to improve the quality of their lives socially and psychologically. Training the women to master their art and educating them in running a microbusiness is the basis of the studio operation. This is done through hiring professional potters to oversee studio activities and to support and facilitate the women's work and through providing special programs not only related to pottery production and sales but also intended to enhance independence and self-esteem. However, there are special challenges in the studio – overcrowding and the mental fragility of the women.

The studio has two kilns, two sinks, four throwing wheels, two workbenches for clay, and one table for glazing. All around the studio walls are shelving spaces where the members store their work. Special shelving is designated for items to be fired and those just out of the kiln. Tucked away in the corner is a desk with a computer for staff members. Although the women work independently on their creations, there are studio operations that are exclusively done by staff members: preparing and reclaiming the clay, preparing the glazes, and operating the kiln. The members are very appreciative of what the staff does for them:

> It helps that they hire someone that is trained to mix clay, so I don't have to mix all that reclaimed clay, which is great! (FG)

The studio is open to the members from 10:00 a.m. to 4:00 p.m., four days a week, and members come when they want, usually staying four to five hours. Some women come every day; others only come some days. They work on their own, but staff members are available to assist them whenever they ask for help and to advise them on what would be marketable. Space is crowded for the number of women using the studio. There is high demand for the potter's wheels, so the members have to sign up on a schedule roster for their use. There is some self-organization by the members (Field Observation [FO]); however, "spacing continues to be an issue as we crowd up to 15 women daily in a studio space that comfortably holds five … and without significant growth in space and resources we'll have to turn many women away" (Doc:SP2009).

The lack of space often leads to tension in the studio; therefore, formal and informal mechanisms are in place to keep the studio running effectively. There is a studio code of conduct that guides the women's behaviour: wheel time is allocated, and women are responsible for cleaning the wheel after use, storing their work, cleaning their space, and generally leaving the studio space ready for the next person to use. More informal methods of keeping the studio running smoothly have been worked out by the women themselves (FO).

Our field observations indicate that the women are generally supportive of each other both in the studio and at sales venues. This is one of the things the women appreciate most about Inspirations – the sense of friendship, family, and community. This does not happen without considerable effort on the part of staff and members. One of the staff's objectives at Inspirations is to give the women a feeling of ownership and responsibility for the studio. This is achieved through monthly meetings attended by members and staff and held in the studio. During these meetings, the women discuss the events that occurred over the last month, particularly the challenges encountered, and suggest possible changes to the studio policies or the code of conduct. They discuss the training they have received and give staff feedback on particular items they wish to learn how to make.

Crowding is not the only source of tension in the studio, and conflict can arise despite the formal mechanisms in place to regulate studio behaviour. There is jealousy among the women, because some are inevitably better artists and are more successful in selling their products. This can lead to copying or stealing ideas. The problem became so serious that the group "came up with an agreement about what copying is" (KI-1):

Everyone got a handout on what copying is and if someone feels that their work is being copied by another person, they will come to a staff member and discuss it with us, and the staff will hold up firing the piece that has been copied. And once that person asks us why their work hasn't been fired yet, we have a discussion around copying. (KI-3)

Sometimes the conflict is self-regulated, and the women resolve the issues on their own. However, often the studio staff has to step in:

If there are two women that are in disagreement, we don't always need to step in. We are all adults and they can work it out on their own. If it escalates to it going somewhere where it shouldn't then I will step in but if they can solve it on their own … (KI-2)

Conflict is often exacerbated by the fragility of the women's mental health. Staff members are not formally trained psychologists or social workers, but they have some experience in these areas, and most often they successfully defuse the situations. Studio members are largely pleased with how the staff helps them and runs the studio; however, there is one area – dealing with disruptive members – in which there was general consensus that improvement was needed:

I don't think they [staff members] have the training to prepare them for what they may need with the some of the clients. (FG)
      I think it is great that they hired [names two staff members] who are trained in ceramics. But I also think they need someone who is trained in social work. Like for example, truthfully [named staff] needs to be consistent when dealing with problems and there are times when she would treat a problem this way and other times she would ignore it. You can't do that. It has to be very, very consistent so there is no question; if you come here and do this, this is the consequence, no two ways about it; this is it. (FG)

Sistering makes training in crisis intervention, mediation, and dealing with hostility available to staff.
Inspirations Studio is constantly striving for quality improvement of the product in order to enhance sales. To this end, Inspirations has enlisted artists to instruct the women:

We have learnt that what works is hiring professional artists to work with the members. The members show immediate respect for and apply the

knowledge these established artists have imparted to them … Since the
beginning of our artist workshop series the members have begun producing more professional work. (Doc:TEF2009)

Other measures to improve the quality of the product are special training sessions for women with weaker output and a buddy system matching Inspirations' veterans with new members. The studio has attempted
to standardize their product in terms of quality, and this has improved
sales. Here, too, the uniqueness of the women artists is evident. For example, one of the better artists refuses to make her product in a variety
of colours, and this affects her sales (KI-1).

Product improvement is not the only thing that Inspirations is pursuing. Sistering and Inspirations are constantly striving to improve their
operations through periodic strategic planning and visioning. One critical issue to be considered through visioning will be a review of the
Inspirations model and the capacity of Inspirations Studio as a social
purpose enterprise to generate more significant income both for members and for studio operations through proactive marketing and contract
sales. Another is to determine how the social purpose enterprise model
fits with Sistering's overall purpose and to what extent Inspirations
should be expanded to other crafts such as knitting, textile arts, and jewellery (the latter two were originally part of Inspirations until space got
too crowded). Of course, the issue of space is critical, and new premises
are being planned.

As more pressure is being put on Inspirations to recoup operating
costs (one funder is decreasing its funding by $5,000 a year), it becomes
more important for Inspirations to grow its own business. In other words,
Inspirations needs to ensure increases in its commissions and clay reclamation. This leads to some tension between its own business needs and
its role as a microbusiness incubator. There is a delicate balance between
managing women's expectations around Inspirations' contract sales –
wherein the women have to participate in sales and give a percentage of
their earned revenue back to the studio – and focusing on strategies to
maximize the income and independence of individual entrepreneurs.
There are women who prefer to find sales venues on their own and do
not have to pay a percentage to the studio or a shop owner:

> To a certain extent, there is a lot of frustration because you look at some of
> the work on the shelf over here [points to a shelf] and you can see it is very
> beautiful work, but the woman does not want to pay 40 per cent, so

automatically when we have new places where we are trying to sell, we don't take her stuff with us. (KI-1)

In this way the women miss out, but the studio misses out as well. Poor health is another disadvantage for Inspirations and its members:

Another factor impeding overall business health is the impact of our members' vulnerable lifestyles on their emotional, physical stability and their ability to participate in the studio. Their struggles often translate into periods of absence from the studio, which results in loss of production time, sales opportunities and revenue. This often compounds their crisis, as the supplemental income they earn through sales is vital for their livelihoods (three meals a day, medicine, clothing and household maintenance). To counter this factor many of the members have begun to build larger inventory so that when they do encounter crises the impact on their sales and their ability to participate is limited. (Doc:TEF2009)

In this section, we have elaborated on how value is created at Inspirations Studio. The focus is to improve the quantity and quality of the product. To this end, experienced and knowledgeable potters were hired to help the women and accomplished artists were engaged to further enhance the women's art. Successful sales and appreciation of artwork by the client enhances self-worth among the women. Other social values are also created in the studio by giving the women responsibility in the studio and giving them a voice through the monthly meetings; encouraging them to participate in studio activities; and arranging for special workshops such as the anti-oppression training. The women are actively involved in maintaining a safe place that can serve as a professional setting for their work. And not least, the women all appreciate the social camaraderie that typifies the studio, which gives them a sense of belonging. This notwithstanding, we have seen some of the problems Inspirations Studio faces because of the fragile nature of the population they serve. Unlike a regular business, a social purpose enterprise engages vulnerable populations whose fragile health can make a deep impact on the revenues of the organization.

Resources and Partnerships

We now turn our attention to the input side of the systems model: what is needed in order to create value in terms of resources and also what

partnerships support the creation of value. Here, too, we will be looking at the resources necessary for the creation of social value as well as
product (material) value. Generally speaking, the input resources are
human, financial, and material.

Of course for any organization, human resources are key because
they provide the core competencies needed to function. Human resources at Sistering/Inspirations can be classified into three groups:
permanent staff, members, and occasional knowledge transmitters.

PERMANENT STAFF

The three permanent staff members are:

a) The social purpose enterprise coordinator, who is in charge not
only of Inspirations Studio but also the other enterprises in Sistering. Her duties include teaching the women with respect to pricing
and business skills; preparing reports about the progress of the
women; finding sales venues; developing partnerships and relationships with funders and clients; managing the revenue stream; keeping the books; writing financial reports for the agency, the women
and for other funders; maintaining a safe studio; and liaising with
Sistering and overseeing the Spun program.

b) The studio facilitator, who maintains the studio. Her duties include
preparing and reclaiming the clay; preparing the glazes; training
and advising the women; creating the lessons for the new women;
loading and firing the kiln; helping with pricing, marketing and studio sales; maintaining a safe studio; helping to arrange trips to local
museums and galleries; and arranging visiting artist workshops.

c) The weekly relief worker, whose role is similar to the studio facilitator, and who comes in on Fridays.

MEMBERS

The members are women who have suffered trauma, poverty, homelessness, and mental health issues – but who have artistic talents. Since its
inception, more than one hundred members have been engaged in the
studio. New members are taken at the beginning of the year. After completing the training, those who demonstrate that they are able to make a
marketable product, work independently, and negotiate the use of space
with the other women are invited to participate. At any one time there
are about twenty-six active members. Currently, Mondays are set aside
to train the new members. Almost anyone with an interest can come to
the studio, but after a few training sessions, there is some self-selection

as some women realize their lack of talent or ability. Some others are encouraged by staff to join Sistering's less challenging social enterprises such as Spun. Only a few women end up as Inspirations members.

OCCASIONAL KNOWLEDGE MOBILIZERS

Consultants – particularly experts in marketing – and professional artists occasionally come to Inspirations Studio to give advice to the studio staff and to teach the women. One year, with some new funding, Inspirations "hired established ceramic artists to conduct product development workshops and consultation with the members. This investment led to increased production and quality and resulted in an increase of revenue by 25%" (Doc:TEF2009). Sistering provides opportunities for Inspirations' staff members to learn skills in dealing with women who have mental health issues and who have suffered from trauma. These outside consultants and artists help to enhance both the social value and the product value.

VOLUNTEERS

Inspirations uses the services of occasional volunteers mostly for studio sales and other shows. There is also a volunteer advisory committee with whom Inspirations staff can consult. As a project of Sistering, Inspirations does not have an independent board. Its interests are represented by the board of directors of Sistering.

FINANCIAL RESOURCES

As Sistering is a non-profit organization with a charitable registration, the main sources of financial input are the funders: government, foundations, and private donors. The funds flow to Inspirations Studio through Sistering. Some are specifically earmarked for Inspirations, but some flow from Sistering's general budget. Inspirations Studio also generates its own income from the commissions from sales and from recouping part of the clay costs from the members. This is represented by the feedback loop in Figure 6.1. Inspirations' goal is to eventually be able to pay all material costs from these sources of income. At present, this income covers 30 to 40 per cent of the costs of the material resources, which include clay, glazes, equipment, rent, electricity, and so on.

PARTNERSHIPS

Sistering and Inspirations have established several partnerships to assist the organization in sustaining its operations. For example, they recently partnered with Parkdale Green Thumb to create forty planters for floral arrangements used as centrepieces for the United Way's Partnering for Community Impact Conference. At the end of the conference, the planters were sold to the attendees (http://inspirationsstudio.org/2012/02/09/inspirations-studios-collaboration-with-parkdale-green-thumb). Inspirations is also an active member of the Toronto Social Purpose Enterprise Network (SPEN).

Sistering also has established partnerships related to the health and well-being of the women. These include Inner City Health Associates, who facilitate weekly visits from a primary health-care physician and psychiatrist, and CCAC (Community Care Access Centre), who send out a community nurse each week to complement basic medical services by offering education to women, giving them referrals to the wider community, and monitoring chronic illnesses that many marginalized women suffer from. Chiropody (foot care) services are also provided by community volunteers (Sistering annual report, 2010).

Cost Structure and Revenue Stream

The overall annual budget of Inspirations in the years 2010 to 2012 is in the $120,000–$130,000 range (Figure 6.2). The middle column presents the percentage breakdown of Inspirations' operating costs. These costs are covered by both input revenue (left column) in the form of grants and donations, and output revenue (right column) in the form of commissions and clay reclamation. Grants from government and other sources account for about 95 to 97 per cent of Inspirations' budget depending on the year. Inspirations' goal is to cover at least the total material costs (i.e., art supplies). As noted, currently commissions and clay reclamation cover about 30 to 40 per cent; however, over its history, there has been a steady growth in the percentage of operating costs paid by revenue generated from Inspirations product.

The rest of the output revenue, which makes up approximately 33 to 40 per cent of the total costs, does not get reinvested into the Inspirations' cost structure. Rather, it is considered part of the women's microbusiness revenue. The women's microbusiness costs include clay purchases, venue rental fees (where applicable), and commission payments to the vendors and Inspirations. For items sold by staff or at consignment venues arranged by Inspirations, the women pay a commission to Inspirations. In the case of consignment sales in shops, most shops charge 50 per cent. In these cases, the total revenue received by

Figure 6.2 Cost Structure and Revenue Streams

Cost Structure and Revenue Streams

Revenue Stream	Cost Structure	Revenue Stream (as a % of costs)
Government Grant.. 62–77% Other Donors 20–35%	Administration & Personnel. 70–80% Office Expenses .... 02% Rent..................................... 06–09% Supports .... 02–03% Art Supplies 08–14%	Total Sales Revenue....33–40% Of this 3–6% is returned to Inspirations as: Commission on Sales..01–03% Clay Reclamation.......02%

Inputs to Inspirations

Donations are the major source for Inspirations accounting for 94-97% of the cost structure. Commissions on sales and clay reclamation account for the rest.

3-6%

Circa 33–40%

To the women's microbusinesses

Inspirations is dispersed to the women. In the case of craft fairs, the women pay 50 per cent of the vendor's fee and Inspirations will pay the other 50 per cent. In the past, some women were unwilling to pay a commission so they sold exclusively on their own. This prompted a change in Inspirations' policy; women now have to participate in at least ten sales brokered by Inspirations, or sell $1,000 worth of goods at these sales. Women can continue to sell on their own, but they must also participate in Inspirations-supported sales.

By fostering "participant engagement, accommodation and ownership within their working studio" (Doc:SP2009), Inspirations is evolving from a single purpose model – as an incubator of individually owned microbusinesses for marginalized women – to a model that also includes aspects of a participant-owned group business enterprise.

Discussion

Using the open systems, value proposition model as the basis for analysis is particularly beneficial in the study of social purpose enterprises because it clearly delineates between the social benefits and the product benefits offered by an organization. In the case of Inspirations, the social value was preeminent in its creation; the microbusiness was merely the means to achieve the social goals of marginalized women earning some income to improve their quality of life and self-worth. However, without creating product value, the achievement of the social goals would be endangered. Thus, in our analysis we focused on both the social value and the product, or the economic, value.

The main beneficiaries of the social values were the women themselves. During the focus group discussion, the women enthusiastically confirmed the economic, social, and psychological benefits. The social values are delivered through various channels, including the work, training, and programs in the studio and at the sales venues where the women see their art being appreciated. Just having a place to go to create items of value to others is probably the main way in which the social values are delivered.

While there is some anecdotal evidence of societal benefit from the improved quality of life of these women, there are no clear data to indicate the overall societal impact of this program. This is an area that may benefit from some controlled longitudinal research. Sistering may want to participate in research of this sort, as the clarification of societal impact may help them pinpoint for their funders the benefits of their enterprise programs.

Much of the work of Inspirations' staff members is focused on improving the quality of the product and expanding the customer base. Product value is delivered in a number of ways: direct studio sales, consignments, special orders, crafts fairs, corporate and non-profit events, store sales, and so on. New marketing efforts, such as expanding into social media, have lately increased the number of client groups as well as the number of sales. Inspirations Studio's main marketing strategy is to pitch the purchase of their product as an opportunity for the buyer to give back to the community and to help others help themselves. Although some of these new marketing strategies are beginning to work, there is dissatisfaction with marketing on the part of both members and staff. With stiff competition, competitive pricing is an important vehicle to achieving sales. Here, too, there are difficulties, as the women's pottery is not always competitively priced. Overall, however, channels of delivery have expanded and have led to increased revenue. In the last few years, Inspirations has been very successful in creating long-term relationships with corporate and non-profit buyers, which has resulted in many repeat purchases.

The creation of value occurs mostly in the studio, and we have presented a detailed picture of how this value is created and also of the challenges faced by Inspirations. The women are constantly learning at many levels – art and business skills and also social skills – both formally and informally. They learn through instruction, interaction, and special workshops. They are independent business owners, using the studio to build their own businesses. They create their art independently and make decisions on pricing and where to sell. For this privilege, they must follow the studio rules and code of conduct, which they had a part in creating and are able to revise collectively as the need might arise. In this way, they have a say in the running of the studio.

Many of the challenges that arise are a result of inadequate studio space and equipment for the level of demand. This, in conjunction with the mental instability of some of the women, can lead to tension and even conflict in the studio and at sales venues. The inconsistent way in which these tense incidents are handled was the only overt criticism expressed in the focus group discussions. Recognizing this shortcoming, Sistering is providing staff with opportunities to learn more about crisis intervention, mediation, and dealing with hostility.

Value cannot be created without sufficient resources: human, financial, and material. We have identified these resources. Inspirations Studio has appropriate and qualified permanent staff and has availed itself of outside experts in the fields of ceramics, marketing, and strategic planning. Use of these experts has been beneficial to the organization, as the quality and delivery of the product have improved. In the case of Sistering/Inspirations, as with other non-profit organizations, financial resources are crucial for survival. Inspirations Studio has shown initiative and agility in attracting the resources it needs to supplement the shortfall from its operations. Over the years, it has managed to find new funders, sponsors, and supporters.

Conclusions

The open systems, value proposition model enabled us to identify the strengths, weaknesses, and challenges of Inspirations Studio. Its strengths are many, and are related to its ability as an organization to constantly learn and renew itself. A small but talented staff, well respected by the members, keeps the studio running smoothly even though there are occasional social interaction challenges among the women. Its greatest challenges lie in the quality of the ceramic output, the uneven rates of production owing to the health of the members, the plan for marketing their product, the creation of meaningful partnerships and, currently, the need to find a new venue for their operations. As are all non-profit organizations, Sistering/Inspirations is dependent on its funders; however, over the years, Inspirations has shown remarkable agility – first in joining Sistering, and later in augmenting its funding sources. As the percentage of government funding decreased, donations from other sources increased.

Inspirations began as an externally funded microbusiness incubator where the emphasis was on helping women to create their independent businesses. But over time, in response to the needs of the studio, the enterprise is taking on some of the characteristics of a participant-owned group enterprise. As such, the women are encouraged to care not only about their own businesses but also about the studio's sustainability. Inspirations is inching up on the ratio of costs that it can cover with the revenue from clay reclamation and commissions.

Although the expectation with this type of enterprise is not to break even financially, the question still arises: is a studio that can only accommodate a relatively small number of women the most efficient way to help women supplement their income and become contributing members of society? Despite limitations in numbers of women served directly, Inspirations has served as a model for other, less restricted enterprises at Sistering such as Spun and On the Path, and a planned fibre-based enterprise. With a new strategic plan in place that sees all of Sistering's social purpose enterprise studios and employment-readiness programs housed under one roof, women with diverse sets of artistic and craft skills will be given a chance to use these skills to supplement their income and to improve their quality of life.

Even when viewed strictly from a cost/benefit analysis, Inspirations Studio's budget is relatively small ($120,000 per year) for an operation of its kind. Although the studio earnings contribute only a small portion of Inspirations' total budget, the support from grants and donations represent an expense of about $3,000 per member per year. If it does nothing else than reduce a woman's hospital use by just a couple of days a year, then it is an expense that pays for itself. But it is not fair to evaluate this enterprise from a dollars and cents perspective. Its strength lies in the chances it offers to women to reverse the downward trend of their lives. And this Inspirations Studio does well and is an example to other social purpose enterprises. As one of the members of Inspirations Studio said:

I would say it saved my life. I mean not literally, but it helped me regain my self-esteem … after working hard all my life and ending up losing everything (FG).

As the well-known saying goes: "Saving one life is considered as if saving an entire world" (translated from Talmud Tractate Sanhedrin 37a).

REFERENCES

Katz, D., & Kahn, R. (1966). *The social psychology of organizations*. New York, NY: John Wiley & Sons.

Meinhard, A., Greenspan, I., Paterson, J., & Livingstone, P. (2007). *Benefits and challenges to people with psychiatric disabilities who volunteer*. Centre for Voluntary Sector Studies Working Paper Series, Vol. 2007(2).

Thompson, J.D. (1967). *Organizations in action*. New York, NY: McGraw-Hill.

Yin, R.K. (1989). *Case study research: Design and methods. Applied Social Research Series* (Vol. 5). London, United Kingdom: Sage.

7 Microentrepreneurs in Economic Turbulence: The Alterna Savings Micro-Finance Program

EDWARD T. JACKSON, SUSAN HENRY,
AND CHINYERE AMADI

Introduction

In order to build the resilience that they need to prevail in difficult economic times, low-income women must have access to capital to create and sustain businesses and jobs for themselves and others. Microfinance is an important tool in making this happen. But microloan programs themselves must navigate in the same economic turbulence. These programs need to generate and utilize real-time, granular knowledge in order to adjust and improve as they proceed forward in uncertain and challenging conditions.

This chapter reviews the five-year experience of a research partnership that sought to create and mobilize new knowledge to analyse and strengthen a microloan program that mainly serves women in the lower-income bracket, many of whom are new immigrants. From 2008 through 2012, Alterna Savings and the Carleton Centre for Community Innovation (3ci) at Carleton University jointly designed and implemented two studies of the effectiveness of Alterna's provision of microcredit in southern Ontario. The first evaluation was undertaken in 2009, at the onset of the global financial crisis, and the second was carried out at the end of this period, in 2012. The findings of these studies were used to better understand the achievements of the microentrepreneurs benefiting from this program, and the evolving challenges they face in the context of a prolonged economic downturn. At the same time, the research was used to adjust, adapt, and strengthen the design and management of the program itself.

Resilience

What is resilience? In everyday usage, the term usually refers to the "ability to recover quickly from illness, change or misfortune," or "buoyancy," or "springing back" (Free Dictionary, 2013). The Rockefeller Foundation (2014) defines resilience as "the capacity of individuals, communities and systems to survive, adapt, and grow in the face of stress and shocks, and even transform when conditions require it." In recent years, *community resilience* has come to mean the "capability to anticipate risk, limit impact, and bounce back rapidly through survival, adaptability, evolution, and growth in the face of turbulent change" (Community and Regional Resilience Institute, 2013.). At a systems level, the Social Innovation Generation initiative argues that: "Resilience is the capacity to experience massive change and yet still maintain the integrity of the original. Resilience isn't about balancing change and stability. It isn't about reaching an equilibrium state. Rather, it is about how massive change and stability paradoxically work together" (Social Innovation Generation, 2010:1). Understood through the lens of complexity theory, and applied to ecosystems, communities, and organizations, this formulation of resilience has gained traction in the fields of social innovation, social enterprise, and social finance.

There is no question that actors at the margins of systems need to be especially resilient in the face of change and turbulence. It is essential that, among other things, they build new skills and knowledge, form meaningful alliances, and continuously learn and adapt as they proceed forward. These imperatives certainly apply to low-income women in the economies of developed and developing nations alike. They apply to smaller financial institutions, such as credit unions, in the fierce competitive environment of financial services, where space is heavily occupied by giant banks and insurance companies. This chapter examines the experience of both low-income women entrepreneurs and a medium-sized credit union during a challenging economic period in two local economies – Toronto and Ottawa.

The Research Partnership

When the two partners convened in 2008, they already shared a common interest in community economic development and microfinance. Alterna Savings had proven itself to be a leader in these areas through a vigorous corporate social responsibility effort, which included the promotion of corporate accountability, financial literacy, environmental sustainability, and community investment. In recognition of its leadership, in 2012 Alterna was honoured with the National Credit Union Community Economic Development Award. For its part, the Carleton Centre for Community Innovation (3ci) is a leading, multidisciplinary knowledge centre for responsible investment and social enterprise with a long track record of engaging with non-profit and social economy organizations in partnered research funded by granting councils, foundations, and government agencies.

Prior to their partnership, representatives of Alterna Savings and 3ci had worked together on policy roundtables and sector networks, but had not cooperated on focused research projects. However, in 2008, the two parties had an opportunity to access research funds from the Social Sciences and Humanities Research Council of Canada (SSHRC) as members of the Social Business Project of the Social Economy Centre at the University of Toronto. Coordinated by senior personnel of each institution, the partnership decided to use these funds to support the work of a graduate student to evaluate Alterna's microloan program operating in Toronto and Ottawa. A joint working group designed and supervised this study, used and disseminated its results, and interacted with the University of Toronto project's community of practice through conferences and networking. In 2011 to 2012, the working group elected to assess the microloan program again, and once more a graduate student was recruited to carry out the work. In the latter part of 2012, the findings of the second study were examined by the partners and led to changes to the microloan program that were instituted by the credit union.

The Economic Context

As these activities proceeded over the five-year period, the economy of southern Ontario remained very weak against the backdrop of a faltering national economy. Indeed, the official unemployment rate for the country rose to 9 per cent in 2009, and since then annual employment growth rates in Ontario have been consistently lower than national averages. Moreover, Statistics Canada data show that an alarming 90 per cent of small businesses that entered the national market during the 2000s did not survive to the end of that decade. At the same time, household debt in both Ontario and Canada continued to climb during the 2008 to 2012 period. Likewise, urban housing prices continued to rise, putting home ownership out of the reach of much of the bottom 40 per cent of income earners and even of many in the middle quintile. As 2013 began, Ontario and Canada faced the prospects of even slower economic growth, higher consumer debt, and a looming housing crisis because of inflated prices. In short, the five years that began in 2008 proved to be a challenging economic period, particularly for low-income individuals and households (see Statistics Canada, 2010, 2012a, 2012b).

In this context, banks and other financial institutions were obliged to tread carefully. With Canada's monetary policy ensuring that interest rates remained low through 2008–12, lenders had to cope with low margins on many lines of business. In order to manage the sustained risk they confronted in both household and commercial markets, banks elected to increase fees, raise the tests for creditworthiness, and monitor all their portfolios more assiduously. In general, the banks became more cautious in their lending practices, preferring to provide more products and services to higher-income households over lower-income ones; they also became even more prudent than usual in lending to businesses (see, for example, Canadian Bankers Association, 2012).

Low-income women, and especially low-income women who were recent immigrants to Canada, were not high-priority market segments for these mainstream financial institutions, to say the least. However, credit unions were found to consistently outperform commercial banks in providing financial products and services to microbusinesses and small businesses during the years of the financial crisis (Bruce & Wong, 2013). Some credit unions, like Alterna, were open to serving low-income immigrant women.

The Microloan Program

One exception to these trends was, and remains, the Micro-Finance Program of Alterna Savings. Operating in the same context as the banks and its other competitors, Alterna had, between 2000 and 2012, loaned out almost $2 million to more than 400 borrowers who had sought to start or expand microbusinesses. Loans range from $1,000 to $15,000 and average at about $5,000. Borrowers are charged the prime rate (which averaged 3 per cent in 2012) plus a 6 per cent risk premium, as well as a small administrative fee that contributes to the management costs of the program. A typical borrower in the program is a female of

African or European descent who has few or no personal assets, an annual income below $30,000, and is on some form of government assistance. Many have been denied loans by mainstream financial institutions. Understanding that credit history may not always be an accurate indicator of an entrepreneur's prospects of success, Alterna focuses on their character instead, and rewards tenacious individuals who have diligently taken the time to receive training and develop sound business plans. Beyond the loans, Alterna assists its borrowers with free tele-classes, networking cafés (that offer professional coaching in informal social gatherings), and business literacy workshops.

In the past, borrowers have been engaged in a variety of business sectors including, but not limited to, construction, manufacturing, health care, retail and wholesale trades, food services, and entertainment. Despite this wide range, many of the microenterprises started by borrowers have been confined largely to the service sector of the Canadian economy. Company data show that, within this sector, businesses that offer professional and technical services involving accounting, information technology, marketing, health, and beauty are popular among microentrepreneurs, and account for some 21 per cent of all businesses started up. Businesses in retail trades, accommodation, and food services also make up significant components of the overall microloan portfolio, accounting for 19 per cent and 12 per cent of enterprises, respectively.

In recent years, Alterna has intensified its cooperation with other non-profit community loan funds, which guarantee 80 to 100 per cent of the microloans that are disbursed by the credit union on their behalf through the Micro-Finance Program. Rooted in the local economies of Toronto and Ottawa, these loan funds have shown that they are capable of reaching individuals in diverse communities who have the temperament to succeed in business. Leveraging this capacity has thus enabled Alterna to expand its microloan portfolio. In turn, the credit union provides loan capital and back-end administrative services in disbursing and managing the loans associated with the community loan funds, and in the process reduces the administrative expenses and improves loan repayment rates of the funds.

Looking back on its years in the microcredit business, Alterna has begun to realize that *women* are the primary – and most effective – users of microfinance products and services. For one thing, women have represented a majority of borrowers in the Alterna microloan portfolio, and that trend continues. For another, their repayment rates are far superior to those of men. This is important because lower arrears and loan loss rates improve the efficiency and sustainability of the microloan program. And this is consistent with international experience, where women have been found by microfinance institutions to be more successful borrowers (see, for example, Cheston & Kuhn, 2002). Furthermore, a number of studies confirm that, compared to men, women spend more of their income on their households, in turn improving the welfare of the whole family (Kennedy & Haddad,1994; Kennedy & Peters, 1992; Quisumbing & Maluccio, 2000; Smith, Ramakrishnan, Ndiaye, Haddad, & Martorell, 2003; Thomas, 1997). There is every reason for Alterna to believe that these same dynamics are at work in the households of women microentrepreneurs in Toronto and Ottawa.

Comparing Findings of the 2009 and 2012 Studies

As noted, Alterna and the Carleton Centre for Community Innovation have cooperated on two evaluations of the credit union's microfinance program. The aim of the 2009 evaluation was fourfold: to inform a revision of Alterna's corporate social responsibility policy; to better understand the drivers of success and failure in the program and how to mitigate unnecessary risks in the loan process; to contribute to the larger debate on the efficacy of microfinance as a poverty alleviation tool; and to garner further government support in order to expand microfinance programs across Canada. Using a mixed-methods approach (both qualitative and quantitative), this first study by the partnership employed a literature review, logic model, survey of borrowers, interviews with case-study borrowers, focus group discussions, and social return on investment techniques. Data were generated through these methods to assess the long-term impacts of the microloan program at the micro (borrower), meso (corporate), and macro (policy) levels. Of the 144 invited study participants in the microloan program, forty-seven borrowers volunteered to participate in this research project – a 33 percent participation rate (Alterna Savings, 2010, Grant, 2010; Jackson & Tarsilla, 2013; Tarsilla, 2010).

Three years later, Alterna and 3ci undertook a follow-up study. Deploying the same set of methods and reproducing the survey questions from the first study, the second research project gathered data from eight longer-term borrowers (out of thirty-one potential participants) who had participated in the earlier study, as well as nineteen newer borrowers (of thirty-seven potential participants) who had joined the program after the 2009 study. At the time of the new study, some of this pool of borrowers had been a part of the microfinance program for three years, while others had only been participants for about two months. The combined samples for the 2012 study totalled twenty-seven respondents

In the second study, therefore, 26 per cent of longer-term borrowers and 51 per cent of newer borrowers opted to participate in the research. Across the two studies, the participation rate averaged about 35 per cent. In terms of gender, 62 per cent of participants in the 2009 study were women. In the 2012 research, 40 per cent of the longer-term borrowers and 89 per cent of the newer borrowers were women. Across the two studies, then, women constituted two-thirds of all respondents. In other words, this research was mainly about women borrowers.

Micro-level Findings

Overall, the micro-level findings of the 2009 study were very positive; however, those of the 2012 study were mixed. In terms of employment status, two-thirds of the 2009 respondents had reported that their microloan-funded business was their primary source of income. By 2012, among the longer-term borrowers, this rate had fallen to 50 per cent, with the other half reporting that their businesses either had not taken off or economic pressures had forced their enterprises to close. In contrast, among the newer borrowers surveyed in 2012, all respondents reported that they were currently self-employed, and 63 per cent indicated that they received their primary income from their microloan-funded business.

The pattern for income gains was similar. That is, in 2009, two-thirds of respondents reported a sustained increase in income for their businesses over an up to eight-year period, yet only half of the sample of this older group studied in 2012 reported an increase in income of $10,000, while the other half reported a decrease of about the same amount. Among newer borrowers surveyed in 2012, however, 38 per cent saw their incomes rise in amounts ranging from $5,000 to $23,000 over an up to two-year period. These mixed results run parallel to the experience of the broader small business sector, where a growing percentage experienced a drop in income and an increase in debt between 2008 and 2012. Moreover, in the Greater Toronto Area (GTA) and Ottawa, the average income gains for small businesses in general between 2001 and 2009 were $3,200 and $6,900, respectively (Canada Mortgage and Housing Corporation, 2011). A good percentage of new borrowers in the microloan program, therefore, appear to have exceeded those average income gains.

Moreover, loan repayment rates in 2012 were not as robust as in 2009. Portfolio analysis revealed that, for all borrowers in the microlending program in early 2012, the average repayment rate was about 75 per cent, a sharp decrease from the 2009 rate of 90 per cent. However, two points are worth making here: first, the 25 per cent of un-repaid loans included a large component of loans classified as "currently in default," but the credit union can and often does recover these loans by working with the affected borrowers to restructure their payment plans. Second, this analysis included borrowers from the community loan funds as well as from Alterna per se, and repayment rates for the Alterna loans were consistently higher than for the community loan funds. In fact, Alterna as a whole tends to perform better in this respect than the study seems to suggest. For instance, in December 2012, the credit union recorded an overall portfolio balance of about $310,000; at the same time Alterna's loan loss was approximately $7,000, as many of the loan funds provide guarantees on the loans. Therefore Alterna's losses over the full portfolio amounted to about 2.25 per cent for the year. The loan loss to its in-house community loan fund for the same period was slightly higher, at 4.7 per cent.

With respect to housing, since receiving their loans, 50 per cent of longer-term borrowers in 2012 reported an improvement in their living arrangements, compared to 70 per cent in 2009. A majority of newer borrowers surveyed in 2012 reported no drastic change in their living circumstances, though 14 per cent indicated that they had moved to smaller accommodation. These findings reflect a continuing rise in housing prices in Toronto and Ottawa during the 2008 to 2012 period, and suggest that microborrowers may have been forced out of the housing market (Canadian Housing and Mortgage Corporation, 2012a). The latest figures from the Canadian Housing and Mortgage Corporation (2012b) indicate that average housing prices in the GTA rose by 7.9 per cent to about $470,000, while those in Ottawa rose by 5 per cent to about $340,000 for the 2010 to 2011 period. These rates of increase in the housing market would seem to have outpaced the growth in the capacity of the borrowers' enterprises to generate net revenues by a considerable margin.

In terms of perceived benefits, again there were important differences between the 2009 and 2012 findings. In 2012, nearly one-third of the newer borrowers claimed that their loan had improved the social and economic status of their households. A borrower identified as Sharon, for instance, said that "the loan [had] enabled [her] to work for [her] self, and also be at home with [her] children at the same time." Another new microentrepreneur identified as Gladys was thrilled with the loan, saying: "because of the loan my business is now growing fast. I am seeing the benefits." Still another borrower, Irene, was also glad that the loan had helped her to expand her business; for instance, she was now able to join a trade fair (CGTA), something she would not have been able to do prior to the boost the loan gave to her business.

Alarmingly, however, only 25 per cent of longer-term borrowers reported that this was the case, while just over 40 per cent of that group had said the same thing in 2009. Significantly, some 75 per cent of longer-term borrowers – while still largely grateful to have received the loan that enabled them to start a business – claimed that the size of their loan was too small to have a sustained impact on their socio-economic status.

The borrowers' perspectives on the challenges they faced are instructive. The following are some examples of what longer-term microentrepreneurs said when asked about the impact of the loan on their social economic status:

- "$5,000 doesn't go that far." – Alan, 2012
- "In addition to my business collapsing, I lost my job in 2009 and [I decided to leave] Toronto [and move] to a smaller town forty-five minutes away. My social economic status at this time is minute." – Morton, 2012
- "The loan I received was too small to impact my social economic status in any way." – Kendra, 2012
- "The broader economy has had a negative impact on my business and my social economic status. My business eventually went bankrupt and so I was forced to close it and relocate to another town to find a job." – Beatrice, 2012

The picture that emerges from the findings of the 2012 study is that conditions following the 2009 study were more difficult for microentrepreneurs and small businesses in general than the period prior to the 2009 study. Furthermore, it is very likely that without the provision of microcredit, borrowers and their households would have had an even more challenging experience. Where the 2009 study highlighted a very positive set of findings at the micro-level, the 2012 study generated findings that were mixed, at best. It is likely that performance on similar indicators by other financial institutions and entrepreneurs in southern Ontario and more broadly across Canada was decidedly mixed, as well (Statistics Canada, 2010, 2012b; Canada Mortgage and Housing Corporation, 2011).

Meso-level Findings

Likewise, findings at the meso-level of the credit union itself were generally positive in 2009, but quite mixed in 2012. In terms of customer loyalty, since its inception, the Micro-Finance Program has catalysed $2 million in additional business for Alterna Savings through the sales of other financial products and services to existing and new members. This is a major achievement, and it has been driven by customer loyalty. However, for longer-term borrowers, the 2012 study found that only 25 per cent stated that Alterna Savings had become their primary financial institution, a decline from the 35 per cent who made this claim in 2009. The apparent reasons for this drop include a perception among longer-term borrowers that Alterna Savings' banking fees were high, though the credit union confirms that their fees are in line with those of other financial institutions. Another disincentive cited by respondents was the relatively sparse availability of automated bank machines in their communities.

Interestingly, in contrast, 100 per cent of the newer borrowers surveyed in 2012 indicated that Alterna Savings had become their primary bank. There may be three reasons for this demonstration of loyalty among newer borrowers. First, it is now Alterna Savings' policy that all microloan borrowers must bank at the credit union. Equally important, for two-thirds of the newer borrowers, Alterna Savings was likely the only financial institution willing to finance their businesses. Indeed, one-quarter of the newer borrowers reported that their loan applications had been denied by between two to five mainstream institutions. A third source of customer loyalty was the other community loan funds that Alterna administers: borrowers who joined the microloan program through a community loan fund often stayed with Alterna Savings because of its relationship with their chosen loan fund.

The following testimonials from microentrepreneurs illustrate this loyalty to Alterna Savings:

"I will definitely keep doing business with Alterna! I really like the attention that I get from the Alterna staff; Jean Barrett [GTA Micro-Loan

Co-ordinator] is always very friendly to me when we talk. I believe she is the reason I was able to get my loan." – Gladys, 2012

"Even though I currently have three bank accounts at other institutions, I will always maintain an account at Alterna because they were the only bank willing to give me a chance. To me, Alterna does not feel like a regular bank; everyone there seems to care about my success." – Josh, 2012

With respect to corporate reputation, the positive evaluation of the Micro-Finance Program in 2009 led to extensive media coverage that enhanced the credit union's image in the community. More than a fifth of newer borrowers indicated that they had been drawn to Alterna Savings' nontraditional banking philosophy. Most newer borrowers had, in fact, been referred to Alterna Savings by local community loan funds. As one said, "I trust Alterna because [the] mentors at [my loan fund] recommended the loan program to me. My experience so far with them has been positive" (Adam, 2012). Others came to the institution on the recommendation of past borrowers and local business development centres. Only 12 per cent of newer borrowers and 20 per cent of long-term borrowers elected to join the microloan program as a result of direct marketing by Alterna Savings.

With regard to marketing exposure, more than 60 per cent of the borrowers surveyed in 2009 said that they had referred new clients – relatives, friends, and colleagues – to the credit union. However, in 2012, that number had dropped to 50 per cent among long-term borrowers. Notwithstanding, 75 per cent of newer borrowers surveyed in 2012 reported that they had referred clients to Alterna Savings. This spike in referrals by newer borrowers could be attributable to their positive experiences at financial literacy sessions organized by the credit union and its community partners, as well as networking events, tele-classes, and workshops. As Nancy said: "Workshops are presented monthly. I attended one really good one a few months ago on sales strategies and learned a lot. I receive notices via email from my contact at Alterna. I also read their newsletter sometimes, and get information from other websites. I occasionally talk to my friends about these events and try to encourage them to consult Alterna about loans and advice."

The findings at the meso-level highlight the dual necessity for the credit union to not only work to retain its current members but also to attract new borrowers to the Micro-Finance Program. Broadly speaking, the findings reported here suggest that Alterna was doing a somewhat better job attracting new customers than retaining long-standing ones. However, the long-term sustainability of the program depends on its staff being able to carry out both tasks vigorously and successfully at the same time.

Macro-level Findings

Comparing the findings of the 2009 and 2012 studies at the macro, or policy, level is also an interesting exercise: in terms of job creation, only 25 per cent of newer borrowers surveyed in the 2012 study reported that they hired at least one new employee after they received their loan. At the same time, about 75 per cent of business owners without permanent employees stated that they occasionally hired workers on a short-term, contractual basis. Note that the majority of businesses owned by newer borrowers were still relatively new, and may be able to hire more full-time workers as the businesses develop. Notably, though, none of the respondents in the longer-term borrower group reported hiring employees for their businesses. In contrast, the 2009 study found that 62 per cent of borrowers had hired multiple workers after they received their loan. On this question, then, the 2012 study underscored that microentrepreneurs were adapting to challenging economic conditions by hiring mainly part-time workers or not hiring employees at all. Despite these more modest results, it is still clear that microborrowers can have some positive job creation effects in their immediate communities. This is important from a policy perspective because it highlights the fact that microfinance, if supported in the appropriate manner, can bolster the local job market and reduce community reliance on government employment programs.

In the area of government assistance, though, the two studies actually yielded similar findings. That is, in 2009, 42 per cent of study participants entered the program on some form of government assistance, usually provincial social assistance (welfare) or federal employment insurance. Upon receiving their loan, this number decreased by half, to about 21 per cent, showing, rather definitively, that microfinance can help reduce social assistance costs to governments and taxpayers. This finding was reinforced in 2012, when *none* of the 75 per cent of longer-term borrowers who had previously received such assistance had returned to government support. Among newer borrowers, the percentage receiving government assistance also dramatically decreased, from 75 per cent prior to receiving their loan to about 13 per cent after receiving their loan. In fact, the 2012 study calculated that this reduction in public support saved governments and taxpayers as much as $1,000 per participant per month. It is also noteworthy that the 2012 study found that newer borrowers reduced their participation rate in government-sponsored mentoring and job-placement programs from 62 per cent prior to joining the microloan program to 14 per cent after they received their loan. This sharp decrease in the use of such public services represents a considerable savings to governments and taxpayers.

The 2009 study had found that tax payments by borrowers had increased substantially as a result of their augmented income; unincorporated business owners paid a combined federal and provincial rate of at least 30 per cent on income earned, whereas owners of incorporated businesses paid a combined rate of just under 17 per cent. However, the 2012 study found that all borrowers surveyed, both longer-term and newer, reported that their tax payments remained unchanged over time. In other words, their income gains were so modest that they rarely had to pay additional tax. This finding speaks to the more difficult conditions faced by borrowers at the beginning compared with at the end of the 2008–12 period. Thus, while the additional contributions to employment and tax payments by the Alterna Savings microentrepreneurs proved to be modest in the latter part of the five years ending in 2012, the gains in savings to governments and taxpayers associated with microloans were substantial and held steady, even under conditions of a sustained economic downturn. This is an important public-policy finding.

Other Findings

The 2012 study yielded other notable findings. It proved difficult to recruit longer-term borrowers for the 2012 study, though newer borrowers were more willing to participate in the research. In light of the experiences of both studies, there appears to be excitement among newer borrowers, but it is evident that this can dissipate over time. This is especially true when there is infrequent contact between borrowers and Alterna program staff in the context of a challenging economic environment.

The longer-term borrowers in particular commented on this infrequent contact and indicated they would be open to more engagement from program staff. A considerable number of longer-term borrowers expressed disappointment that their interest rates on subsequent loans did not improve after they had successfully paid off their initial loan.

They suggested that the credit union lay out a "roadmap for success" that makes it clear how they could work towards obtaining a better interest rate on their next loan. As a borrower identified as Morton said in 2012: "[It would be better if the credit union] lowered the interest rates for borrowers who have [successfully] paid off their loan and are [now] on to the second or third loan."

The report of the 2012 study included recommendations in regard to these and other issues. In particular, it was recommended that the microloan program's portfolio of borrowers be evaluated on an annual basis to enable the program to learn and adapt rapidly. It was also recommended that borrowers who leave the program be surveyed in order to monitor longer-term impact and to maintain contact with these entrepreneurs. Further, the study included a recommendation that the Alterna program institute a quarterly or biannual electronic newsletter to increase the frequency and efficiency of its communication with all borrowers. The newsletter could feature inspiring stories of microborrowers, testimonials of successes and challenges, business advice, and updates of statistics on the program (e.g., average savings rates of members, reductions in dependence on government programs, et cetera). Finally, the 2012 report recommended that the credit union offer more appealing interest rates to borrowers who successfully meet agreed-upon benchmarks with their first loan.

Program Changes

The mixed, sobering findings of the 2012 study prompted the credit union, in the last quarter of that year, to make some important changes to the microloan program. These actions were informed by the recommendations contained in the 2012 study. Two major changes are worth noting: a flexible, sliding interest rate and a community development department.

Flexible, Sliding Interest Rate

Responding to the recommendation of the 2012 report prepared by the Carleton Centre for Community Innovation, Alterna Savings has introduced a sliding interest rate that, once implemented, will be tied to borrowers' Beacon scores. Beacon scores are single numbers that summarize the credit risk of a potential borrower. They range from 300 to 900, with 750 and above considered a good score. Factors used in determining an individual's Beacon score include previous payment history, current level of indebtedness, length of credit history, and types of credit being accessed currently. It is hoped that this measure will not only serve as an added incentive for entrepreneurs to join the program but also improve their credit scores during the period in which they participate in the program. The table below illustrates more clearly how the sliding interest rate will be applied:

Table 7.1 Terms of the New Sliding Interest Rate for Microloan Borrowers

Borrower's Beacon Score	Interest Rate
750+	Prime +2.00%
680–749	Prime +3.00%
649–679	Prime +4.00%
Under 649	Prime +6.00%

In a further effort by Alterna to increase the incentive for entrepreneurs to join the program, the introduction of this new sliding interest rate has been coupled with a reduction in administrative fees. In the past, a microentrepreneur would be expected to pay an administrative fee equivalent to 6 per cent of their loan amount. Now, all borrowers will only be required to pay a flat fee of $100. Alterna calculates that this policy change will result in savings of up to $800 per loan for microentrepreneurs.

New Community Development Department

A second significant change was organizational in nature. In 2013, the microloan program moved from its location, then in Alterna's marketing department, and became part of a new community development department, which focuses on promoting community economic development. With particular reference to the microloan program, the new department will pursue three priority areas: expanding outreach activities and targeted initiatives to improve financial growth for the credit union and microborrowers; improving internal processes – particularly for loan procedures and borrower follow-up – to increase client retention rates and community awareness of the program; and managing risk and reducing default rates through a mix of methods, such as more frequent and meaningful interactions between staff and borrowers, increased provision of business advisory services, and free marketing assistance through an electronic newsletter.

It is too soon to determine whether these changes will deliver real results. However, it is clear that, in instituting these measures, Alterna is attentive to the feedback from its microlending program and it is committed to developing it further. It is likely that most of Alterna's microloan borrowers will continue to be low-income women. All businesses must adapt and evolve, and try to continuously improve, in the midst of a changing environment. This is as true for a medium-sized financial enterprise like Alterna as it is for a woman-owned microbusiness in Toronto or Ottawa – or anywhere else, for that matter. Through these surveys of its microborrowers, Alterna is mobilizing knowledge for its own resilience and that of its portfolio entrepreneurs.

Implications

Clearly, the 2012 research put into bold relief that the longer-term borrowers in the microloan program were feeling the pressure of the economic downturn; this was true both in terms of running a viable business and of maintaining their relationship to the credit union. While Alterna Savings could, and perhaps should, have done more to communicate with and support these members, much of what the borrowers faced during 2008–12 was caused by forces in the environment that challenged all small business owners in southern Ontario and across Canada. Indeed, it is possible that without the provision of microfinance for self-employment, these borrowers would have fared far worse in the downturn. This is a question that could be investigated empirically. It should be reiterated, too, that, in spite of intense economic pressures, the reduced reliance on government assistance among borrowers held steady for the whole period under study for both longer-term and newer microcredit recipients. Why this occurred is also an important question for future research.

Taken together, the two studies confirm that microcredit and microenterprise can be important tools for building resilience among low-income borrowers – who are predominantly women – in the face of economic turbulence. Moreover, the self-employment created by these tools proved to be a durable solution that enabled most borrowers to cope with the economic storm in southern Ontario. But this solution has its limits, and this group of stakeholders has serious economic vulnerabilities. As noted, one strategy that may be beneficial is for the organizations working to strengthen the resilience of low-income microentrepreneurs to engage with them more, and to more rapidly adapt programs to the changing needs and conditions of this group. In other words, resilience must be built not only at the micro-level of the individual microentrepreneur but also at the meso-level of support programs for these actors. The research reported here also shows that new knowledge creation is critical for institutions to make informed and targeted changes to such programs.

What this research did not probe in detail, however, is how, on a daily basis, the women entrepreneurs in the microloan program adjust their business and household strategies to respond to evolving challenges and opportunities. But both studies have identified successful borrowers whose experiences could be examined at a more granular level in future research. This type of research could yield useful further insights on how low-income women and their families adapt, learn, bounce back from adversity, and keep moving forward – in other words, how they build resilience.

As it happens, the management team responsible for implementing the microloan program is comprised solely of women. This is appropriate given the gender composition of the portfolio. As they codirected the 2009 and 2012 studies in conjunction with Carleton University personnel, they learned much about their program and took action on the knowledge produced by that research. And, in introducing significant changes to the program in late 2012, the Alterna team demonstrated that they, like their microentrepreneur customers, were (and are) women building resilience. By ensuring that the program adapts and improves – that it remains resilient as conditions in the environment evolve – these changes can enable individual women entrepreneurs to more effectively navigate the economic turbulence of the times.

There are implications for the research partnership, as well. First, the partnership must walk a fine line between reporting the findings of these studies in a frank and open manner and, at the same time, maintaining Alterna Savings' reputation in a very competitive sector. Because the issues faced by microborrowers matter not only to the credit union but also to Ontario and Canada, the partnership has engaged this challenge – and is committed to continuing to do so. Second, the partners are planning future action research on the microloan program to monitor progress, to improve operations and results, and to measure the value created by microfinance. And it seems likely that this next phase of joint knowledge creation will be undertaken against a

backdrop of sustained – and perhaps even worsening – economic challenges for the province and the country.

Conclusion

This chapter has reported on two studies of borrowers in a microloan
program in southern Ontario, which were undertaken at the beginning
and end, respectively, of the five-year period ending in 2012. The chapter
has used this research to assess the experiences of individual microentrepreneurs and that of the program delivering capital and other support to them. The research indicated that pressure from the economic
downturn of these years intensified, especially for longer-term borrowers in the portfolio, and that borrowers faced real challenges in maintaining viable businesses during the period. Nonetheless, overall, most
borrowers made it through the period with their businesses intact and
did not return to government assistance. The tools of microcredit and
microenterprise enabled them to navigate the economic storm. And there
is some evidence to suggest that they did so more successfully than other
small business owners in Ontario and Canada during the same period.

The studies also showed that the microloan program itself should be
adapted to respond to the new conditions faced by its borrowers. In late
2012, Alterna Savings made significant changes to its Community
Micro-Finance Program that were aimed at enabling its members to
more effectively build resilience in the years ahead. A clear majority of
these members in the program are women. The credit union is committed to accompanying these women and men in the next phase of their
entrepreneurial efforts, while expanding the microloan portfolio. At the
same time, the next phase of the work of the research partnership between Alterna Savings and Carleton University will create new knowledge to assist the credit union with further learning and adaptation. For
all the parties involved, this important journey continues.

REFERENCES

Alterna Savings. (2007). *2006–2007 Accountability report.* Retrieved from https://
   www.alterna.ca/AlternaSavings/AboutUs/Governance/CorporateReports/
Alterna Savings. (2010). *Community Micro-Loan Program report.* Retrieved
   from https://www.alterna.ca/AlternaSavings/AboutUs/Governance/
   CorporateReports/

Bruce, D., & Wong, Q. (2013). The battle of the banks. *Canadian Federation of Independent Business, Montreal*. Retrieved from http://www.cfib-fcei.ca/english/article/5171-battle-of-the-banks-how-small-businesses-rate-their-banks.html

Canada Mortgage and Housing Corporation (CMHC). (2011). *Canadian housing observer*. Retrieved from https://www.cmhc-schl.gc.ca/en/corp/about/cahoob/upload/Chapter_1b_EN_dec21_w.pdf

Canada Mortgage and Housing Corporation (CMHC). (2012a). *CHS: Housing costs – Price indices*. Retrieved from: https://www03.cmhcschl.gc.ca/catalog/productDetail.cfm?lang=en&cat=55&itm=4&fr=1359477353268

Canada Mortgage and Housing Corporation (CMHC). (2012b). *Canadian housing observer*. Retrieved from *https://www03.cmhcschl.gc.ca/catalog/product Detail.cfm?cat=122&itm=24&lang=en&fr=1359478175687*

Canadian Bankers Association (2012). Bank lending to business: Backgrounder. Retrieved from http://www.cba.ca/en/media-room/50-backgrounders-on-banking-issues/128-business-credit-availability

Cheston, S., & Kuhn, L. (2002). Empowering women through microfinance. In S. Daley-Harris (Ed.), *Pathways out of poverty: Innovations in micro-finance for the poorest families* (pp. 167–228). Bloomfield, CT: Kumarian Press.

Coyle, M., Wehrell, R., & MacDonald, J. (2006, November). Small is beautiful, big is necessary: Canada's commercial and cooperative answers to the global challenge of microfinance access. Paper presented at the Global Microcredit Summit, Coady International Institute, Halifax, NS.

Grant, T. (2010, April 28). Small loans yield big returns. *The Globe and Mail*. Retrieved from http://www.theglobeandmail.com/report-on-business/small-business/sb-money/business-funding/small-loans-yield-big-returns/article4258978/

Jackson, E.T., & Tarsilla, M. (2013). Mixed methods in social accounting: evaluating the micro-loan program of Alterna Savings Credit Union. In L. Mook (Ed.), *Accounting for social value* (pp. 117–138). Toronto, ON: University of Toronto Press.

Kennedy, E., & Haddad, L. (1994). Are preschoolers from female-headed households less malnourished? A comparative analysis of results from Ghana and Kenya. *Journal of Development Studies, 30*(3), 680–695. http://dx.doi.org/10.1080/00220389408422332

Kennedy, E., & Peters, P. (1992). Household food security and child nutrition: the interaction of income and gender of household head. *World Development, 20*(8), 1077–1085. http://dx.doi.org/10.1016/0305-750X(92)90001-C

Quisumbing, A., & Maluccio, J. (2000). Intrahousehold allocation and gender relations: new empirical evidence from four developing countries (FCND Discussion paper No. 84). Washington, DC: IFPRI.

Smith, L.C., Ramakrishnan, U., Ndiaye, A., Haddad, L., & Martorell, R. (2003). The importance of women's status for child nutrition in developing countries (Research Report No. 131). Washington, DC: IFPRI.

Social Innovation Generation. (2010). *Adaptability and resilience.* Toronto, ON. Retrieved from http://www.sigeneration.ca/home/resilience-and-adaptability/

Statistics Canada (2010). *Employment services bulletin.* Retrieved from http://www.statcan.gc.ca/pub/63-252-x/63-252-x2012001-eng.pdf/

Statistics Canada. (2012a). *Labour force survey estimates (LFS), supplementary unemployment rates by sex and age group, annual* (CANSIM Table 282–0086).

Statistics Canada. (2012b). *Labour force survey, November 2012.* Retrieved from http://www.statcan.gc.ca/daily-quotidien/121207/dq121207a-eng.htm/

Tarsilla, M. (2010). *Social impact evaluation of the Alterna Savings Micro-Loan Program.* Ottawa, ON: Carleton Centre for Community Innovation.

The Free Dictionary. (2013). Resilience. Huntington Valley, PA: Farlex, Inc. Retrieved from http://www.thefreedictionary.com/

The Rockefeller Foundation. (2014). Resilience. New York. Retrieved from http://www.rockefellerfoundation.org/our-work/current-work/resilience

Thomas, D. (1997). Incomes, expenditures and health outcomes: evidence on intrahousehold resource allocation. In L. Haddad, J. Hoddinott, & H. Alderman (Eds.), *Intrahousehold resource allocation in developing countries* (pp.142-165). Baltimore, MD: Johns Hopkins University Press.

8 Canadian Immigrants and Their Access to Services: A Case Study of a Social Purpose Enterprise

MARLENE WALK, ITAY GREENSPAN, HONEY CROSSLEY, AND FEMIDA HANDY

Introduction

The purpose of this chapter is to investigate facilitating factors and barriers to service utilization for an immigrant-dominated, low-income population. Using a case study of a social purpose enterprise that offers employment and skills-training programs to Canadian immigrants, we assess the factors that influence service seekers' utilization of such training programs. We are especially interested in the utilization patterns of programs offered by, and managed as, a social purpose enterprise that competes in the marketplace with for-profit companies for clients and resources. This case study focuses on the Academy of Computer & Employment Skills (A.C.E.S.), a Toronto-based social purpose enterprise operated by Working Skills Centre (WSC). Launched in 2008, A.C.E.S. offers training programs in office administration, computerized accounting, medical reception, and supply chain administration for a mostly low-income immigrant population.

Service utilization is the extent to which people make use of services available in the community or in a specific organization. A number of studies across Canada, the United States, and Britain have found that service utilization is more difficult, and utilization rates are lower, for marginalized people when compared with the general population. Most often service utilization obstacles have to be overcome by the elderly (Wolinsky et al., 1983), immigrants (Derose, Bahney, Lurie, & Escarce, 2009; Derose, Escarce, & Lurie, 2007), and especially by older immigrants (Jang, Kim, & Chiriboga, 2005; Lai & Chau, 2007) and female immigrants (Kouritzin, 2000; Sword, Watt, & Krueger, 2006). Areas of underutilized services by immigrants include health care and mental health care (Reitz, 1995).

While health-care underutilization by immigrants has been widely documented (Derose et al., 2009; Derose et al., 2007; Fenta, Hyman, & Noh, 2007; Jang et al., 2005; Lai & Chau, 2007; Sword et al., 2006). Little research has been conducted on other services that immigrants might seek in their efforts to integrate into the host country – for instance, skill training that potentially improves employment chances. Indeed, as Reitz (1995, Ch. 2, para. 6) articulates:

> There is a need to measure and analyze actual rates of service utilization, and barriers to utilization, experienced by members of clearly defined minority population groups, to establish degrees of inequity in access to specific types of services experienced by such groups, and to measure the impact that these inequities have on the well-being of the groups or parts of the groups.

Our study examines the effectiveness of programs that aim to help immigrants to better settle and integrate into their host societies. Equal and effective utilization of employment training services for immigrants is a matter of concern for non-profit managers in numerous countries dealing with the challenges of global migration. Social outcomes are critical for programs designed as social purpose enterprises (see Chapter 1 in this book). Social purpose enterprises may compete with for-profit companies and hence need to justify their not-for-profit status, which affords them access to income subsidies and tax exemptions. Accordingly, our main research question is: What are the factors that foster or hinder enrolment (that is: service utilization) in employment training programs that operate as social purpose enterprises run by a non-profit organization?

The chapter begins with a short background discussion on immigrants and service utilization. It then lays the theoretical framework of the analysis, drawing on the Behavioural Model of Healthcare Utilization (Andersen & Newman, 1973). Following description of the case study and the methods of investigation, the study results are presented. Finally, we discuss what recommendations can be offered based on the study findings.

Background: Immigrants and Service Utilization

Service Utilization among Immigrants

Immigrants are a highly heterogeneous population in terms of their legal status, skills, professions, and other socio-economic factors that influence their ability to access services in their host countries (Lai & Chau, 2007). Generally, scholars point to a variety of barriers to immigrants' access to services. The most widely acknowledged barrier is the lack of services provided in the native language of the service-seeking immigrant, and the low level of language proficiency in the host country's official language(s) (Derose et al., 2009; Lai & Chau, 2007). Numerous studies have focused on the utilization of health care services among immigrants in health-care settings, limited language proficiency can lead to problems in understanding medication instructions and dosage information, which can result in additional health problems (Wilson, Chen, Grumbach, Wang, & Fernandez, 2005).

Similarly, cultural differences between the host country and the predominant culture of the country of origin might be a barrier to utilization. For instance, immigrants may hold different perceptions of health-care provision as compared to the prevalent views in North America, such as the appropriate relationship between care providers and recipients, which is culturally determined (Fenta et al., 2007).

Besides the language and cultural barriers, immigrants' socio-economic background, educational attainment, level of occupation, earnings, legal status, and residential location were identified as influential parameters in immigrant health-care utilization (Derose et al., 2007). Despite the variations in educational attainment among immigrant groups, those with lower educational levels, lower income, or low-skill jobs tend to face more obstacles in health-service utilization (Derose et al., 2007). Immigrants' legal status, too, influences the rate of health-care utilization. Undocumented immigrants usually do not have health insurance; therefore, they tend to seek services only when it will directly improve their health condition (Derose et al., 2007; Lai & Chau, 2007). In countries like the United States that do not have universal health care, lack of health insurance immediately reduces the likelihood of using health-care services (Kaiser Commission on Medicaid and the Uninsured, 2000). Residential location can be influential depending on the newness of the destination. If a place is already established as an immigrant destination, networks of immigrants with similar backgrounds might be available to help newcomers access information about services (Derose et al., 2009; Derose et al., 2007).

While the above review points to barriers to immigrants' health-care utilization, little is known about utilization of other services that immigrants might seek in their efforts to integrate into the host country. This chapter adds to the existing literature by focusing on utilization of job and skills-training services that can potentially improve immigrants' employability in the host country's labour market. Data show that two-thirds of the immigrants arriving in Canada between 2000 and 2001 planned to pursue continuing education on their arrival (Statistics Canada, 2003). Among surveyed immigrants, further education and training is widely regarded as the key to successful labour market entry. The most commonly hoped for forms of education were a university degree (40 per cent) followed by language instruction (28 per cent) and job-related training courses or seminars (25 per cent). After six months in Canada, 12 per cent of immigrants had in fact taken some form of job-related training (Statistics Canada, 2003).

When asked about their ability to access further education and training, 40 per cent of immigrant respondents stated that they encountered barrier(s) along the process. Language and finances were the most commonly cited problems (Statistics Canada, 2003). Other barriers cited were qualifications gained outside Canada that were not accepted, limited spaces in desired training courses, and lack of time. Aycan and Berry (1996) similarly regarded a lack of language competency to be the major difficulty in getting credentials and accreditations, thus contributing to an inability of immigrants to fully integrate into the labour force. Because of the need to understand these barriers, this case study examines immigrants' ability to access services and to utilize professional development and skills training offered by a social purpose enterprise.

Immigrants to Canada

In 2010, over 280,000 people in Canada received permanent resident status (CIC, 2011, p. 3), making them legal immigrants to Canada. They originated from Asia and Pacific (48 per cent), Africa and the Middle East (24 per cent), Europe and the United Kingdom (15 per cent), and the United States and South and Central America (13 per cent) (CIC, 2011). Of these immigrants, 67 per cent spoke some English, although English was the mother tongue of only 9 per cent of these people.

About 18 per cent of Canadians (roughly 6.1 million people, most of whom are first-generation immigrants) have a language other than English or French as their first language (Statistics Canada, 2003). According to the 2006 Canadian census, legal immigrants to Canada account for 20 per cent of the Canadian population (Statistics Canada, 2006). Over the past decade, it is believed that undocumented migration to Canada

Table 8.1 Recent Immigrant Population and the General Canadian Population
(Aged 25–64 Years) by Level of Education, 2006 (%)

Population	Without high school diploma	High school diploma	Some post-secondary	College or trade certification	University degree
Canadians	23	20	8	30	19
Recent immigrants	9	15	9	16	51

Note. Adopted from Statistics Canada (2008).

has been rapidly increasing. Even though accurate numbers are missing, it is estimated that there are 20,000 to 500,000 undocumented immigrants living in Canada (Magalhaes, Carrasco, & Gastaldo, 2010).

Immigrants to Canada are highly educated (Table 8.1). Of those who immigrated between 2001 and 2006, 51 per cent hold a university degree, compared to only 19 per cent of Canadian citizens, while only 15 per cent of immigrants hold a high school diploma compared to 20 per cent among Canadian citizens (Statistics Canada, 2008). This difference reflects Canada's immigration policy, which prioritizes highly educated immigrants, such as engineers and health-care professionals, who can fill required occupations in the Canadian economy (Aydemir & Sweetman, 2006).

Theoretical Framework

Drawing on Andersen and Newman's (1973) Behavioural Model of Healthcare Utilization, we investigate various factors that might explain immigrants' access to and utilization of job and skills-training services in a social purpose enterprise. Originally developed for health-care settings the model was widely tested and applied among various immigrant populations (Derose et al., 2009; Fenta et al., 2007; Jang et al., 2005). We adapt this model to the context of immigrants' utilization of skills-training services. Given the similarities in the process of using services, this model provides a good framework for studying those who search for job training and skills development services.

Andersen and Newman (1973) present two overarching factors that might explain individuals' service utilization, or lack thereof. *Predisposing factors* consist of an individual's socio-demographics, the social structure in which the person is embedded, and his/her beliefs. *Enabling* (or impeding) factors are the means individuals have that help them to *access* services (Andersen & Newman, 1973; Derose et al., 2009), including aspects of their families and communities. They point out that their model serves as a *guide* to the selection of variables rather than as a rigid framework.

In the predisposing factors, following Andersen and Newman (1973), we include age, gender, marital status, and language as sociodemographic variables. Social structure variables consist of an individual's educational attainment and immigration status. Beliefs are measured by an individual's assessment of self-efficacy. As enabling factors, we include income and quality of life as measures of *family aspects,* and diversity of friendships and faith-based engagement as measures of *community aspects.* Figure 8.1 illustrates the theoretical framework and key concepts for this study. The operationalization of the measures is discussed in the method section.

The Case Study

Working Skills Centre

This study focuses on the case of Working Skills Centre (WSC) and its social purpose enterprise – Academy of Computer & Employment Skills (A.C.E.S.). Founded in 1978, WSC is a Toronto-based non-profit agency dedicated to the advancement and empowerment of immigrants, primarily women, through helping them to access Canadian employment. Initially, WSC supported only women from Spanish- and Portuguese-speaking countries, but soon after it opened up its services to women who immigrated to Canada from any country (Working Skills Centre, 2012a). Since 2005, the agency has served all unemployed individuals – men or women, immigrants or not – with the majority (83 per cent) of the clientele still being immigrant women. WSC's support programs consist of settlement services, work experience and job placement, and professional development and skills training – the latter program is the focus of this chapter. Funded in part by the Canadian Ministry of Citizenship and Immigration (CIC), WSC assists as many as 3,200 individuals annually. Given the highly diverse population that WSC serves, the agency emphasizes the importance of being culturally sensitive. For example, WSC staff and board members speak sixteen different languages and represent different ethnic, cultural, and religious orientations (Working Skills Centre, 2012c).

Figure 8.1 Theoretical Framework Adapted from Andersen and Newman (1973)

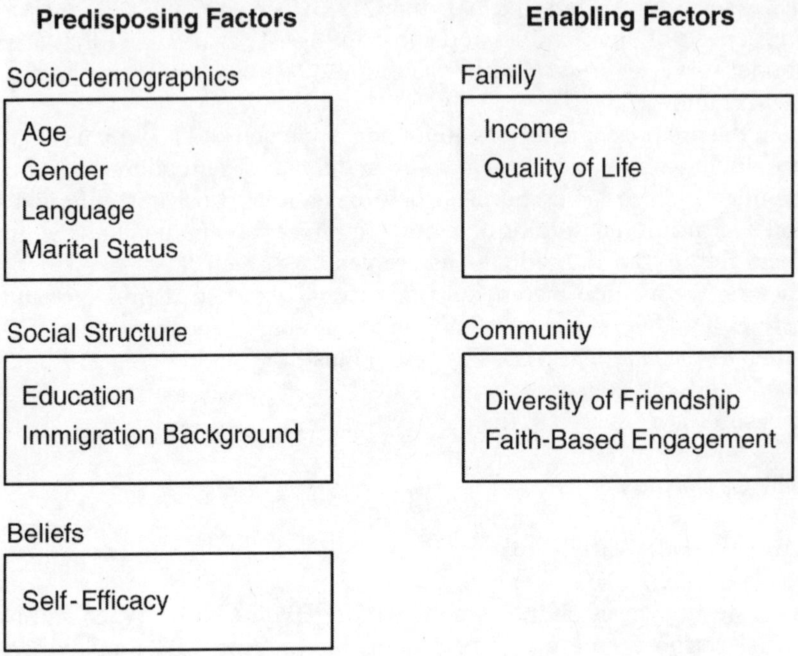

Predisposing Factors	**Enabling Factors**

Socio-demographics

Age
Gender
Language
Marital Status

Family

Income
Quality of Life

Social Structure

Education
Immigration Background

Community

Diversity of Friendship
Faith-Based Engagement

Beliefs

Self-Efficacy

Academy of Computer & Employment Skills (A.C.E.S.)

A.C.E.S. is a social purpose enterprise, established by WSC in 2008, when WSC transformed its long-standing community-based training into a private career college that operates in accordance with Ontario's Private Career Colleges Act of 2005 (Ministry of Training, Colleges and Universities). This employment and skills-training enterprise awards diplomas for a variety of training courses, such as office administration, supply chain administration, computerized accounting, and medical reception. A.C.E.S. is an income-generating enterprise embedded within WSC as a parent non-profit organization, and therefore falls under the definition of a social purpose enterprise (see Chapter 1). Most of the program's revenue stems from third-party contracts (e.g., City of Toronto) and is supplemented by fee-paying students. Corporate and individual donations help to fund WSC scholarships and bursaries that are awarded to selected A.C.E.S. students. The training programs usually take six months, or six hundred hours of training, to complete (Working Skills Centre, 2012d). Hands-on workshops and small class sizes ensure that the students receive plenty of personal instruction in an environment that mirrors a professional work setting (Working Skills Centre, 2012b). On completion of the academic program, graduates can choose to attend an unpaid internship for six weeks, through which they gain practical experience and apply the skills learned during the program. This is followed by a six-month support period, where WSC counsellors work with graduates, providing job search and job maintenance assistance. With an annual average of 320 participants, agency records suggest that graduates have a success rate of 73 per cent in finding employment following program completion (Working Skills Centre, 2012a).

Information sessions about available programs and services are held weekly to potential clients, and clients decide which programs interest them most. Because A.C.E.S. is a vocational program that aims towards employment, eligibility requirements have to be met on enrolment. In that sense, some filtering of service utilization is done by the agency rather than as a result of the client's choice. Students need to be eighteen years or older, commit to attend the entire training, have English language proficiency and basic computer literacy, and hold at least a secondary school graduation diploma (SSGD) or its equivalent. Interested clients must complete English, math, and computer literacy assessments. In addition, WSC employment counsellors assess potential clients' job readiness and employability during a scheduled interview. If eligibility criteria are not met, WSC refers clients to other programs or agencies. An admissions team makes the final decision for enrolment, since demand constantly exceeds supply. Spaces in the training programs are offered to those candidates who are most likely to be successful.

Candidates face various barriers when considering program enrolment. Practical barriers include, for example, cost of childcare and transportation. While those on social assistance get financial aid for transportation (lowering the scope of the transportation barrier), recent cutbacks have decreased affordable daycare, increasing the burden of this barrier, especially for single mothers, as indicated by WSC client records. Clients' immigration status can be another barrier, especially for refugees who need to have a work permit before accessing diploma programs (although they can access settlement support services and language classes immediately). Lastly, language barriers often hinder training attendance of interested participants. WSC tries to support these candidates with language training or by referring them to free ESL programs. Some A.C.E.S. programs are offered part-time, evening or weekends, allowing further flexibility for those working in other jobs or fulfilling family responsibilities (Working Skills Centre, 2012d). From a supply side perspective, the limited availability of sponsored seats is the program's biggest barrier. While government grants cover the costs of about eighty to ninety people annually, over five hundred express interest in attending in an average year, and for fee payers, the costs are often either a hardship or a deterrent.

Community-University Collaborative Research: The project was carried out as a collaborative effort between WSC, the parent organization of A.C.E.S., and an academic team from the University of Pennsylvania. Typical of research collaborations between academia and the community, we experienced both the benefits and challenges of aligning our distinct interests, expectations, schedules, and priorities (Orr & Bennett, 2012). At times, it felt as if the teams were speaking two different languages, which is a common challenge in collaborative projects (Orr & Bennett, 2012). Other times, the research team tried to mitigate difficulties through regular conference calls and personal visits at the research site. Despite these minor difficulties, the research experience was mutually helpful, as benefits certainly offset the challenges.

Methods

Design

We use a cross-sectional study design with a convenience sample of potential clients who intended to utilize job-training services. First, a sample was drawn from a population of job-seeking immigrants and second-generation immigrants to Canada who attended the weekly information sessions about A.C.E.S. programs held at WSC. From this population, some enrolled in the training programs and others did not. The study compared between these two groups: service users and non-users.

Recruitment and Data Collection

WSC staff and volunteers facilitated recruitment and data collection. Data were collected from two sources. First, administrative data, including demographics, employment, and education information, were collected using an intake form from *all* potential candidates who attended open information sessions at WSC. The agency collects these data routinely, unrelated to the research project. Second, all information session attendees from December 2010 to June 2012 were asked to voluntarily fill out an additional survey, before the decisions about acceptance to the training program were made. The administrative data are available for a greater number of individuals because not all information session attendees chose to fill out the survey. Accordingly, sample sizes of Models 1 and 2 below, which rely on administrative data, are higher compared to sample sizes of Models 3 to 5, which rely on survey data.

The survey contains two components: social and personal-behavioural. The social component focuses on participants' social and political integration into Canadian society. The personal-behavioural component includes measures of participants' quality of life, self-efficacy, and empowerment.

Variables

The analysed variables were obtained from both administrative and survey data using matched unique identifiers. In light of several challenges in the matching process, we use in this chapter only reliable matched cases, as described below.

1) PREDISPOSING FACTORS – SOCIO-DEMOGRAPHICS
Predisposing factors, adapted from Andersen and Newman (1973), are personal characteristics that existed prior to service utilization and consist of socio-demographic, social structural, and attitudinal-belief variables. As socio-demographic variables, we used participants' information from the agency's intake forms. These included age, gender, native language, and marital status. Age is a continuous variable measuring clients' year of birth. Gender is dichotomized for female and male (female = 1, male = 0). Language was assessed by asking participants about their native language. This variable was recoded as a dummy variable with "English = 1" for native English speakers and "not English = 0" for those whose first language is not English. Marital status was dichotomized, too, for "Single" (yes = 1, no = 0).[1]

2) PREDISPOSING FACTORS – SOCIAL STRUCTURE
Social structure variables reflect the status of the individual in society (Andersen & Newman, 1973). We operationalized social status using

the clients' educational attainment. Educational attainment (hereinafter "Education") was treated as continuous variable.[2]

3) PREDISPOSING FACTORS – BELIEFS

Andersen and Newman (1973) argued that beliefs are not a direct reason for service utilization, but could lead to differences in the extent to which individuals are inclined to use services. In this study, individuals' attitudes and beliefs were operationalized using a measure of self-efficacy. We draw on Bandura (1997), who defines self-efficacy as "beliefs in one's capabilities to organize and execute the courses of action required to produce given attainments" (Bandura, 1997, p. 3). Those beliefs also impact motivation by forming aspirations, influencing choices of behavioural action, and furthermore, shaping the expected outcome of personal efforts (Bandura, 1997; Chen, Gully, & Eden, 2001). Using a validated scale known as the New General Self-Efficacy Scale (Chen et al., 2001), participants were asked about their "overall ability to perform successfully in different situations" and about their confidence in the effectiveness of their actions. All scale items were aggregated into a continuous variable of *self-efficacy*.[3]

4) ENABLING FACTORS – FAMILY

Enabling factors positively contribute to the access of services (Andersen & Newman, 1973). We measure both "family" and "community" aspects in this study. We use *income* and *quality of life* to measure "family" as one important enabling factor. Income was assessed by asking participants about their current source of income. In the analysis the income variable was a dummy variable of whether or not participants receive income security.[4] We conceptualized "quality of life" as global quality of life that encompasses general satisfaction and happiness with life (Oleson, 1990). One item measuring Happiness was taken from the European Social Survey (Safi, 2010) and nine items were taken from The Manchester Short Assessment of Quality of Life (MANSA) (Priebe, Huxley, Knight, & Evans, 1999). MANSA is not specifically illness-related, thus it allows for comparisons with the general population, which is appropriate in our case (Oliver, Huxley, Priebe, & Kaiser, 1997). Some of the items on this scale pertain to an individual's relationship with his or her family. For this reason, we include this measure under the family factor (asking questions such as, "How satisfied are you with your relationship with your family?") The variable was operationalized as an aggregation of a ten-item scale.[5]

5) ENABLING FACTORS – COMMUNITY

Certain aspects that are prevalent in a person's community could potentially enable or hinder a person from utilizing services. We measured aspects of community using *Social Capital,* a multidimensional construct that we define as "the resources available to actors as a function of their location in the structure of their social relations" (Adler & Kwon, 2002, p. 18). For our analysis we used the Social Capital Community Benchmark Survey (SCCBS), which is based on Robert Putnam's theoretical construct of social capital (Roper Center for Public Opinion Research, 2000). Out of ten indices of social capital that were initially developed, we measured six: electoral politics, protest politics, civic leadership, faith-based engagement, diversity of friendships, and charitable behaviours, with two items each for a total of twelve. Analysis for internal consistency suggested that in our data only two of these measures – faith-based engagement and diversity of friendship – have high-enough internal consistency; therefore, these were the two subscales that we used to operationalize "community" as an enabling factor.[6]

Table 8.2 summarizes the descriptive characteristics (means and standard deviations) and the factor score (Cronbach's α) for the measured scales used in our analysis: self-efficacy, quality of life, and the social capital subscales. Study participants' self-efficacy was high. Overall, participants rated their quality of life as decent, with scores ranging above the midpoint. Looking at faith-based engagement and diversity of friendships, we found that both scores range above the midpoint.

Table 8.2

Descriptive Characteristics of Measured Scales

Variables (measures)	Range	Mean	SD	α
Self-efficacy (Beliefs)	1–5	4.08	0.59	0.89
Quality of Life (Family)	1–7	4.82	1.09	0.89
Faith-based Engagement (Community)[a]	1–5	3.20	1.39	0.80
Diversity of Friendships (Community)[a]	1–5	2.83	1.33	0.88

Note. [a] Items were log-transformed for analysis; original values are reported here.

Sample Description

Our data are comprised of two different samples: (1) The first sample was a full census of all potential WSC clients (N = 890) who attended information sessions during the years 2010 to 2012, and it included their demographic data and enrolment information. For these data, we tested to what extent demographic and social structural factors (as two parts of predisposing factors) play a role in using training services. (2) The second sample was a subset of the 890 WSC clients (N = 378, or 42.5 per cent of the potential pool of respondents), who agreed to take the additional survey that had questions on their attitudes and beliefs, quality of life, and available social capital and was designed to determine to what extent beliefs, family, and community factors influence utilization of services. This group was subdivided into two: those who participated in A.C.E.S. programs (N = 145 or 38 per cent of the 378 who took the additional survey), and those who did not participate in A.C.E.S. programs (N = 233 or 62 per cent of the 378 who took the additional survey).

Looking at the entire sample (N = 890): 82 per cent were female; the average age was forty years (SD = 10) and 20 per cent were under the age of thirty; 62 per cent reported that English was not their native language; 57 per cent were Canadian citizens; and 64 per cent had a college degree or more. Thus the sample can be considered well educated, which mirrors the general image of immigrants to Canada (Table 8.1; Statistics Canada, 2003).

Data Analysis

First, independent two-sample t-tests and chi-square (χ^2) analyses were conducted to test if diploma program students differed from non-students in their demographic characteristics (Table 8.3). Second, drawing on Andersen and Newman's model, a series of logistic regression analyses were conducted with service utilization in A.C.E.S. training programs as a binary outcome variable. Model 1 contains only the socio-demographic information (age, marital status, gender, and English language skills) as independent variables. Model 2 consists of demographic and structural factors. In Model 3, the predisposing beliefs variable (self-efficacy) was added, and Model 4 consists of family variables (income, quality of life) as part of the enabling factors. The final model, Model 5, is the full model, and it includes the community variables

Table 8.3 Descriptive Statistics Comparing Students and Non-Students

Variables		N	Diploma Student	N	Non-student	Test of Independence
Age	20–69	216	39.06 (11.00)	599	39.89 (10.06)	$t(813) = 1.00$, $p = .31$
Gender	Female	185	85.3	543	81.5	$\chi2(1) = 1.56$, $p = .21$
	Male	32	14.8	123	18.5	
Marital Status	Single	116	54.5	282	47.2	$\chi2(1) = 3.29$, $p = .07$
	Not Single	97	45.5	315	52.8	
Language	English	102	50.5	207	34.3	$\chi2(1) = 16.72$, $p \leq .0001$
	Not English	100	49.5	396	65.7	
Education	≤ to high school	87	41.4	205	33.7	$\chi2(2) = 4.42$, $p = .11$
	≤ college	62	29.5	190	31.3	
	≥ university	61	29.1	213	35.0	
Immigrant Status	Yes	146	68.9	517	82.3	$\chi2(1) = 17.26$, $p \leq .0001$
	No	66	31.1	111	17.7	
Income	Income Security	165	80.9	423	69.7	$\chi2(1) = 9.60$, $p = .002$
	Other	39	19.1	184	30.3	
Self-efficacy	1–5	133	4.16 (.48)	220	4.04 (.65)	$t(351) = -1.74$, $p = .08$
Quality of Life	1–7	124	4.86 (1.01)	210	4.81 (1.13)	$t(332) = -.44$, $p = .66$
Faith-based Engagement[a]	1–5	139	3.37 (1.34)	221	3.09 (1.42)	$t(358) = -1.84$, $p = .07$
Diversity of Friendships[a]	1–5	140	2.74 (1.29)	215	2.88 (1.36)	$t(354) = 1.00$, $v = .32$

Note. Sample size changes due to missing data on some variables. Values for age, self-efficacy, quality of life, social participation, and engagement are means and standard deviations. Other values are percentages.

[a] Items were log-transformed for analysis; original values displayed here.

(diversity of friendships, faith-based engagement) alongside all the other variables.

Missing data were not problematic (< 7%) for Models 1 and 2, and were thus deleted listwise (Allison, 2009). However, for the measures on quality of life, faith-based engagement, diversity of friendships, and self-efficacy, missing data ranged from 0.3 per cent on six variables to 26 per cent of missing values on one variable; therefore, in Models 3, 4, and 5, we imputed the data using multiple imputation by chained equations (Allison, 2010; Rubin, 1987). All analyses were done using STATA 11.2.

Results

Bivariate Analysis

Unpaired two-sample t-tests and chi-square (χ^2) analyses were conducted on all variables of the full sample to test for differences between students (service utilizers) and non-students (Table 8.3). Significant differences were found for language, immigrant status, and income. Those with first language other than English and immigrants to Canada were less likely to utilize the training service, but people receiving income security were slightly more likely to start a diploma program. Those findings correspond with A.C.E.S. eligibility criteria: those receiving income security are eligible for subsidies and can participate in the diploma programs at almost no cost; in some cases they only pay for books and materials (Working Skills Centre, 2012d). Concerning the survey measures, we find that the two groups are similar with regard to the diversity of their friendships, faith-based engagement, quality of life, and self-efficacy.

Multivariate Analysis

To test to what extent clients' predisposing factors and enabling factors influence their ability to access services at A.C.E.S., a series of logistic regression analyses were conducted with service utilization as binary outcome (dependent) variable (Table 8.4). Model 1 contains the socio-demographic variables (age, marital status, gender, and language). We find that the odds of being accepted into one of A.C.E.S. programs are twice as high for English-speaking candidates compared to individuals whose first language is not English ($OR = 2.17, p \le .0001$).

Table 8.4 Logistic Regression Predicting Service Utilization

Independent Variables	Model 1	Model 2
Predisposing Factors		
Demographics		
Age	0.99	0.99
Female	0.97	0.91
Single	0.88	0.80
English	2.17****	2.20****
Social Structure		
Education	–	0.91
Beliefs		
Self-efficacy	–	–
Enabling Factors		
Family		
Income Security	–	–
Quality of Life	–	–
Community		
Diversity of Friendships	–	–
Faith-Based Engagement	–	–
Total N	728	708
LR^2	18.39***	19.97**
Degrees of freedom	4	5

Note. Entries are odds ratios. Results are based on the full sample using listwise deletion to handle missing data. +$p \leq$ .10, *$p \leq$ .05, **$p \leq$ .01, ***$p \leq$ .001, ****$p \leq$ .0001.

This finding is not surprising, given that A.C.E.S. eligibility criteria state that students have to meet a certain English proficiency language benchmark. Furthermore, this finding is consistent with the research literature indicating that immigrants with lower levels of language proficiency are less able to utilize different kinds of services (Derose et al., 2009; Kouritzin, 2000; Lai & Chau, 2007; Sword et al., 2006). When social structural factors, in the form of education, are added to the model, we find essentially the same results ($OR = 2.20, p \leq$ .0001).

Data for Models 3, 4, and 5 have been imputed through multiple imputation using chained equations based on five imputations (Allison, 2010; Rubin, 1987) (see Table 8.5). Beliefs in the form of self-efficacy as

Table 8.5 Logistic Regression Predicting Service Utilization

Independent Variables	Model 3	Model 4	Model 5
Predisposing Factors			
Demographics			
Age	0.99	0.99	1
Female	1.11	1.11	1.13
Single	0.96	0.92	0.89
English	1.86*	1.85*	1.80*
Social Structure			
Education	1.05	1.07	1.07
Beliefs			
Self-Efficacy	1.38+	1.35	1.33
Enabling Factors			
Family			
Income Security	–	1.38	1.51
Quality of Life	–	1.04	1.03
Community			
Diversity of Friendships	–	–	0.79
Faith-Based Engagement	–	–	1.50*
Total N	378	378	378
Degrees of freedom	717.2	316.1	3331.7

Note. Entries are odds ratios. Data were imputed using multiple imputation by chained equations on the basis of 5 imputations. + $p \leq .10$, *$p \leq .05$, **$p \leq .01$, *** $p \leq .001$.

a third component of the predisposing factors were added to Model 3. English is still statistically significant ($OR = 1.86$, $p = .015$), and self-efficacy approaches statistical significance ($OR = 1.38$, $p = .099$). Similar to Models 1 and 2, clients whose native language is English were 1.86 times more likely to enrol in training programs. For self-efficacy, the odds that a client will be accepted into the program increase by 38 per cent; thus clients who have more self-efficacy – a greater belief in their opportunities for success – are more likely to achieve service utilization. Model 4 considers enabling factors in form of family variables (income, quality of life). None of these additional variables assists in explaining immigrants' service utilization. Findings from

Model 3, however, are confirmed with similar effect sizes. English language is still a significant predictor for program enrolment ($OR = 1.85$, $p = .017$). The full model, Model 5, adds community factors (diversity of friendships and faith-based engagement) to the utilization model. Interestingly, we find that faith-based engagement is statistically significant ($OR = 1.5$, $p = .046$). Clients' odds of accessing training services at A.C.E.S. are 50 per cent higher when they are more engaged in faith-based activities (such as donating money to religious causes and attending religious services) in their communities.

Discussion and Conclusion

The main objective of this study was to investigate the facilitating factors and barriers that an immigrant-dominated population of job seekers face when trying to utilize training services. To carry out this task, we examined one social purpose enterprise, which is run by a non-profit organization. The study provides some interesting findings on facilitators and barriers to immigrants' service utilization in a less explored field – that of job-training and employment services.

In terms of access to services, we consistently find that English language proficiency is a significant predisposing factor for accessing services. This finding is consistent with A.C.E.S.'s eligibility criteria and with previous research that indicates that the lack of services provided in the first language of the service-seeking immigrant is a major barrier to service utilization (Aycan & Berry, 1996; Derose et al., 2009; Kouritzin, 2000; Lai & Chau, 2007; Sword et al., 2006).

Service-seekers with English as their second language were less likely to access diploma programs compared to those who speak English as their first language. While this eligibility criterion is a business strategy, the challenge for a social enterprise is to discover how to create both financial and social outcomes. This strong preference for English speakers shows that eligibility requirements to the diploma programs are a hurdle for immigrants seeking services. The application process seems to be rigid, reflecting a desire to select the most suitable clients in the highly demanded diploma programs. The application process is aligned with A.C.E.S.'s for-profit competitors, a rational move by a social purpose enterprise in a competitive environment. The language proficiency prerequisite ensures that the students enrolled in the program have a common foundation to start the training, making both teaching and learning easier. Furthermore, if students are selected carefully, the likelihood that they will succeed is higher. Achieving positive outcomes is crucial for A.C.E.S., because this signals to both government and private financial supporters that the social purpose enterprise is running effectively and that future funding is a good investment.

However, narrow eligibility criteria artificially push up success rates while leaving a large share of interested clients without these services. A remaining question is whether A.C.E.S. can meet the social and financial expectations simultaneously and equally. From the clients' perspective, those programs are regarded as an important and necessary step for future entrance into the host country's job market. Being denied training can be (another) frustrating experience for immigrants – an additional hurdle on their route to social integration. This is an important finding because social purpose enterprises are often dependent on outside funding and the funders' criteria for success. This might leave individuals who are more vulnerable and more disadvantaged unable to benefit from social purpose enterprises.

A.C.E.S. might think about a combined approach between professional development and skills training and language acquisition. Given the fact that WSC staff members are highly diverse and fluent in many languages, there might be a way to offer skills training in languages other than English in order to speed up skill acquisition, while having the students take English language classes at the same time. Skills training might be taught in English at a later time, when students have the necessary language skills. This might prolong the length of the training program, but if such an idea is implemented and students successfully complete both language and professional training, they will have acquired all of the skills needed for entering the labour market. This strategy could also better fulfil the social purpose of such an enterprise.

The English language proficiency barrier is a major concern for the service provider (WSC), but its inability to accept immigrants with lower language skills perhaps points to the fact that A.C.E.S. has to abide by the rules of the market as well as the rules of the regulator (the government agency that give licenses to vocational programs). It indicates that a social purpose enterprise, by its conscious decision to enter the marketplace and compete with for-profit businesses, is willing to accept more limits on its operation compared to non-profits that can determine the eligibility for service provision more freely. In this, our research adds to the knowledge of social purpose enterprises in an important way. Most often, only the positive aspects of social purpose enterprises are documented and researched. More problematic aspects are rarely mentioned. In order to support the ongoing research in this area, however, it is important to consider both positive and negative externalities of social purpose enterprises.

A second important finding is that clients' self-perception can influence their ability to utilize services. Even though only marginally significant, we find that a client's self-efficacy (the belief that one is able to use a skill well; Bandura, 1997) positively relates to service utilization. Since self-efficacy reflects one's beliefs rather than his or her actual skill, different people with similar skills or the same person in various circumstances may very well behave and perform differently. Acting effectively requires skills as well as belief in one's self-efficacy. Thus, if clients perceive themselves to be capable of accessing services, they might perform better in the various tests during the application process.

Part of the A.C.E.S. recruitment process, as noted above, is a personal interview with a career counsellor. This part of the application process is not given the same attention by A.C.E.S.'s for-profit competitors and is the one aspect that sets the social purpose enterprise apart from competing private career colleges. During this assessment interview, counsellors evaluate personal and social aspects of applicants' lives and determine whether candidates should be admitted to A.C.E.S. or be referred to another program. Once again, the candidates' self-perceptions are taken into account during the assessment interview for the training program, because self-efficacy is an important determinant of successful employment outcomes, and consequently financial stability.

Third, we find that social capital potentially plays a role with regard to access to and utilization of job-related training. One aspect of the social capital measure, faith-based engagement, plays a significant role in predicting service utilization at A.C.E.S. Clients who are more engaged in faith-based activities in their community are 50 per cent more likely to access job-training services, while controlling for all other variables in the model. This finding might occur for several reasons. For instance, those attending religious services have broader social networks and might also be more likely to have access to knowledge of such training programs through dissemination efforts in their place of worship. Another possibility is a direct relationship between faith-based activities and an individual's personal beliefs related to potential success. Future research should investigate this relationship further in the context of service utilization.

The lack of other significant variables attests to the nondiscriminatory practices of the organization with respect to offering training to immigrants, regardless of their income, age, marital status, or education. While religious affiliation might be a significant variable, this information was not available to the organization on intake; therefore, it is not part of the decision making. Hence, immigrant' access to services primarily depends on their language skills, and perhaps also their engagement in other organizations that help disseminate information about the availability of services.

Finally, we find that Andersen and Newman's (1973) Behavioural Model of Healthcare Utilization is applicable and appropriate to investigate the access to job-skills trainings by an immigrant-dominated population. It is important to note, however, that health-care utilization differs from utilization of job-related skill training, given that not every immigrant has the need for such services. The population that this study focused on is interested in job-related services and needs employment or better employment opportunities.

This study is not without limitations. Even though we find Andersen and Newman's (1973) model appropriate for a study of immigrants' ability to access services, future research should add more variables to account for a broader spectrum of possible influential factors. For instance, variables of interest may be length of time in the host country, expectations of the service (e.g., clients' perceptions about the outcome of the training programs), availability of transportation, and the number and age of children, as well as the availability of daycare. We are also aware of the fact that measuring whether English is the clients' first language or not is only a proxy for English proficiency level. Future research should investigate to what extent more proficient speakers achieve service utilization as compared to less fluent speakers as indicated by language proficiency level. In addition, actual participation in the survey was likely affected by level of language proficiency, as individuals whose first language was not English might have been more likely to decline participation.

Furthermore, we find only adequate internal consistency in the three subscales of social capital (civic leadership, political interest, and protest politics). Future research should continue to investigate reliability of those scales used on an immigrant-dominated population. Generally, social desirability might have played a role when collecting survey data, given the fact that most of the clients participating in information sessions wanted access to highly desired program seats.

Finally, this study looks at only one organization. It is unclear to what extent our findings can be generalized across organizations. We therefore suggest the replication of our study in other organizations that provide job-related, skills-training services to immigrants. Despite its limitations, this study provides some new insights into the barriers and facilitators that immigrants to Canada face when searching for job-related training.

In closing, this chapter suggests that as a social purpose enterprise, A.C.E.S. achieves a valuable return to society because its clients are being prepared to function more fully and independently in the job market. However, this can only be verified for clients who were able to access their training services – it cannot be verified for other immigrants and for Canadian job seekers.

NOTES

1 Marital status was initially assessed using five response options: single, married, separated, divorced, and widowed. Using "single" as reference category, no significant differences between the other categories could be found ($X^2(4) = 4.57$, $p = .33$); therefore, we collapsed the variable into a dummy variable "single" (yes = 1, no = 0).

2 Education was assessed by asking participants about the highest education level they had completed with five options: public / primary school, high school, college, university, and additional training. Participants did not fall in the first or last category. A likelihood ratio test between models treating education as continuous and categorical variables was not significant (LR $X^2(1) = 0.11$, $p = .74$); therefore, education was treated as continuous variable.

3 Eight items were taken from the New General Self-Efficacy Scale (e.g., "When facing difficult tasks, I am certain that I will accomplish them") (Chen et al., 2001). Response options were on a 5-point Likert-scale ranging from *strongly disagree* to *strongly agree*; higher scores indicate higher self-efficacy. Internal consistency for this scale in previous studies was high ($\alpha = .85$) and content as well as predictive validity have been established. For our data, we also find high internal consistency ($\alpha = .89$).

4 Options for *source of income* were: employment, savings, social services, employment insurance, family support, and "other." Social services and employment insurance were combined into one category called *income security* services. All other options were not considered income security.

5 Respondents were asked: "We want to learn about your quality of life, your well-being, and the level of satisfaction in different situations in your life," and were given ten previously validated related statements. Response options ranged from *could not be worse* to *could not be better* on a 7-point Likert-scale. All items collapsed onto one component when using principal component analysis, and achieved high internal consistency (α = .89).

6 Responses to the social capital items were originally given in an ordinal scale, ranging from *never* to *weekly*. Following Sinha, Greenspan, and Handy (2011), we recoded, averaged, and log-transformed these items into a new continuous variable by approximating the number of days per year for each activity: never (0 days/year), less than once a month (7/year), once a month (12/year), more than once a month (32/year), and weekly (52/year). The log-transformed variables had a correlation of $r = 0.91$ with the ordinal variables that only calculated the means of the twelve original items. After log-transforming the items, they were subjected to principal component analysis, whereby five distinct components emerged. One item ("How many times in the last 12 months have you volunteered?") had to be excluded following Comrey's (1988) rule for multiple loaders. The remaining item from the initial charitable behaviour dimension ("How many times in the last 12 months have you donated money to non-religious causes?") loaded on one component together with the two items measuring faith-based engagement. Internal consistency for this three-item scale, however, was inadequate; we therefore removed this item due to low item-total correlation (Spector, 1992), retaining the component faith-based engagement. Of the five distinct components, internal consistency was high for only two: faith-based engagement (α = .80) and diversity of friendship (α = .88), but low for the other three: civic leadership (α = .38), protest politics (α = .46), and political interest (α = .36). Only the first two components were thus included in our model.

REFERENCES

Adler, P.S., & Kwon, S.W. (2002). Social capital: Prospects for a new concept. *Academy of Management Review*, 27(1), 17–40.

Allison, P. (2009). *Logistic regression using SAS: Theory and application* (2nd ed.). Cary, NC: SAS Press.

Allison, P. (2010). Missing data. In J.D. Wright & P.V. Marsden (Eds.), *Handbook of survey research* (2nd ed., pp. 631–657). Bingley, United Kingdom: Emerald Group.

Andersen, R., & Newman, J.F. (1973). Societal and individual determinants of medical care utilization in the United States. *Milbank Memorial Fund Quarterly, 51*(1), 95–124. http://dx.doi.org/10.2307/3349613

Aycan, Z., & Berry, J.W. (1996). Impact of employment-related experiences on immigrants' psychological well-being and adaptation to Canada. *Canadian Journal of Behavioural Science, 28*(3), 240–251. http://dx.doi.org/10.1037/0008-400X.28.3.240

Aydemir, A., & Sweetman, A. (2006). *First and second generation immigrant educational attainment and labor market outcomes: A comparison of the United States and Canada* (IZA Discussion Paper, No. 2298). Retrieved from http://papers.ssrn.com/sol3/papers.cfm?abstract_id=932037

Bandura, A. (1997). *Self-efficacy. The exercise of control.* New York, NY: Freeman.

Citizenship and Immigration Canada. (2001). *Canada – Facts and Figures. Immigration Overview – Permanent and Temporary Residents.* Retrieved from http://www.cic.gc.ca/english/resources/statistics/menu-fact.asp

Chen, G., Gully, S.M., & Eden, D. (2001). Validation of a new general self-efficacy scale. *Organizational Research Methods, 4*(1), 62–83. http://dx.doi.org/10.1177/109442810141004

Comrey, A.L. (1988). Factor-analytic methods of scale development in personality and clinical psychology. *Journal of Consulting and Clinical Psychology, 56*(5), 754–761. http://dx.doi.org/10.1037/0022-006X.56.5.754

Derose, K.P., Bahney, B.W., Lurie, N., & Escarce, J.J. (2009). Review: Immigrants and health care access, quality, and cost. *Medical Care Research and Review, 66*(4), 355–408. http://dx.doi.org/10.1177/1077558708330425

Derose, K.P., Escarce, J.J., & Lurie, N. (2007). Immigrants and health care: sources of vulnerability. *Health Affairs, 26*(5), 1258–1268. http://dx.doi.org/10.1377/hlthaff.26.5.1258

Fenta, H., Hyman, I., & Noh, S. (2007). Health service utilization by Ethiopian immigrants and refugees in Toronto. *Journal of Immigrant and Minority Health, 9*(4), 349–357. http://dx.doi.org/10.1007/s10903-007-9043-0

Jang, Y., Kim, G., & Chiriboga, D.A. (2005). Health, healthcare utilization, and satisfaction with services: Barriers and facilitators for older Korean Americans. *Journal of the American Geriatrics Society, 53*(9), 1613–1617. http://dx.doi.org/10.1111/j.1532-5415.2005.53518.x

Kaiser Commission on Medicaid and the Uninsured. (2000). *Immigrants' health care: coverage and access.* Washington, DC.

Kouritzin, S. (2000). Immigrant mothers redefine access to ESL classes: Contradiction and ambivalence. *Journal of Multilingual and Multicultural Development, 21*(1), 14–32. http://dx.doi.org/10.1080/01434630008666391

Lai, D.W.L., & Chau, S.B.Y. (2007). Predictors of health service barriers for older Chinese immigrants in Canada. *Health & Social Work, 32*(1), 57–65. http://dx.doi.org/10.1093/hsw/32.1.57

Magalhaes, L., Carrasco, C., & Gastaldo, D. (2010). Undocumented migrants in Canada: A scope literature review on health, access to services, and working conditions. *Journal of Immigrant and Minority Health, 12*(1), 132–151. http://dx.doi.org/10.1007/s10903-009-9280-5

Oleson, M. (1990). Subjectively perceived quality of life. *Image, 22*, 187–190.

Oliver, J.P.J., Huxley, P.J., Priebe, S., & Kaiser, W. (1997). Measuring the quality of life of severely mentally ill people using the Lancashire Quality of Life Profile. *Social Psychiatry and Psychiatric Epidemiology, 32*(2), 76–83. http://dx.doi.org/10.1007/BF00788924

Orr, K., & Bennett, M. (2012). Public administration scholarship and the politics of coproducing academic–practitioner research. *Public Administration Review, 72*(4), 487–495. http://dx.doi.org/10.1111/j.1540-6210.2011.02522.x

Priebe, S., Huxley, P., Knight, S., & Evans, S. (1999). Application and results of the Manchester Short Assessment of Quality of Life (MANSA). *International Journal of Social Psychiatry, 45*(1), 7–12. http://dx.doi.org/10.1177/002076409904500102

Reitz, J.G. (1995). A review of the literature on aspects of ethno-racial access, utilization and delivery of social services. Toronto, ON: Ontario Ministry of Community and Social Services. Retrieved from: http://www.ceris.metropolis.net/Virtual%20Library/other/reitz1/reitz1.html

Roper Center for Public Opinion Research (2000). Social Capital Community Benchmark Survey. Retrieved from http://www.ropercenter.uconn.edu/data_access/data/datasets/social_capital_community_survey.html

Rubin, D.B. (1987). *Multiple imputation for non-response in surveys*. New York, NY: Wiley. http://dx.doi.org/10.1002/9780470316696

Safi, M. (2010). Immigrants' life satisfaction in Europe: Between assimilation and discrimination. *European Sociological Review, 26*(2), 159–176. http://dx.doi.org/10.1093/esr/jcp013

Sinha, J.W., Greenspan, I., & Handy, F. (2011). Volunteering and civic participation among immigrant members of ethnic congregations: Complementary NOT competitive. *Journal of Civil Society, 7*(1), 23–40. http://dx.doi.org/10.1080/17448689.2011.553409

Spector, P. (1992). *Summated rating scale construction*. Newbury Park, CA: Sage.

Statistics Canada (2003). *Longitudinal survey of immigrants to Canada: Process, progress and prospects* (Catalogue no. 89–611-XIE). Retrieved from http://www.statcan.gc.ca/pub/89-611-x/89-611-x2003001-eng.pdf

Statistics Canada (2006). *Immigrant status and period of immigration.* Retrieved from http://www12.statcan.ca/census-recensement/2006/dp-pd/hlt/97-557/T403-eng.cfm?Lang=E&T=403&GH=1&SC=1&S=0&O=A

Statistics Canada. (2008). *Educational portrait of Canada, Census 2006.* Retrieved from http://www12.statcan.ca/census-recensement/2006/as-sa/97-560/pdf/97-560-XIE2006001.pdf

Sword, W., Watt, S., & Krueger, P. (2006). Postpartum health, service needs, and access to care experiences of immigrant and Canadian-born women. *Journal of Obstetric, Gynecologic, and Neonatal Nursing, 35*(6), 717–727. http://dx.doi.org/10.1111/j.1552-6909.2006.00092.x

Wilson, E., Hm Chen, A., Grumbach, K., Wang, F., & Fernandez, A. (2005). Effects of limited English proficiency and physician language on health care comprehension. *Journal of General Internal Medicine, 20*(9), 800–806. http://dx.doi.org/10.1111/j.1525-1497.2005.0174.x

Wolinsky, F.D., Coe, R.M., Miller, D.K., Prendergast, J.M., Creel, M.J., & Chavez, M.N. (1983). Health service utilization among the noninstitutionalized elderly. *Journal of Health and Social Behavior, 24*(4), 325–337. http://dx.doi.org/10.2307/2136399

Working Skills Centre. (2012a). About us. Retrieved from http://workingskillscentre.com/about-us/

Working Skills Centre. (2012b). Diploma Programs. Retrieved from http://workingskillscentre.com/training/diploma-programs/

Working Skills Centre. (2012c). Settlement Services. Retrieved from http://workingskillscentre.com/settlement-services/

Working Skills Centre. (2012d). Training - A.C.E.S. Retrieved from http://workingskillscentre.com/training/aces/

9 Well-Being of Childcare Workers at The Learning Enrichment Foundation: A Toronto Community Economic Development Organization

ANDREA CHAN, ROBYN HOOGENDAM, PETER FRAMPTON,
ANDREW HOLETON, EMILY POHL-WEARY, SHERIDA RYAN,
AND JACK QUARTER

Employees of childcare centres are paid poorly, both in Canada and internationally (Cleveland & Hyatt, 2000; Cleveland & Krashinsky, 2004; Cleveland, Forer, Hyatt, Japel, & Krashinsky, 2007; Payscale, 2012). Their salaries and benefits are not commensurate with their level of schooling or the importance of their work. Data for 2012 from the website, *Living in Canada*, indicates that the average wage for childcare workers in Greater Toronto, the location of this study, is $16.21 per hour, and the range is from $11.22 to $23.78. Data for 2012 from *Payscale*, a website of self-reported salaries by industry and country, posts the following hourly wage levels for workers in the sector and uses national data to recommend the following wage levels (per hour): childcare worker, $12.84; childcare assistant, $11.50; daycare teacher, $13.05; and early childhood educator (ECE), $14.21. These are low wages, especially for people living in Canada's cities, where most childcare centres are located. To put these wages in perspective, in Ontario, the minimum hourly pay is $10.25 per hour, scarcely different than the pay of $11.50 for some childcare assistants. In addition to low wages, childcare workers experience high staff turnover and dissatisfaction (Cleveland & Hyatt, 2000; Cleveland & Krashinsky, 2004; Cleveland, Forer, Hyatt, Japel, & Krashinsky, 2007). There are periodic campaigns to increase wages, but generally these have not solved the problem.

This study focused on childcare workers at The Learning Enrichment Foundation, and in particular, attempted to understand what impact The Learning Enrichment Foundation's childcare program had on its workers. We attempted to understand whether the childcare workers believe that their well-being has improved in comparison to their situation before working at LEF – and if so, why.

The Learning Enrichment Foundation (LEF)

The Learning Enrichment Foundation is a community economic development organization operating in Toronto's inner suburbs. The organization's website describes its mission as follows:

> The Learning Enrichment Foundation provides integrated and holistic community responsive initiatives that enable individuals and families to become valued contributors to their community's social and economic development.

LEF has been operating since 1978 with a focus on integrated supports to employment as a key economic development tool. These supports include childcare, employment, settlement, entrepreneurship assistance, and skills and language training. The organization is within one of the lowest-income pockets in the city (City of Toronto, 2011), and one that attracts a disproportionate share of new immigrants. LEF has training programs for various forms of industry: childcare centres, bicycle shops, cooking, and food services. These programs may be viewed as social purpose enterprises (see Chapter 1). LEF not only trains its clientele but also assists with employment through its relationships with employers, networks, and language training. In addition, LEF is a local employer, and one of its industries is childcare. LEF's involvement in childcare started in the early 1980s. Currently, there are sixteen childcare centres and thirteen before-and-after-school programs located across the former City of York and in North Etobicoke, serving about 1,100 children from infancy to age twelve. LEF's childcare centres employ approximately 180 childcare workers, about 72 per cent of them full-time. LEF also trains childcare workers through its early childhood assistant training program, some of whom are employed at LEF and others of whom are employed elsewhere.

The demographics of LEF childcare workers are as follows: with few exceptions, all are women. Eighty-six per cent are between thirty years old and fifty-nine years old, and their ages are almost evenly distributed through that range. Only 24 per cent were born in Canada, and the others are first-generation immigrants from many different countries, but predominantly from the Caribbean islands, southern Asia, and countries such as Iran and Afghanistan. In other words, they are from countries where wages were much lower than in Canada. Sixty per cent of the childcare workers identify themselves as from visible minority groups. Those who are first-generation immigrants came to Canada between 1955 and 2008, but the majority came in the mid-1980s onwards – that is, they are recent immigrants. Just over half have English as a first language. Among the others, there are nineteen different languages of origin, with Spanish being the largest grouping. LEF childcare workers have relatively high levels of schooling: about 80 per cent have some level of college, including 14 per cent who have university degrees and 7 per cent who have graduate degrees. The largest group – 56 per cent – has a college diploma. Just under half of the LEF childcare workers have a certificate from LEF's early childcare assistant program, and just under half had a diploma in early childhood education from a college. Nearly three-quarters were employed prior to joining LEF, predominantly in Canada. About half were employed previously as an early childcare professional. Of those who were unemployed, they were either supported by their families or through a government program such as employment insurance. The current childcare workers at LEF have been employed, on average, ten-and-a-half years with the organization.

Of part-time and full-time childcare workers at LEF, 48 per cent earn between $30,000 and $39,999 and another 19 per cent earn over $40,000. If only full-time childcare workers are considered, the proportion increases to 53 per cent who earn between $30,000 and $39,999, and 22 per cent who earn $40,000 and above. As such, 75 per cent of full-time childcare workers at LEF earn $30,000 and above annually. This compares favourably to the average wage of $16.21 per hour (or just over $31,000 per year) earned by childcare workers across Toronto.[1] The childcare workers support not only themselves; three-quarters have children, and the average age of these children is sixteen, suggesting that the LEF childcare workers have dependents who need their support. About 40 per cent of the childcare workers do not have a spouse, and 38 per cent are single parents with children.

Methodology

To assess the impact of employment for childcare workers at LEF, we used mixed methods in two stages, starting with a survey and followed by a semistructured interview (Creswell & Plano Clark, 2007; Greene & Caracelli, 1997; Tashakkori & Teddlie, 2003). The survey was of 86 workers at sixteen[2] LEF childcare centres. The centres were selected by the LEF management, and the childcare workers were volunteers who agreed to participate in the study. Of the eligible childcare workers at the centres, 74 per cent volunteered to take a survey to assess the impact of their LEF experience. Of those who took the survey, six agreed to an in-depth interview that explored the issues raised through the data analysis of the survey items.

Survey

The survey (see http://www.socialeconomycentre.ca/business-done-differently-research-instruments) consisted of a combination of background items about the demographic characteristics of the sample and an asset matrix that asked participants to indicate whether there has been a change in their life from before working at LEF to the present. The matrix (see Figure 9.1) included thirty-five items divided into five categories: Financially; Personally; Access to Services; Physically and Mentally; Friends and Family. A variation of the asset matrix originated with the Sustainable Livelihoods model produced for international development work by the Department for International Development in the United Kingdom (DFIT, Guidance Sheets, http://www.eldis.org/go/topics/dossiers/livelihoods-connect/what-are-livelihoods-approaches/training-and-learning-materials). This model looks at its target (community, individual) as possessing a set of assets and provides a framework for the evaluation of these assets. Through this tool, strengths and weaknesses are visible and interventions can be developed working within a specific context. The benefit of this framework is that it looks at its target from a position of strength, rather than one of deficit. The matrix was adapted and simplified for the purpose of this study (see Figure 9.1).

Interviews

The interview format was semistructured. The interviewer proceeded with a set of questions that explored the themes arising from the responses to the data, but gave the interviewees space to raise their own issues. The exact interview questions can be found at http://www.socialeconomycentre.ca/business-done-differently-research-instruments. The issues addressed through the interviews were:

• Economic Well-Being: has there been an improvement in your economic well-being, and if so, what explains it?

- Self-Confidence: has there been an improvement in your self-confidence, and if so, what explains it?
- Access to Services: has there been an improvement in access to services, and if so, what explains it?
- Skills (Human Capital): has there has been an improvement in your skills, and if so, what do you think explains it?
- Family and Community Relations: has there has been an improvement in your family and community relations from before you worked at LEF, and if so, what do you think explains it?

Figure 9.1 Asset Matrix

OVERALL LIFE CHANGES

We are looking to find out how the following aspects of your life have changed over time. Please rank the categories below on a scale of 1 to 5. A ranking of 1 would mean your satisfaction in that area is very low and a ranking of 5 would mean it is very high. If they don't apply, enter "n/a" (not applicable).

For example, someone who worked at LEF for **12** years might answer like this:

	Prior to LEF	Now
Financially		
Income	2	4
Savings	3	3

How has your life changed:

	Prior to LEF	Now
Financially		
Income		
Savings		
Access to Credit		
Personally		
Motivation		
Confidence		
Ability to Speak Out on Concerns		

Figure 9.1 Asset Matrix (*cont.*)

Access to Services
Child/Elder Care
Secure Shelter
Library
Internet
Banking
Groceries
Affordable Transportation
Family Doctor
Education

Physically and Mentally
Skills
Knowledge
Ability
Employability
Earning Power
Good Health
Leadership Abilities

Friends and Family
Work Networks
Neighbours
Leisure
Family Support
Friendships
Trusting Relationships
Political Participation
Issues of Violence (Domestic, etc.)
Live in Community with High Crime
Live in Community Where You Feel Fearful
Time Spent with Children
Health of Children
Access to Pediatrician/Other Needed Specialist

We also attempted to learn how these various factors impact on each other and the impact of their particular form of childcare training on each of these factors. In addition, the interviews explored areas of improvement and barriers to improvement. The interviews were conducted by phone, recorded, and later transcribed for data analysis.

Results

Converting the Asset Matrix to Scales

The first step in the data analysis was to determine whether the thirty-five items in the asset matrix could be grouped into scales. The designers of the matrix organized the items within five groups, but there was no evidence that the groups had the statistical properties of a scale. Using the responses from the participants in this study, a Cronbach's alpha test was undertaken of the items in the matrix to determine whether they could be grouped into five larger constructs: Financial Well-Being; Self-Confidence; Access to Services; Human Capital; and Family and Community Relations. These construct names differ somewhat from those used when the data were collected (Figure 9.1); in particular: "Financially" was changed to Financial Well-Being; "Personally" to Self-Confidence; "Access to Services" stayed the same; "Physically and Mentally" was changed to Human Capital; and "Friends And Family" became Family and Community Relations.

Cronbach's alpha test was conducted for the prior scores and now scores separately. For all five groups of items, both before and now, the Cronbach's alpha scores were higher than .7, and therefore were viewed as meeting an adequate standard for a scale (see Table 9.2). As such, the items of these five groupings were combined and the scales were created and used in subsequent analyses.

For each scale, a new score was created for each individual childcare worker by taking the mean on the item scores belonging to the scale. Means were only computed for childcare workers where there were scores on more than half the number of items belonging to that scale. If a childcare worker were missing more than half the scores on one scale, then no score would be generated for the scale.

"Prior to LEF" and "Now" Differences

Using the responses from the LEF childcare workers, paired-samples *t*-tests were conducted to determine whether there is a difference

Table 9.2 Cronbach's Alpha Scores for the Items in the Asset Matrix: Prior to LEF and Now

Scale	Cronbach's Alpha	
	Prior to LEF (*n*)	Now (*n*)
Financial Well-Being	.78 (58)	.73 (60)
Self-Confidence	.89 (57)	.73 (60)
Access to Services	.93 (36)	.93 (37)
Human Capital	.90 (52)	.86 (52)
Family and Community Relations	.76 (26)	.79 (28)

between the prior to LEF scores and the now scores on each of the five scales: Financial Well-Being; Self-Confidence; Access to Services; Human Capital; and Family and Community Relations (see Table 9.3).

For all five scales, there is a statistically significant increase from prior to LEF to now, suggesting that the childcare workers at LEF experienced an improvement in their lives, according to the Sustainable Livelihoods framework. For four scales, the increase is considered moderate and for Human Capital, the increase is strong.

Impact of Background and Demographic Variables on the Five Asset Matrix Scales

The background and demographic variables included in the analysis were: gender; age; born in Canada or elsewhere; length of time in Canada; whether English is first language; visible minority; schooling; early childhood education training; previous employment; marital status; having children; housing and the number of times moved; full-time or part-time at LEF; number of years employed at LEF; salary at LEF; adequateness of salary; perception of job security at LEF; proximity between workplace and home; participation in the surrounding community (i.e., volunteering, both formal and informal). For the exact wording of the survey items, see http://socialeconomycentre.ca/business-done-differently.

Analyses of covariance were conducted to determine if scores on the background, demographic, and community-related variables were significant predictors of the outcome variables (i.e., the "now" scores on the five scales) after controlling for the prior score. We present the significant relationships for each outcome variable in turn.

Table 9.3 Paired Samples T-Tests on the Five Asset Matrix Scales

Scale (n)	n	Prior to LEF M (SD)	Now M (SD)	t	Cohen's d (Effect Size)
Financial Well-Being	65	2.22 (0.87)	2.91 (0.84)	t = –5.07*	0.63 (moderate)
Self-Confidence	61	3.00 (1.08)	3.85 (0.78)	t = –5.82*	0.75 (moderate)
Access to Services	58	3.10 (1.04)	3.63 (0.97)	t = –4.98*	0.65 (moderate)
Human Capital	60	3.21 (0.96)	4.01 (0.72)	t = –7.35*	0.95 (large)
Family and Community Relations	54	3.20 (0.81)	3.59 (0.64)	t = –4.09*	0.56 (moderate)

Note. * p < .001

Financial Well-Being

Two variables were significant predictors of the feeling of Financial Well-Being now: current level of salary and number of children.

CURRENT LEVEL OF SALARY

Controlling for prior Financial Well-Being, current salary was a significant predictor of current Financial Well-Being for childcare workers. Current salary accounted for approximately 14 per cent of the variance of Financial Well-Being now scores for childcare workers. One would expect that the higher the income, the greater the perceived Financial Well-Being. However, the relationship proved not to be linear. Those who made $30,000–$39,999 had a significantly higher (adjusted) mean perceived Financial Well-Being than those who made $0–$29,999, but perceived Financial Well-Being did not increase for those who earned $40,000–$49,999. The relationship between current salary and perceived Financial Well-Being will be considered further in the final discussion.

HAVING CHILDREN

Controlling for prior Financial Well-Being, the data show that childcare workers with children to support experience less Financial Well-Being than those without children. The response is understandable, as children cost money to support. However, this relationship is weak: only 6 per cent of the variance (partial $\eta2$ = .06) on current Financial Well-

Being is accounted for by having children as a predictor, holding constant prior Financial Well-Being.

Self-Confidence

Self-Confidence was the second scale in the asset matrix. Organization membership in the community was the only significant predictor of Self-Confidence now.

ORGANIZATION MEMBERSHIP

Controlling for Self-Confidence prior to LEF, those who were members of organizations in the community had a significantly higher mean Self-Confidence now score than those who were not, but the effect was small. When holding constant prior Self-Confidence, membership in organizations in the community accounted for approximately 7 per cent of the variance (partial $\eta 2 = .07$) on current Self-Confidence of childcare workers sampled.

Access to Services Now

Access to Services now was the third scale in the asset matrix. Two variables were significant predictors: level of schooling and membership in organizations.

LEVEL OF SCHOOLING

Controlling for Access to Services prior to LEF, level of schooling was a significant predictor (accounting for almost 15 per cent of variance) of current Access to Services for childcare workers. The group with college diplomas had a significantly higher mean Access to Services now score than those who did not, but there was no indication that additional schooling beyond the college diploma strengthened the relationship.

MEMBERSHIP IN ORGANIZATIONS IN THE COMMUNITY

ANCOVA was not performed as the homogeneity-of-slopes assumption was not observed. Instead, separate simple main effects tests were conducted for three groups: those with low, medium, and high Access to Services scores prior to joining LEF.[3] Controlling for low prior Access to Services scores, those who are members of organizations in the community reported significantly greater Access to Services now as compared to those who are not; this relationship was strong, accounting for 18 per cent of the variance in current Access to Services now scores.

Controlling for the mid Access to Services score prior to LEF, those who are members of organizations again had greater Access to Services now as compared to those who are not members; the relationship accounted for 9 per cent of the variance in current Access to Services now. For those with high Access to Services prior to LEF, the membership in organizations was not a significant predictor of Access to Services now scores.

Human Capital

There were three significant predictors of Human Capital now, the fourth scale in the asset matrix: type of early childhood care training, current level of salary, and membership in organizations.

TYPE OF TRAINING

Controlling for Human Capital prior to LEF, the type of childcare training workers received was a significant predictor of Human Capital now scores, accounting for 9 per cent of the variance. The group with ECE/Mothercraft as their highest level of childcare training had a significantly higher mean score on Human Capital now as compared to those with only ECA training.

CURRENT LEVEL OF SALARY

The ANCOVA test could not be performed for this variable as the homogeneity-of-slopes assumption again was not met. As such, three separate simple main effects tests were conducted at low, medium, and high scores on Human Capital prior to LEF, respectively. For those with a low Human Capital score prior to LEF, level of current salary was a significant predictor and accounted for 35 per cent of the variance in Human Capital now. Controlling for the low prior Human Capital score, those whose current salary is $30,000–$39,999 and $40,000–$49,999 had a significantly higher mean Human Capital now score than those whose current salary is $0–$29,999. However, there was no significant difference between the $40,000–$49,999 and the $30,000–$39,999 groups.

For those with a mid Human Capital score prior to LEF, level of current salary accounted for 24 per cent of the variance in Human Capital now. Controlling for the mid Human Capital prior to LEF, again those whose current salary is $30,000–$39,999 and $40,000–$49,999 had a significantly higher mean Human Capital now score than those whose current salary is $0–$29,999. However, there was no significant difference between the $40,000–$49,999 and $30,000–$39,999 groups. For those with a high Human Capital score prior to LEF, current salary level was not a significant predictor of Human Capital now scores.

MEMBER OF COMMUNITY ORGANIZATIONS

The ANCOVA test again could not be performed due to treatment by covariate interaction. Simple main effects analysis was used to assess differences between those who are members of community organizations and those who are not, at three different levels of prior to LEF scores for Human Capital. Controlling for the low prior Human Capital score, those who were members of organizations in the community had a mean current Human Capital score that was significantly higher than those who were not members; the relationship accounting for 19 per cent of the variance in Human Capital now.

Controlling for the medium prior Human Capital score, those who were members of organizations in the community had a mean current Human Capital now score that was significantly higher than those who were not members; the relationship accounting for 10 per cent of the variance in Human Capital now. For those with a higher Human Capital score prior to LEF, membership in community organizations was not a significant predictor of Human Capital now scores.

Family and Community Relations

The fifth scale in the asset matrix, Family and Community Relations, had the largest number of statistically significant predictors: self-identified as a member of a visible minority; level of schooling; part-time versus full-time employment; current level of salary; and volunteering.

SELF-IDENTIFIED AS VISIBLE MINORITY

Controlling for Family and Community Relations prior to LEF, those who identified as belonging to a visible minority group had a lower mean Family and Community Relations now score compared to those who did not, the relationship accounting for 8 per cent of the variance in current Family and Community Relations scores.

LEVEL OF SCHOOLING

Level of schooling was grouped as follows: those who did not have a college diploma, those who had a college diploma, and those who had more than a college diploma, and this accounted for almost 18 per cent of variance on Family and Community Relations now for those sampled, holding constant the prior score. The only significant relationship was that those with college diplomas had a significantly higher mean Family and Community Relations now score than those who did not. Possibly, the group with more than a college diploma experienced frustration about not having higher income given the amount of their schooling, and this might have had an adverse effect on their Family and Community Relations score.

PART-TIME VS FULL-TIME EMPLOYMENT

Holding constant the variable Family and Community Relations prior to LEF, those who worked full-time had a significantly higher mean Family and Community Relations now score that those who worked part time, the relationship accounting for 16 per cent of the variance in current Family and Community Relations scores. Possibly people who worked part time did not do so by choice, and they experienced frustration that affected their Family and Community Relations score.

CURRENT LEVEL OF SALARY

Holding constant the prior score, those whose current salary is $30,000–$39,999 and $40,000–$49,999 had a significantly higher mean Family and Community Relations now score compared to the group in the $0–$29,999 salary range, accounting for around 21 per cent of variance in Family and Community Relations now scores for those sampled. However, there was no statistical difference in Family and Community Relations now score between the $40,000–$49,999 and $30,000–$39,999 groups.

VOLUNTEERING

There were a larger number of incomplete responses for this item, so the sample size was reduced. Controlling for prior score, the mean score for current Family and Community Relations for the group that increased its volunteering since working at LEF was significantly higher than those who had decreased their volunteering since LEF, accounting for a sizable 41 per cent of variance on Family and Community Relations now for those sampled. Current Family and Community Relations did not differ between the group that did not change their volunteering and either of the two other groups. Volunteering could be viewed as one indicator of community participation, and it stands to reason that persons with higher scores on the Family and Community Relations scale would be associated with a large increase in volunteering.

Qualitative Findings

The purpose of the interviews was to explore in greater depth the quantitative findings from the survey, in particular, the significant results. The transcripts were initially coded, segment-by-segment, then sorted and categorized as concepts under the five primary areas of interest of this study.

Financial Well-Being

The quantitative data shows that LEF childcare workers experienced a significant improvement in their Financial Well-Being. Significant improvement should not be misconstrued, as their profession is low paid, something that the interviewees noted in their comments. Of the six interviewees, four obtained their early childhood assistant certificate (ECA) at LEF, and this led to a financial improvement. Two others had college diplomas from the start, and one had been promoted at LEF. The interviewees' comments highlight the improvement in their conditions:

> I didn't take the ECE course; they [LEF] trained us. And I was getting paid $5.25 an hour. The salary range now is much different.
>
> We have sick day benefits … I compare this and other companies, I think we are okay.
>
> There's a big gap between private daycare and non-profit organization. Because over there, they give you whatever they want to pay. I remember I was there before going for my last maternity; I couldn't survive with the money I was getting during the maternity leave. So instead, going back to work within six months after my birth to be able to reach my basic needs.
>
> Once I was hired I realized I was making $2 more an hour. That was a lot, I thought. Because when you add it up, it does make a difference.
>
> I'm able to hold the job of a supervisor, as opposed to being in a classroom. So there is a big, well I don't know if it's big, but there's a $10,000 difference in salary, and I certainly feel a lot more comfortable now with that pay cheque than with the one I had before.

Two variables were significant predictors of Financial Well-Being at LEF: current salary and number of children. For current salary, the quantitative data showed that persons in the $30,000 to under $40,000 bracket experienced greater Financial Well-Being than those whose salary was less than $30,000. Interestingly, the same was not true for those whose salary was greater than $40,000. The interviews attempted to explore this finding, which on the surface was paradoxical, as one might expect that the subjective experience of Financial Well-Being and salary would have a linear relationship – that is, the higher the salary, the greater the experience of satisfaction.

The interviewees' responses on this matter shed some light on this relationship. First, the interviewees note that the experience of Financial Well-Being depends not only on how much is earned but also on the ability to manage expenses within that income. With respect to the ability to manage expenses, having children is an obvious consideration. With children, there are greater expenses.

> In order for me to stay [at] a level of stability, I would just have to cut down my expenses, right? So I don't overuse the money I get. I use it wisely, so I will be able to survive.
>
> People always want more money. I compare this and other companies, I think we are okay. But maybe we need some improvement. I don't know. Just more money, like everyone.
>
> The amount of money changes depending on our needs.

Most of the interviewees refer to the cost of children, but one views them as a potential financial benefit: "I'm waiting for my son to get a job, and we can ... my son, his wife, me, we can combine money."

From the interviews, it is challenging to understand why persons in the $40,000-plus income range do not experience a greater sense of Financial Well-Being than those who earn less than $30,000. One can only speculate that persons in that range have taken on additional expenses like a mortgage or car, and possibly they have more financial dependents. It could also be that their expectations have increased, or as one interviewee says, "*$50,000–$60,000 a year, is where I'd be more comfortable.*" It would appear that the subjective feeling of Financial Well-Being represents a combination of actual salary and expectations.

Level of schooling is a consideration in childcare workers' income. Those in the $40,000-plus range would have college diplomas and perhaps other degrees and might expect more. Those in the $30,000 range would be predominantly early childhood education assistants, who prior to receiving that training may have been on the margins of the workforce or collecting social assistance. At LEF, their incomes may be low, but they have job security – or, as one interviewee states: "Being employed at LEF is better than not working or being on social assistance or whatever. That is the only income me and my family are based on. We are able to cater for them, based on this income; so I think I've improved in life based on LEF."

Self-Confidence

The quantitative data shows that LEF childcare workers experienced a significant improvement in their Self-Confidence from before. The interviewees primarily attribute their increase in self-confidence to improvements in economic well-being, skills development, and workplace experience. Confidence is gained by being able to make ends meet, and becoming successful and effective at work (e.g., by successfully implementing workshop learning in the classroom and improving interpersonal skills through increased interaction with parents and children). The interviewees appear to be experiencing greater security.

> My economic well-being has improved my self-confidence, because if you have peace of mind to pay bills, you'd be better.
> The money, yes. To make your own, you are more assured.
> I think you learn during work hours; with staff, you become more confident.
> Of course, you get experience. You get more practice. You get to know more people, more parents, more children ...You get to feel more confident.

Supervisors as well as instructors and coworkers were mentioned by participants as people who play substantive roles in encouraging and developing the self-confidence of staff at LEF. One participant expressed a lack of confidence in her language skills even at the time of the interview. It would be ten years working as an ECA before she decided, at the encouragement of her supervisor and others, to pursue ECE certification: "I maybe should have gone early, but I didn't have the confidence. But my supervisor, she pushed me. She encouraged me. She said go, go, go ... And obviously when I start, I was comfortable with this experience ... I really appreciate she was pushing me."

From the survey, participation in community organizations had been a predictor of Self-Confidence. Although a connection was drawn in different ways between community participation and self-confidence during the interviews, it may be that self-confidence influences participation in community organizations and events, and not vice-versa. Feelings of insecurity can prevent a person from becoming engaged in community or social events. One interviewee expressed "shyness" from participating in community-organized groups and events because she felt not as "plugged in" and up-to-date on current events and community activities as other group members. Another interviewee expressed insecurities over her language skills, which served as a barrier to participating in social events organized even within LEF. "And I was the one who was avoiding, because of language. If I go to this [LEF] party, I have to talk. My language, they needed ... time, they have to take time with me to understand what I want to say."

Access to Services Now

The response from childcare workers to the survey indicated that they experienced an improvement in their access to services from before LEF to now. According to participants, services where there had been improved access include healthcare (eye care, dental care, prescription drugs), as these were part of the employee benefit package. Interviewees noted that they had experienced greater access to credit, as it depends on a consistent income and stable employment history. Through working at LEF, childcare staff members gain access to information about various services that they can access. Sometimes the information is intended for parents, but has relevance to childcare workers themselves (e.g., free computer and yoga classes, and free income tax clinic). As one interviewee stated: "To have this information for the parents make me understand more how I can use this information for myself."

It was not simply access to services that improved but rather the ability to use services. For example, the library is a community resource accessed for work: "Being at work with the children at LEF makes it more necessary to go to the library to get books."

The Internet has made it possible to facilitate information getting to the childcare centres that is dispersed through a broad area: "They're always opening lines of communication between centres. Emailing the supervisors to explain to us what is going on."

The responses to the survey showed that those without college diplomas experience relatively lower access to services. One indication of this from the interviews was that for the ECAs (early childhood assistants), completing their apprenticeship hours was very burdensome, and they had less time to do anything else. One can also speculate that college qualification increases the probability of being in a supervisory role and that position may lead to lead to greater information about access to services. This issue will be explored more fully in the final discussion, but it appears that some of the most consistent predictors are items that may enhance social capital, such as membership in organizations.

Human Capital

In response to the survey, human capital or skills improved strongly from before LEF to now. All of the interviewees indicated that their skills improved since joining LEF. One of the predictors of Human Capital now is early childhood education training. Half of those interviewed have formally advanced their childcare training since joining LEF, moving from early childhood assistants to early childhood educators with college qualifications. This finding suggests why both early childhood education training and income are predictors of Human Capital now. The theme of continuous learning and skills development ran throughout the discussions with participants.

> We were told about learning and given opportunities to attend workshops. Because that really helps to be better at your profession. Only a fool would say, no thanks, I don't need it. Workshops help you to improve in your skills and to put them into play.
>
> LEF has workshops like teamwork and dynamics, first aid and food handling. They have actually helped me to know more about my program.

Skills were learned within the day-to-day work environment, from the interaction with children: "Children are the best teachers." Peer interactions were also of importance: "over the years as an ECA, I have gained a lot of knowledge by working alongside the ECEs."

The interviewees also referred to the importance of community resources such as the library, which can be used to develop skills that are relevant to their childcare work: "I learn things from the librarian, on how to make things more interesting when you do storytelling. Little things like that helped me. And I come in and try it with the children in the classroom. So that has helped me feel good, like yeah, I tried something new."

Another interviewee spoke about the learning on the job: "And of course, I have learned a lot: in managing the behaviour of children; in planning activities; and implementing them for child development. Knowing the different culture of children, because we are multicultural. I have learned a lot, yes, and I try to apply the skills to my every day job."

For interviewees whose first language is not English, the day-to-day work experience has also served as an opportunity to improve their language skills: "You talk, you read and you sing, and it even helps you build up strong English language skills, especially for someone like me who was not born here."

The motivation behind improving skills relates in part to the desire to improve job performance, as illustrated by an ECE interviewee: "I'm improving myself. I'm studying in Seneca, an inclusion program, for children with special needs, to help me in my job. I have had children with special needs, and I wanted to learn more. To help them better; to know more specific things. I have learned a lot."

Another motivation for skills development and additional schooling is salary improvement:

> So just like I was telling a couple of years ago to a co-worker, "you know what, it's going to be a sacrifice, but do it. The pay cheque that you're going to get. You're just going to feel a lot better."

Family and Community Relations

Like the four other asset categories, the childcare workers responding to the survey experienced an improvement in their family and community relations. However, in the interviews, the response was more ambiguous. For example, some interviewees indicated a lack of leisure time and decreased community involvement due to their busy schedule; others mentioned increased volunteering in the community and participation in church since having joined LEF. Increased volunteering and community participation was one of the predictors of Family and Community Relations now. One way that the interviewees did this was through LEF-organized events such as the Santa Claus parade and the organization's Christmas party: "I participate in the Santa Clause parade in the city every year. And I even go with my children. And it's being done by LEF. I go with my children to also have fun with me, and help giving out books and candies. So when it comes to volunteering, I want to even include my children in it."

In addition to LEF, church was an important influence on community participation: "I just always go to church. This takes time. For two-and-a-half years I was busy with school in the evening. I lost a little bit [of] connection, but now I go back again to my church."

Church participation led to increased volunteer community outreach activities, including visiting nursing homes and hospitals, as well as helping her neighbour with snow removal: "My neighbour, her sight is not there. At times when the snow comes, I will just do both driveways."

The survey data suggest that there is a positive relationship between level of salary and working full-time and experiencing positive family and community relations, a point that is substantiated to a degree by the interview data. As one interviewee says: "If you're happy at work, you're happy at home." The interviewees perceived their family and work lives as intertwined in different ways:

> My training in childcare has very big impact in my life. Because working in childcare you need to be loving, caring, you need to have patience with children. But children are children. So as a mother, working with them has really trained me to be more passionate.
>
> I'm a parent of young children. I bring those ideas to working with other children.

Awareness and access to community programs have benefited both the interviewees' own children and the children at work: "I would get out there to learn more about the children's programs, because I work in the field and I want to know what's out there to offer to parents. And also on the personal side, because I'm a parent, I want to see what's there in the community for my child." The interviews suggest that work life interacts in many ways with home and community life.

General Discussion

The responses to the asset matrix show that the childcare workers at LEF experienced improvement in their well-being on five distinct dimensions: Financial Well-Being; Self-Confidence; Access to Services; Human Capital; and Family and Community Relations. For all five scales, the response pattern is clear and unequivocal. What is less clear is why this improvement has occurred.

Neither the responses to the surveys nor the interview data provide a compelling explanation of the reasons that the study's participants perceived an improvement in their well-being. Of the items that were predictors in the survey, most did not explain a large part of the variance for the five well-being scales. Of the predictor items, two items were significant predictors for three of the well-being scales: Current Salary and Membership in Organizations.

Current Salary was a significant predictor for Financial Well-Being, Human Capital, and Family and Community Relations. Membership in Organizations was a significant predictor for Self-Confidence, Access to Services, and Human Capital. The only other predictor that was significant for more than one scale was Level of Schooling, with the scales on Access to Services and Human Capital.

Put simply, the predictors could be subdivided into those that were primarily economic in orientation – Current Salary and Level of Schooling – and those that were social in orientation – Membership in Organizations and Volunteering. We shall discuss these in turn.

Economic Predictors

It is clear from both the survey data and the interviews that economic factors were of importance to the well-being of the childcare workers. Their salaries, while good by the standards of their profession, were low relative to Canadian norms and to what is needed to live comfortably in a city like Toronto. The average Canadian salary is $46,500 and the average hourly wage is $23.53 (Statistics Canada, 2012). Nevertheless, there is evidence to suggest that the childcare workers in this study are experiencing upward mobility: 26 per cent of the childcare workers (about one in four) were without a paying job prior to joining LEF. That group was mostly supported by their family, but some were receiving income either through Employment Insurance or Ontario Works, government programs that support people without jobs. For this group, their entry point into LEF was generally to pursue an early childhood assistant (ECA) certificate. This was an entry point into a low-paying job, but one with a fixed salary and benefits, an improvement from their pre-LEF circumstances. It provided job security, a point referred to by the interviewees. Job security could be explored in detail in subsequent research, as it may have been as important as or even of greater importance than the childcare workers' salary.

Those who came to LEF as early childhood educators (ECE) may have experienced a promotion. Therefore, a sizable part of the sample could be characterized as upwardly mobile, albeit still in relatively low-income jobs and living in a relatively high-cost city. Their experience of upward mobility is reflected in their response to the Financial

Well-Being scale. However, their experience of improved salary is not only a predictor of Financial Well-Being, but also Human Capital and Family and Community Relations. In other words, it bears on several facets of their being, as one might expect.

An anomaly in the data for the predictor current salary is that there is a consistent difference between those in the middle-salary group – $30,000 to $39,999 – and those whose salary was lower; however, no consistent difference between those whose salary was $40,000 and greater and those in the $30,000 range. In other words, the pattern isn't linear, as one might expect. Possibly, the people in the $30,000 salary range on average experienced greater mobility than those in the $40,000 range. The latter group may be coming up against a ceiling effect for the profession, and might experience greater frustration about their salary. Also, the latter group is likely to have college diplomas and, as a result, may expect more. Our data did not lend itself to using social mobility as a predictor, but perhaps this is something that could be studied in subsequent research.

Another possible explanation for the response pattern of current salary as a predictor is that persons in the $40,000 salary range may take on additional expenses such as a mortgage or car purchase, and realizing that they may have financial challenges could be frustrating. Some of the interviewees refer to the need to control expenses.

Level of Schooling does not directly predict Financial Well-Being, but it does predict Access to Services and Family and Community Relations – those with a college diploma scoring higher in both cases. The relationship to Access to Services may provide a clue not only of greater use but also of greater cost, as many services involve an expense. That relationship may give a clue as to why childcare workers in the $40,000-plus range are not experiencing greater financial well-being than those in the $30,000 range.

Social Predictors

The social predictor most consistently related to the scales in the asset matrix was Membership in Organizations. This, and the predictor Volunteering, could be viewed as measures of social capital. Membership in Organizations was related to three of the scales: Self-Confidence; Access to Services; and Human Capital. Volunteering, another indicator of organizational participation, was related to Family and Community Relations. In fact, Volunteering predicted a large 41 per cent of the variance for Family and Community Relations. That relationship was stronger than any other in the analysis.

The variables, Membership in Organizations and Volunteering, are indicators of social capital. There is a body of evidence that suggests a significant relationship between social capital and economic success (Putnam, 1993, 2000). Our study does not show that relationship, but it shows that social capital variables are strongly related to the other four of the matrix scales. The relationship between social capital measures and Self-Confidence, Access to Services, Human Capital, and Family and Community Relations seems logical, as all of these measures involve human engagement, a central characteristic of social capital. The fact that these measures are unrelated to Financial Well-Being may suggest that they are too far removed from it. The organization that most interviewees mentioned was their religious congregation, and participation in a congregation may be too tangential to Financial Well-Being to be an important predictor.

Conclusion

This study of childcare workers at The Learning Enrichment Foundation indicates that their well-being has improved on five scales of the asset matrix: Financial Well-Being; Self-Confidence; Access to Services; Human Capital; and Family and Community Relations. The experience of improvement in these five domains was consistent and clear. Less evident was the reasons for the improvement. The variables that predicted improvement were divided into two groupings: economic and social. The primary economic variable was Current Salary; the primary social predictors were Membership in Organizations and Volunteering.

NOTES

1 The average hourly wage of $16.21, for 37.5 hours a week for 52 weeks, amounts to an annual salary of $31,610.
2 Since the completion of the survey, LEF has closed one of their childcare centres.
3 ANCOVA was not performed as the homogeneity-of-slopes assumption was not observed. The assumption requires that the regression lines relating the covariate (i.e., scores on Access to Services prior to LEF) and the dependent variable (i.e., scores on Access to Services now) are parallel across all comparison groups (i.e., organizational membership). Instead,

simple main effects tests, which allows for heterogeneity of slopes (or unparalleled lines) were conducted at low, medium, and high values on covariate (i.e., 1 SD below the mean, mean, and 1 SD above the mean, respectively).

REFERENCES

City of Toronto. (2011). Profile of low income in the City of Toronto. Retrieved from http://www1.toronto.ca/city_of_toronto/social_development_finance__administration/files/pdf/poverty_profile_2010.pdf

Cleveland, G., & Hyatt, D. (2000). *Education, experience, job tenure, and auspice.* Toronto, ON: University of Toronto.

Cleveland, G., & Krashinsky, M. (2004). *The quality gap: A study of nonprofit and commercial child care centres in Canada.* Toronto, ON: Childcare Resource and Research Unit, University of Toronto.

Cleveland, G., Forer, B., Hyatt, D., Japel, C., & Krashinsky, M. (2007). *An economic perspective on the current and future role of non-profit provision of early learning and child care services in Canada.* Retrieved from http://www.childcarepolicy.net/wp-content/uploads/2013/04/final-report.pdf

Creswell, J.W., & Plano Clark, V.L. (2007). *Designing and conducting mixed methods research.* Thousand Oaks, CA: Sage Publications.

Greene, J.C., & Caracelli, V.J. (1997). *Advances in mixed-method evaluation: The challenges and benefits of integrating diverse paradigms: New directions for evaluation (No. 74).* San Francisco, CA: Jossey-Bass.

Living in Canada. (2012). *Early childhood education salary.* Retrieved from http://www.livingin-canada.com/salaries-for-early-childhood-educators-and-assistants.html

Payscale. (2012). *Hourly rate for industry: Child care / day care.* Retrieved from http://www.payscale.com/research/CA/Industry=Child_Care_or_Day_Care/Hourly_Rate

Putnam, R. (1993). *Making democracy work: Civic traditions in modern Italy.* Princeton, NJ: Princeton University Press.

Putnam, R. (2000). *Bowling alone: The collapse and revival of American community.* New York, NY: Simon and Schuster. http://dx.doi.org/10.1145/358916.361990

Statistics Canada. (2012). *Average hourly wages of employees by selected characteristics and profession.* Retrieved from http://www.statcan.gc.ca/tables-tableaux/sum-som/l01/cst01/labr69a-eng.htm

Tashakkori, A., & Teddlie, C. (Eds.). (2003). *Handbook of mixed methods in social and behavioural research.* Thousand Oaks, CA: Sage Publications.

SECTION C

Urban Poor and Immigrants

The social purpose enterprises in Section C – FoodShare (Chapter 10), Furniture Bank/Furniture Link (Chapter 11), and the Northwood Translation Bureau (Chapter 12) – address the needs of the urban poor and immigrants.

FoodShare, a leader in the promotion of healthy foods and related issues, houses a number of social purpose enterprises. The focus of this research was the **Good Food Market**, which sells quality produce, purchased from local farmers, to low-income neighbourhoods in the GTA.

Furniture Bank/Furniture Link is a social purpose enterprise, founded in 1998, that obtains quality furnishings from individuals and businesses and makes them available to low-income families in need. It also employs people with low incomes to provide its services.

Northwood Translation Bureau operates within Northwood Neighbourhood Services in the northwest part of the GTA, and employs recent immigrant professionals in providing translation, notarization, and interpretation services.

Unlike the enterprises in Sections A and B, FoodShare and Furniture Bank focus not on their workforces per se, but on serving the broader community. FoodShare's focus is on poor neighbourhoods that lack access to quality foods at reasonable prices within walking distance. Subsidies are needed to make its model workable. The research looks at the effectiveness of FoodShare's approach. Furniture Bank/Furniture Link provides furnishings for people in severe financial difficulties; it transfers furnishings from the well-to-do to the poor. Furniture Bank serves as an intermediary, and includes within its services a fee-for-service furniture pickup and delivery system offered through its social purpose enterprise, Furniture Link. Northwood Translation Bureau focuses on immigrants who are attempting to make a living from using their linguistic skills. The participants are self-employed, but highly marginalized.

10 Doing Markets Differently: FoodShare's Good Food Markets

MICHAEL CLASSENS, J.J. MCMURTRY,
AND JENNIFER SUMNER

Raj Patel's (2007) observation that roughly two billion people face catastrophic health issues related to food – half because they eat too few calories, and half because they eat too many – remains one of the most concise and compelling indictments of our contemporary food system. Patel is, of course, only one among a growing number of people who point out the pathologies built into the ways humans produce, distribute, and consume food (see, for example, Barndt, 2002; Corrigan, 2011; Das, Steege, Baron, Beckman, & Harrison, 2001; Friedmann & McMichael, 1989). From financial instability and marginalization (Corrigan, 2011; Qualman, 2011), to the erosion of labour rights (Barndt, 2002; Das et al., 2001), socio-ecological destruction (McMichael, 2006), and negative health consequences (Patel, 2007), the contemporary food system creates a wide variety of fundamentally unsustainable crises.

The challenges that the contemporary food system pose to social and environmental sustainability have not gone unnoticed, and activities rising up around these issues constitute, in aggregate, one of the most important social movements today (Morgan, 2009). In reality, there is no single, cohesive, and integrated "food movement," but instead a range of social networks gathered around loosely bound thematic issues. Food sovereignty (Desmarais, 2007), civic agriculture (Lyson, 2004), food democracy (Hassanein, 2003), foodsheds (Kloppenburg, Hendrickson, & Stevenson, 1996), foodscapes (Johnston & Baumann, 2010), fair trade (McMurtry, 2009), and locavores (Elton, 2010) are just the beginnings of a list capturing the diversity, energy, and rich character of a broad collection of alternative food initiatives (see Levkoe, 2011). Social purpose enterprises, such as FoodShare's Good Food Markets (GFMs), are one of the ways in which social economy actors have tried to address the food crisis.

Intersections between alternative food initiatives and the social economy have been of particular importance to the broader milieu of contemporary alternative food politics (see McMurtry, 2009; McMurtry, 2010; Sumner, 2012; Sumner & Llewelyn, 2010). This chapter explores some of the issues and tensions, as well as promises and pitfalls, of one such union between the social economy (specifically social purpose enterprises) and food-animated social change. More specifically, we discuss a two-year research project on FoodShare Toronto's GFM program, a modest program with ambitious goals: to reshape food distribution patterns in some of Toronto's most marginalized communities, to challenge geographies of hunger, and to educate, animate, and engage citizens in social change in and through the food system.

Importantly, we intentionally highlight the most basic material and logistical dynamics of the GFM program. Invoking the language of social change can often have the effect of steering analysis away from the practicalities of social economic organizing – of skirting the messiness of specificity in favour of more manageable generalities. However, we suggest here that the potential for social change to occur through the GFM program is inevitably predicated on quotidian details. The everyday concerns of the program, such as how many hours volunteers commit to the program, how satisfied market visitors are, how market leaders deal with leftover produce, and the like, are key to the very survival of the program. As is discussed in more detail below, the success of the GFM program is irrevocably fused to these most basic considerations. Without painstaking attention paid to these and other details, the GFM program would collapse, and along with it any hope of animating social change through it.

This perspective did not emerge ex nihilo but is instead a function of the collaborative nature of the project. We worked closely with FoodShare staff throughout the study period, and crucially, our research questions were crafted in concert with managerial and executive staff members of the organization. The study thus reflects the concerns the organization had about the challenges of the GFM program and their desire to discover practical solutions. Drawing on the extensive experience of FoodShare's agents of social change ultimately makes this a richer and more practically applicable project.

In the section immediately following this brief introduction, we provide pertinent details about FoodShare and the GFM program, including the specific workings of the program, its intended outcomes, and the context within which the program operates. Following this, we describe the variety of qualitative methods employed for the study and discuss the collaborative nature of the project. Next, we report on our findings and highlight some of themes emerging from a variety of GFM stakeholder groups. We conclude this chapter with some observations about the promises and pitfalls of food-related social change efforts, and make suggestions for future academic and on-the-ground work.

Toronto's FoodShare and the Good Food Market Program

Launched in the fall of 1985 with a $20,000 grant from Metro Toronto and a three-month mandate to coordinate the burgeoning food bank system in Toronto, FoodShare has grown into a multimillion-dollar organization and a key presence in the alternative food politics of the city.[1] A broad-stroke historical summary of the confluence of conditions that resulted in the organization's formation and subsequent direction provides some insight into the shifting terrain of food-based community organizing and activism in Toronto. In short, the GFM program was an inconceivable intervention when FoodShare was launched – but, as a combination of social economy principles and organizational innovation developed in response to a deepening food crisis, the GFM program has rapidly become an important, if high-maintenance, program in Toronto.

The growth of the GFM can be viewed in the context of the strategies that have evolved to address hunger, one of which is an elaborate system of food banks. Though easily conceived of as timeless institutions, the first food bank in Canada was launched in Winnipeg in 1981. One year after this, the Daily Bread Food Bank Foundation, a support organization for food banks, was established in Toronto. Hunger certainly was a problem in Canada before the early 1980s; however, the rapid rise of food bank infrastructure during the 1980s is testament to the significant political and economic restructuring that was underway. In this early era of rollback neoliberalism (Peck & Tickell, 2002), protections of the welfare state were vanishing and food concerns were emerging in historically unprecedented ways in many of Canada's large cities. By 1983, there were an estimated forty-five agencies in Metro Toronto alone providing food in some way for those living in poverty (Laws, 1988). As this infrastructure was being put into place in response to devolution of state responsibility, the immediate need of those without enough food was the main concern for community-based organizations that were filling the gap. Simply put, responding to the increase in poverty caused by federal-level funding cuts through either resisting state restructuring or intentionally planning urban- and community-level initiatives was overshadowed by the need to provide hungry people with food.

What emerged from this crisis-response environment in Toronto in the early 1980s was a patchwork of organizations providing stopgap food services, with little or no coordination or cooperation between them. A report in 1983 identified this lack of coordination among the forty-five food-provisioning agencies in Toronto as a significant imped-iment to a more effective community response (Laws, 1988). By 1985, the issue was still unresolved, and the mayor of Toronto, Art Eggleton, called for the development of an emergency food coordinating appara-tus: "I am introducing, with those already involved in fighting the problem [of hunger], a concept called FoodShare Toronto. It will be an information service and clearing house designed to direct people in need, as well as co-ordinate offers of donations and services from the community" (Eggleton, 1985, cited in Laws, 1988, p. 443).

Eggleton recommended that FoodShare Toronto be funded by Metro Toronto City Council through a one-time provision of $20,000, and that the service commence in October 1985 and end three months later. The original intent was to fund a short-term City Hall "hunger hotline" that would connect those who had food or resources to donate to social economy organizations and have the collateral benefit of raising aware-ness about the issue of hunger in the city. FoodShare was never meant to last beyond three months.

In January of 1986, one month after its planned disbandment, Food-Share was holding citywide food drives (Harvey, 1986). By April of that year, it had moved well beyond simply coordinating food services in the city and was lobbying the provincial government to reinvest in affordable housing and social assistance payments (Monsebraaten, 1986). In 1987, FoodShare called on the federal government for $200,000 to fund "alternative solutions" to the problem of hunger in Toronto (Flavelle, 1987). The organization was proposing to use the money to, among other things, design programs meant to "encourage low-income groups to start their own co-operative grocery stores, food-buying clubs and gardens ... [which] ... help build community pride and indi-vidual skills" (Donna MacDonald, quoted in Flavelle, 1987, A6). The executive director of FoodShare, Donna MacDonald, went on to argue,

"Lining up for food isn't going to change anything. It's just going to make people more helpless and dependent" (Donna MacDonald, quoted in Flavelle, 1987, A6).

By 1992, though still running the hunger hotline, FoodShare began organizing "food stores" in the lobbies of the properties of Canada's largest public housing provider, the Metro Toronto Housing Authority, in an effort to increase the accessibility of fresh produce to tenants (Reid, 1991). FoodShare began purchasing fresh produce from local farmers through the Ontario Food Terminal and delivering the produce to low-income communities across the city, with the intention of "changing the political and economic situation as it affects 'food security' [while] overhauling the food distribution system in the city" (Kane, 1993, B1).

Within a few years, FoodShare had transformed itself from what was meant to be a three-month effort to raise awareness about hunger and build some initial coordinating infrastructure into a multifaceted community-based agency – an advocacy organization, a non-profit food distribution service, and a coordinator of food-provisioning services with the capacity and resources to bring its demands to both the provincial and federal governments. Currently, FoodShare continues to operate in much the same way – though its revenue stream has increased from the original $20,000 to over $5.5 million in 2011. It has also diversified away from 100 per cent reliance on government funding. In 2009, 32 per cent of revenues came from social enterprise sales and services, and its program offerings had increased and expanded in scope (FoodShare, 2009). FoodShare had transformed from a gap-filling organization operating on a shoestring budget into a multifaceted organization that included the social purpose enterprise, the Good Food Market (McMurtry, 2010).

FoodShare sought a strategy for increasing the food security of people in need. At the same time, the program was designed around principles of the social economy, aiming to build a non-profit food distribution network based on community solidarity that would be under the collective control of marginalized populations in Toronto. The program, no longer confined to the lobbies of public housing units, has expanded operations to eleven communities within the Greater Toronto Area and draws on a variety of neighbourhood spaces, including community centres and community service agencies. The number of GFMs operating across the city has varied over the two-year study period. At times there were as many as sixteen markets in operation. The changing number of markets is partly a function of the fact that some are seasonal and only run in the summer months. However, it is also an indication of the precarious existence of many markets, due to a variety of reasons that will be discussed in greater detail in the results section. Exploring the basic elements of the markets in the GFM program – those that contribute to the markets' successes as well as to their challenges – is essential to better understanding the program and its potential to contribute to broader social change.

The concept of the GFM program is quite simple: FoodShare is able to procure relatively inexpensive fresh produce through bulk purchasing at the Ontario Food Terminal and from farmers in the region. Market organizers[2] are responsible for the on-the-ground organizing of the markets within their communities, making weekly orders for produce based on typical volume of sales, resident requests, and availability, and FoodShare delivers the order to the host market. These organizers buy the produce that they order from FoodShare at cost – a price that does not include, for example, the cost of delivery. By only charging organizers for the cost of the food, FoodShare indirectly subsidizes the program and ensures that the produce sold at the markets remains as inexpensive as possible. In addition, FoodShare provides training and networking opportunities for organizers as well as providing support as determined by the needs of the particular host community. In this way, the GFMs are social purpose enterprises that are heavily subsidized by their parent organization, FoodShare.

In addition to increasing access to inexpensive, fresh produce, the GFM market program also attempts to build place and strengthen community. The strategy of having local residents organize the markets is a conscious attempt to imbue each market with local autonomy and flavour, so that each market "uniquely reflects its community and is a vibrant and important gathering place" (FoodShare, 2012).

This latter aspect of the GFM program – the attempt to enhance a sense of place and community through fostering and showcasing local autonomy and vibrancy – must be understood as a central element of the GFM program. It reflects FoodShare's broader understanding of the fact that acute hunger and food insecurity tend to occur in particular neighbourhoods in Toronto. Accordingly, FoodShare does not attempt to build this sense of place and community just anywhere – instead, it targets lower-income and marginalized communities, bringing fresh and affordable produce to places "where it might not otherwise be available, and where [conventional] farmers' markets are not viable because sales are too low to cover farmers' costs" (FoodShare, 2012).

The GFM program illustrates FoodShare's evolving understanding of the complex nature of food issues, neighbourhood development, and social and economic marginalization. FoodShare's strategy simultaneously attempts to address hunger as well as the social and economic processes that produced the conditions of that hunger. But the strategy of the GFMs goes beyond the particular neighbourhood-based tactics they have developed for the distribution of affordable food to areas of need in Toronto. By procuring the food distributed at the GFMs from local farmers, FoodShare is also attempting to forge an alternative food network – one that is disentangled from the globalized and overly commodified conventional food system – while reinscribing more localized producer-consumer linkages in the Toronto-region's foodscape. Operating both within and outside of the conventional food system, the GMF program takes on the double task of building a more sustainable and just food distribution network, while at the same time building place-based capacities within marginalized communities – no small task for one program. As will be discussed below, despite many challenges, the GFM program has made an indelible imprint on some of Toronto's most marginalized neighbourhoods and provides a clear example of an innovative social purpose enterprise.

Methods

Members of the research team were assembled during the summer of 2010, and included staff members from FoodShare, one faculty member and one graduate student from the Ontario Institute for Studies in Education at the University of Toronto, and one faculty member and two graduate students from York University. From the outset, the project was driven by the principles of collaboration and emphasized the synergistic potential of community organization and academic partnerships. The project reflected concern, on the part of FoodShare staff, about lower-than-expected levels of success with the GFM program. Many markets were struggling to attract and retain a sufficient customer base to maintain sales at a break-even margin. In addition, staff at FoodShare designated to facilitate the GFM program were finding that they needed to spend much more time at each market than they had originally anticipated. This involved much daily and weekly organizing. Not only was this creating an additional drain on FoodShare's internal resources, but it also meant that FoodShare was less successful than it had intended in building community capacity.

To address this problem, the team worked together to design a two-part research strategy that included a review of academic and non-academic literature related to programs similar to the GFM and a short, semistructured survey of various key informant groups including market visitors; competitors; volunteer leader; volunteer non-leaders; community members; and FoodShare staff and volunteer. Near the end of the research process, it was determined that a special-focus group discussion with volunteer (leaders) would also benefit the research strategy and provide market organizers with a forum for a more in-depth discussion of issues, challenges, and successes. Finally, the research team presented initial findings to executive, staff and board members of FoodShare and received valuable feedback, which is reflected in these pages. A brief definition of each interview group and an overview of the questions posed to them follows.

Market Visitors

Market visitors were defined as people at the GFM at any time a researcher was present. From this group, the researchers were interested in finding out what motivates people to attend the markets, what might enable and encourage them to attend more often, how much they usually spend per visit, and what they might like to see changed about the markets.

Competitors

Competitors were defined as both independently owned, or nonfranchised, and corporately owned and franchised vendors who sell fresh fruit and vegetables within the general vicinity of the GFM. It is worth noting that the label "competitor" is used with some caution, because (a) FoodShare is sensitive to the potential that the GFM program might itself be seen as a competitor to smaller fresh-food retailers, who likely cannot compete with the price of produce offered at the GFMs; and (b) FoodShare refers to other produce vendors as partners rather than competitors in a broad food landscape. The questions posed to the competitor group seek to tease out some of the complexity of this dynamic through asking questions about how the competitors perceive the GFM program in their neighbourhood and whether or not they see any opportunity to work with the GFM program.

Volunteer Leaders

The volunteer leaders group is defined according to the role the person plays within the GFM. Typically, each market has one person who is the lead liaison with FoodShare, manages the financial side of the market, and generally spends a greater number of hours participating in the organizing tasks of the market than do other volunteers. From this group, the researchers sought to discover a number things, including what they like about being a volunteer leader, what kinds of supports from FoodShare are most effective, what further supports would they like to see, and how many hours they commit to the market.

Volunteer Non-leaders

The volunteer non-leaders were defined as all other volunteers at the GFM. Typically, there are a number of volunteer non-leaders at each market who are responsible for a range of duties, including receiving the produce shipments from FoodShare and setting up the market space. From this group, the researchers were interested in finding out how long they had been a volunteer, what they like best about being a volunteer, what challenges they face as a volunteer, what supports they receive from the volunteer leader, and what additional supports they might like to see.

Community Members

This group was defined as those who live, learn, work, or worship within the neighbourhood in which the GFM is located who were not at the market at the time of questioning. Research partners at FoodShare were interested to find out more about the broader community's general level of awareness of the GFM. Community members were approached in the streets, parks, and other public spaces around the market space. From this group, the researchers were interested in finding out whether or not the community members knew or had heard about the market, whether or not they had been to the market, how they found out about the market (if they knew about it), and whether or not they planned on attending the market.

FoodShare Employees/Support Staff

There are three distinct, though not mutually exclusive, subset categories of FoodShare employees and support staff: management/coordinator staff, distribution staff/volunteers, and community animators. The management team and coordinators are those with leadership positions within the organization who have some aspect of the GFM program as part of their job description. The distribution staff and volunteers are the employees or volunteers at the warehouse from which the produce is prepared, packaged, and shipped. The community animators are the staff members responsible for providing training, support, and mentorship to market organizers within the various communities served by Food-Share. The questions to these three groups generally attempted to solicit feedback on the strengths and weaknesses of the GFM program from their perspective within the organization, asking what supports might help reduce the weaknesses while building on the strengths.

The short, semistructured surveys were conducted between November 2010 and December 2011. Importantly, the markets were visited throughout the year – both during the summer and fall when the markets took place outside and there was typically more local produce offered, and during the winter and spring season when the markets were inside and there was generally less local produce offered. The researcher would generally arrive at the market about a half hour before the market opened and remain until about a half hour after the market had closed. Each market generally remained open for three to four hours, with most running between noon and six o'clock.

The season, time, or day of the week that the market was offered did not seem to impact the overall number of visitors. While there was variability in attendance between the different markets, each market tended to have fairly stable attendance. All of the markets tended to have the most visitors within the first hour of opening, with a significant drop-off during the remaining two to three hours. While the survey did not include questions asking about this, it is likely that visitors (most of whom are repeat visitors) knew that the selection of produce at the market diminishes rapidly. Unlike commercial grocery stores, the GFMs do not have the facilities or capacity to store an abundance of food on site (more on this below).

In total, eight markets were visited, two to three times each. The number of markets operating on a weekly basis fluctuated during the research period. The eight markets visited were the only ones that seemed to be held consistently throughout the duration of the project. During the visits, seventy-four people were interviewed, including twenty-seven market visitors, eighteen community members, seventeen volunteer non-leaders, eight volunteer leaders, four competitors, and two Food-Share program managers. Most of the competitors were unwilling to participate in the survey. Follow-up work might include redesigning a research strategy better able to engage this demographic.

Results

While only two FoodShare managers were interviewed for this project (the distribution manager, who is responsible for the distribution logistics, and the community manager, who is responsible for the community development mandate), their combined experience and expertise with the GFM program justifies an extended consideration of their comments.

Both managers see a number of strengths to the GFM program. First, they both feel that the program does a better job of offering more culturally appropriate and affordable food than FoodShare's other programs. They also feel that the program does well at promoting community by creating public spaces within which neighbours gather to socialize. The community manager summed up this sentiment well in suggesting that the program addresses issues of both "food deserts" and "community space deserts." She also suggests that the GFMs promote the development of local capacity (through volunteerism, et cetera) as well as provide an alternative to the mainstream food system. Importantly, she argues that the GFMs have an under-realized potential to be strong public spaces within the community.

Both managers also see a number of key challenges for the GFM program. These challenges ultimately dilute the ability of the GFM program to achieve its ambitious social change agenda. The first of these has to do with the amount and kind of work individual volunteers must do to maintain each market. Market organizers (many of whom are volunteers) must commit a significant amount of time to coordinating the markets, and must also have a wide array of skill sets – fiscal management and accounting skills, communication and marketing abilities, fundraising savvy, and volunteer management skills, among others. In some cases, organizations within the various communities host the GFMs and provide support and services to help run the markets, taking a significant burden off particular market organizers.

However, it has been challenging for FoodShare to find organizations willing to provide this support in all GFM communities.

The community manager identified a related – and significant – challenge. She said that FoodShare staff members are, at times, doing too much of the weekly organization of individual markets, which creates two problems. First, this tends to monopolize the time of the FoodShare staff, who are meant to be working with other community initiatives, and not only the GFM program. Second, opportunities to build local capacity are lost when staff members are doing the majority of the market organizing.

Another key challenge both managers see is using the produce left over after the market. Each market makes weekly produce orders from FoodShare, and the distribution staff at FoodShare delivers these orders. The market organizer usually pays for the produce on receiving it from the FoodShare delivery staff. Market volunteers (usually, the organizers) are responsible for any unsold produce left over after each market. It seems that, in many cases, this produce is simply given away, creating a potential for revenue loss. Both managers wonder if there are more productive ways of using this surplus produce, perhaps by turning it into a revenue stream (such as through selling the surplus produce to local soup kitchens).

The distribution manager sees another challenge. FoodShare delivers the weekly produce orders directly to each market, while making a significant effort to be flexible in terms of delivery time and place. This puts considerable pressure on FoodShare resources (both human and financial) because the delivery team must travel across the GTA, often during rush hour. This takes a significant amount of staff time and increasingly means a higher fuel cost. He also suggests that the level of flexibility FoodShare offers in terms of produce type and amount also puts strain on the distribution staff. FoodShare receives full cases of produce – though the GFMs can order half cases or quarter cases. It takes the distribution staff a considerable amount of time to create half and quarter cases, and it would be much easier and time effective to simply send full cases to markets. At the same time, the manager understands that the markets very rarely would be able to actually sell an entire case of any given fruit or vegetable. In short, the flexibility built into the program and the level of support that FoodShare provides for the GFM coordinators puts considerable strain on FoodShare's own internal resources.

In order to address these challenges, both managers would like to see more financial support from FoodShare for the GFM program. The distribution manager would also like to see more training and support for the GFM volunteers, especially for issues related to volunteer-retention strategies, social enterprise knowledge and management, and strategies for "place making," which in this case means fostering a sense of community and belonging through the GFM program. The community manager sees a more fundamental challenge by suggesting that Food-Share has not provided a clear programmatic vision for the GFM program. She suggests that, on the one hand, FoodShare wants to operate the GFM program as a social purpose enterprise – as a means of creating revenue (however meagre) for the individual markets, for Food-Share, or for both. On the other hand, FoodShare also wants the GFM program to facilitate low-income and marginalized populations to more easily access affordable produce. She sees a fundamental incompatibility between these two initiatives, and seems to suggest that FoodShare must choose to run either a revenue-generating (or at least a cost-recovery) program or a program that provides low-cost, accessible produce to marginalized communities.

Two themes emerged from conversations with market visitors – dedication and discernment. Those who attend the markets tend to do so regularly, with 84 per cent of respondents saying that they attend the weekly markets at least two times per month. 40 per cent of market visitors attended the market every week. The reasons for attending the markets varied a great deal, though almost half can be categorized as concerning quality or freshness and price of the produce on offer. Many respondents suggested that the produce at the GFMs was generally of higher quality and lower priced than that available at conventional grocery stores. While the GFMs seem to excel in this respect, they tend to do less well in being able to offer an acceptable number and variety of products. Almost 60 per cent of market visitors said that they would spend more money at the GFM if there were a greater number and variety of products. This is a key tension within the program: shoppers are used to seeing overflowing shelves with a large variety of products. The modest GFM programs clearly cannot compete with the familiar scene in most grocery stores.

The key challenge for the GFMs is that many markets do not have the capacity or infrastructure to productively deal with leftover produce, creating a disincentive to providing the kind of offering many market visitors would like to see. While some of the larger markets (generally supported by a high-capacity organization) are able to find ways of using surplus produce within their other operations (such as in their cafeterias or kitchen programs), many of the smaller markets do not have this option,[3] and end up giving away leftover produce to volunteers, staff, and so on, meaning that they are losing money on a weekly basis. For this reason, market leaders are hesitant to increase their weekly orders, despite the fact that it may entice visitors to buy more.

Many of the market visitors (about one-third of responses) also stated that community building and ambiance were a motivation for attending the market. In other words, people attend the GFMs as a means of attaining high-quality, low-cost food, but they also attend because it gives them a chance to engage with their community – to build a sense of place. Many respondents mentioned that they looked forward to seeing the market volunteers and other shoppers on a weekly basis because it gave them a chance to chat and catch up with them. Others explicitly identified that the market was helping to build a sense of community within their neighbourhood, and that the market had become a known gathering place in the community.

The market volunteers, both leaders and non-leaders, are dedicated and determined. The volunteers universally take pride in their role in making the GFM available within their communities and are specifically motivated by the challenge of making healthy and affordable food accessible within their communities. Most non-leaders contribute about five hours per week to the market, while most leaders contribute five to fifteen hours per week. The tasks vary from market to market, but generally include ordering the produce, setting up and taking down the market, accounting, and outreach and advertising. Some of the larger markets have integrated some specialized tasks, such as accounting and marketing, into the organizations' existing accounting and marketing departments. This is a very good way of leveraging existing internal capacities (see more on this concept below) and taking pressure off market volunteers; however, not all of the markets have access to this level of expertise.

Most market volunteers are also motivated to increase the number of people attending the market on a weekly basis. One key way of achieving this is by offering products and services above and beyond the produce provided by FoodShare. Some markets provide breads, baked goods, and preserves. Others provide novel experiences for market visitors, including pizza bake ovens, story readings for children, and craft tables. In any event, these kinds of value-added products and services are major contributors to the amount of time volunteers (both leaders and non-leaders) spend on the market.

Discussion

While the research for this project did not focus specifically on the impacts of the GFM program on the people who shop at the markets or the neighbourhoods in which the GFMs are located, it is worth emphasizing that the program does seem to be producing some positive outcomes. Anecdotally, the field researcher for this project noted how happy and vibrant market visitors always were. Often visitors would stop to chat with market volunteers and other shoppers, and many markets have designed areas to specifically foster friendly conversations. At a minimum, the weekly GFMs provide people with an important opportunity to meet up with friends and neighbours. Feagan and Morris (2009, 236) observe that these kinds of "embedded" attributes of farmer-market interfaces, such as increased social interaction between vendors and shoppers, provide a counterpoint to conventional grocery stores.

In more concrete terms, FoodShare reports that among market shoppers, 47 per cent say that they have met more of their neighbours through the GFMs, and an overwhelming 98 per cent say that the GFM has made their neighbourhood a better place to live. In terms of food access, 52 per cent of market shoppers say that they are eating more fruits and vegetables, and 37 per cent say that they feel significantly healthier as a result (FoodShare, 2012). A recent case study of one particular GFM (Booth, 2012) found a number of positive impacts. First, the GFM gives people an opportunity to socialize:

> For many GFM customers, the market is a social event; they see their friends and get to know people in their neighbourhood. Many GFM customers are seniors, living on their own, and the market provides them an opportunity to get out of the house and socialize. (Booth, 2012, p. 95)

Second, the GFM provides customers greater access to food, both geographically and monetarily. In terms of geography, its central location makes it easy for them to walk, which saves on transportation costs: "The GFM is located in a food desert; as such, many customers mentioned the benefit of having a weekly produce market in the neighbourhood" (Booth, 2012, p. 96). In monetary terms, customers also benefited from affordability, with price being the major reason why people preferred the GFM. "All the customers were satisfied with the prices at the GFM, and many cited lower prices in response to questions about the advantages of the market" (Booth, 2012, p. 96). Third, the GFM offers high-quality produce to customers:

> Customers overwhelmingly prefer the quality of GFM produce over that of mainstream grocery stores. Every single interviewee without exception mentioned feeling satisfied with the quality of the fruit and vegetables on offer at the GFM, and many stated that it's better than what they have access to elsewhere. (Booth, 2012, p. 98)

Fourth, the GFM saves customers money not only because of its low prices but also through the voucher cards given to volunteers. Fifth, the GFM helps customers save time because of its proximity to their homes. And, sixth, the GFM induced dietary changes in customers, encouraging them to eat more fruits and vegetables.

While the Booth (2012) case study only dealt with one of the GFMs, it is clear that many of these positive impacts would pertain to other GFMs as well, given the basic similarities among them.

However to focus exclusively on these positive individual impacts reported by FoodShare (2012) and Booth (2012) would betray the fact that the GFM program continues to struggle. This, in part, points to the necessity of reshaping the distribution networks of the contemporary food system to serve low-income populations. But it also speaks to the even more difficult work of subverting the modus operandi of the contemporary food system – what Lappé (2011) calls the "one-rule economy" based on profit – to other, more sustainable and just outcomes. These challenges stem from the fact that this modest program – with its alternative vision of food provision, its insistence on community building, and its social economic perspective – is superimposed on the far more robust geography and ideology of the globalized corporate food system. The bad news is that the corporate monopoly of the food system is almost total, with 95 per cent of the foods Americans eat coming from what can be considered a "corporate" source (McMichael, 2000). However, the good news is twofold: First, there are many precedents for dramatic social change being animated through food (see for example,

Dalton, 2012; Heynen, 2009, 2010). Gandhi, for example, framed a mass march important in ending British rule in India around the seemingly simple issue of access to affordable salt (Dalton, 2012), while the Black Panther Party contributed to their civil rights efforts through a school breakfast program (Heynen, 2009). Second, there is a stunning array of other broadly defined alternative food initiatives – some smaller and some larger than the GFM program – that are similarly layered over the terrain of global capitalism. Taken together, initiatives of the social economy provide a patchwork of possibility that may, when stitched together, create a means of overcoming the one-rule economy and lead towards a more just and sustainable food system. In order to have any hope of animating social change, these lofty goals must take into account the nuts and bolts of social economic organizing. In other words, the fundamental mechanics of social change initiatives must be sound.

The GFM program also offers an inspiring example of how some of the problems experienced in the social economy sector can be resolved. It is well known, but often overlooked in the literature, that small-scale, non-profit economic initiatives struggle to be self-funding or even long-term without significant outside funding and support. Unfortunately, the discourse surrounding social enterprises often masks both this reality and the central role that state and community support plays in facilitating the social economy. As McMurtry has pointed out, without a values-based, democratic practice that is focused on community need, the social economy tends to experience mission drift (McMurtry, 2010). FoodShare, however, has begun to develop responses to these problems based on three principles – linkages, leveraging, and logistics.

Loxley (2007) argues that we can understand the success of a community-based economic activity through the links it establishes to other community-based activities. In this way, both social and economic space is developed in meaningful ways. FoodShare has from the beginning been working, if unconsciously, towards linkage by bringing government to the "food table" to discuss and fund food issues alongside farmers, social economy organizations, and communities. FoodShare has also been central in linking community-focused organizations by creating social and economic spaces where actors can gather, discuss community issues, and build alternatives.

Along this line, FoodShare has also leveraged its position in the community to create more opportunities for communities and the undernourished to develop capacities within an unsupportive capitalist environment. This leveraging of existing skill sets and social capital in the service of a broader community is crucial for marginalized neigh-bourhoods. It is bringing civil commons organizations into dialogue with each other to put forward a larger range of possibility for the communities within which it operates (Sumner & Llewelyn, 2010). Further, this form of "ethical value added" activity is crucial to realizing both the value-based goals of the social economy and, more importantly, the basic groundwork of alternative economic systems on which our social future may well depend (McMurtry, 2009).

Finally, FoodShare has begun to innovate in the area of logistics with a recently launched food truck program. In its efforts to introduce affordable and healthy food to marginalized communities unable to sustain a GFM, FoodShare is in the early stages of offering a program that provides a mobile GFM for fresh fruits and vegetables to some of Toronto's most entrenched areas of need. While the program is still evolving, the general concept is that a refrigerated truck, stocked with fresh produce, makes weekly scheduled stops at existing neighbourhood meeting places (community centres, churches, et cetera). The mobile service sells the produce at prices marginally above cost, while providing a value-added, community-enhancing event meant to bolster already-existing infrastructure. This strategy follows the neighbourhood GFM program in that the cost of transportation and storage is largely absorbed by FoodShare.

Although dominant economic theory makes arguments around the economies of scale, very little work has been done on the possibility for "federated" economic activity among small, independent community organizations, in order to realize both social and economic value. While there are tantalizing examples in Mondragon in Spain and the Emilia Romagna region in Italy, the academic and practitioner social economy communities in Canada generally have not engaged in developing this possibility. By serving as a logistics hub for a variety of communities and organizations, FoodShare is opening up this opportunity and continuing its historical pattern of innovation in this area in the marginalized neighbourhoods of Toronto. More importantly for this collection, it is clear that the Good Food Market is an exemplary example of a social purpose enterprise, defined in the introduction as "a market-based entity founded and supported by a non-profit organization for the purposes of the economic and social benefit of persons on the social margins who are employed in or trained through the enterprise." The Good Food Market brings quality food to low-income neighbourhoods in the

Greater Toronto Area at prices that the residents can afford. In order to do this, the GFM is heavily supported by its parent organization, FoodShare, and it is a product of FoodShare's vision of addressing food insecurity in the Greater Toronto Area.

NOTES

1 For more information on FoodShare, visit their website at http//www.foodshare.net/index.htm.
2 In the original design of the program, "market organizers" were meant to be citizen volunteers with the time and capacity to organize a GFM. However, as the program evolved it became apparent that the amount of work, skill, and resources it takes to run a market are often beyond what volunteers can offer. While there are still some markets that are run by volunteers, the majority of markets are now hosted by existing community service agencies that provide paid staff, space, advertising, and other in-kind donations in support of the GFMs. This and other related issues are further discussed in the Results and Discussion sections.
3 FoodShare has recently introduced a new protocol requiring all GFMs to find a community partner to purchase any weekly leftovers.

REFERENCES

Barndt, D. (2002). *Tangled roots: Women, work and globalization on the tomato trail.* Toronto, ON: Second Story Press.

Booth, A. (2012). *How good is the Good Food Market: An exploration of community food security* (Unpublished master's thesis). Adult Education and Community Development Program, OISE/University of Toronto, Toronto, ON.

Corrigan, M. (2011). Growing what you eat: Developing community gardens in Baltimore, Maryland. *Applied Geography (Sevenoaks, England), 31*(4), 1232–1241. http://dx.doi.org/10.1016/j.apgeog.2011.01.017

Dalton, D. (2012). *Mahatma Gandhi: Nonviolent power in action.* New York, NY: Columbia University Press.

Das, R., Steege, A., Baron, S., Beckman, J., & Harrison, R. (2001). Pesticide-related illness among migrant farm workers in the United States. *International Journal of Occupational and Environmental Health, 7*(4), 303–312. http://dx.doi.org/10.1179/107735201800339272

Desmarais, A. (2007). *La via campesina: Globalization and the power of peasants.* Halifax, NS: Fernwood Publishing.

Eggleton, A. (1985, Sept 26). A statement by Mayor Art Eggleton announcing FoodShare Toronto. A concept of community to help fight hunger in Toronto. Toronto, ON: City of Toronto.

Elton, S. (2010). *Locavore: From farmers' fields to rooftop gardens – how Canadians are changing the way we eat.* Toronto, ON: HarperCollins Publishers.

Feagan, R., & Morris, D. (2009). Consumer quest for embeddedness: A case study of the Brantford farmers' market. *International Journal of Consumer Studies, 33*(3), 235–243. http://dx.doi.org/10.1111/j.1470-6431.2009.00745.x

Flavelle, D. (1987, April 14). Give $200,000 to ease plight of hungry, Ottawa urged. *Toronto Star*, pp. A6.

FoodShare. (2009). *Annual Report 2009.* Toronto, ON: Author. Retrieved from http://www.foodshare.net/annual-report

FoodShare. (2012). *Good Food Markets.* Toronto, ON: Author. Retrieved from http://www.foodshare.net/good-food-markets

Friedmann, H., & McMichael, P. (1989). Agriculture and the state system: The rise and decline of national agricultures, 1870–present. *Sociologia Ruralis, 29*(2), 93–117.

Harvey, R. (1986, January 28). FoodShare starts blitz to feed Metro poor. *Toronto Star*, p. A2.

Hassanein, N. (2003). Practicing food democracy: A pragmatic politics of transformation. *Journal of Rural Studies, 19*(1), 77–86. http://dx.doi.org/10.1016/S0743-0167(02)00041-4

Heynen, N. (2009). Bending the bars of empire from every ghetto for survival: The Black Panther Party's radical antihunger politics of social reproduction and scale. *Annals of the Association of American Geographers, 99*(2), 406–422. http://dx.doi.org/10.1080/00045600802683767

Heynen, N. (2010). Cooking up non-violent civil-disobedient direct action for the hungry: "Food Not Bombs" and the resurgence of radical democracy in the US. *Urban Studies (Edinburgh, Scotland), 47*(6), 1225–1240. http://dx.doi.org/10.1177/0042098009360223

Johnston, J., & Baumann, S. (2010). *Foodies: Democracy and distinction in the gourmet foodscape.* New York, NY: Routledge.

Kane, M. (1993, July 7). Groups try new ways to share the fare. *Toronto Star*, p. B1.

Kloppenburg, J., Jr, Hendrickson, G., & Stevenson, G. (1996). Coming in to the foodshed. *Agriculture and Human Values, 13*(3), 33–42. http://dx.doi.org/10.1007/BF01538225

Lappé, F.M. (2011). *Ecomind: Changing the way we think, to create the world we want.* Cambridge, MA: Small Planet Media.

Levkoe, C. (2011). Toward a transformative food politics. *Local Environment,*
    16(7), 687–705. http://dx.doi.org/10.1080/13549839.2011.592182

Loxley, J. (2007). *Transforming or reforming capitalism: Towards a theory of com-*
    munity economic development. Halifax, NS: Fernwood.

Lyson, T. (2004). *Civic agriculture: Reconnecting farm, food, and community.*
    Medford, MA: Tufts University Press.

McMichael, P. (2000). The power of food. *Agriculture and Human Values, 17*(1),
    21–33. http://dx.doi.org/10.1023/A:1007684827140

McMichael, P. (2006). Peasant prospects in the neoliberal age. *New Political*
    Economy, 11(3), 407–418. http://dx.doi.org/10.1080/13563460600841041

McMurtry, J.J. (2009). Ethical value added: Fair trade and the case of Café
    Feminino. [Special Issue]. *Journal of Business Ethics, 86*(1), 27–49. http://
    dx.doi.org/10.1007/s10551-008-9760-x

McMurtry, J.J. (2010). *Living economics: Canadian perspectives on the social econo-*
    my, co-operatives and community economic development. Toronto, ON: Emond
    Montgomery Publications.

Monsebraaten, L. (1986, April 2). FoodShare seeks province's help in crusade
    against hunger in Metro. *Toronto Star,* p. A6.

Morgan, K. (2009). Feeding the city: The challenge of urban food planning.
    International Planning Studies, 14(4), 341–348. http://dx.doi.org/10.1080/
    13563471003642852

Patel, R. (2007). *Stuffed and starved: Markets, power and the hidden battle for the*
    world's food system. Toronto, ON: Harper Collins.

Peck, J., & Tickell, A. (2002). Neoliberalizing space. *Antipode, 34*(3), 380–404.
    http://dx.doi.org/10.1111/1467-8330.00247

Qualman, D. (2011). Advancing agriculture by destroying farms? The state of
    agriculture in Canada. In H., Wittman, A. Desmarais, & N. Wiebe (Eds.),
    Food sovereignty in Canada: Creating just and sustainable food systems
    (pp. 20–42). Winnipeg, MN: Fernwood Publishing.

Reid, S. (1991, November 5). Food store's bounty masks hunger hotline.
    Toronto Star, p. A1.

Sumner, J. (2012). Dining on the social economy: Challenges and opportuni-
    ties for local, sustainable food policy in a global context. *Canadian Review of*
    Social Policy, 67(1), 30–43.

Sumner, J., & Llewelyn, S. (2010). Organic farmers and the social economy:
    Positive synergies for community development. In L. Mook, J. Quarter,
    & S. Ryan (Eds.), *Researching the social economy* (pp. 289–311). Toronto, ON:
    University of Toronto Press.

11 Stakeholders' Stories of Impact: The Case of Furniture Bank

ANDREA CHAN, LAURIE MOOK, AND SUSANNA KISLENKO

Introduction

This chapter explores the impact of a hybrid social enterprise/social purpose enterprise through the eyes of its stakeholders. We were interested in understanding the impacts of the organization from different perspectives as well as garnering these stakeholders' ideas for increasing that impact. The case study is organized in five sections: theoretical approach; a description of the organization; methodology; findings; and discussion.

Theoretical Approach

In order to frame our research approach, we have synthesized concepts from stakeholder theory and crowdsourcing. Traditional stakeholder theory is a theory of management that considers the interests, or "stakes," of different groups involved in running an organization. It emphasizes that understanding the relationships an organization has with groups other than just its owners is important for the success of a business. In order to identify stakeholder groups, we used the definition proposed by Freeman (1984): those who affect or are affected by the organization. In the corporate world, stakeholder groups have been identified as employees, customers, shareholders, suppliers, governments, local communities, competitors, media, and special interest groups (Clarkson, 1995). In the non-profit world, the situation is slightly different. First, there are no owners or shareholders. Second, there are additional stakeholder groups like funders, clients, and volunteers to consider (LeRoux, 2009, Mook, Quarter & Richmond, 2007). Our study also pays attention to collaborators, such as community agency partners working in tandem with Furniture Bank, in order to address a particular issue.

Many organizations focus on stakeholder relationships in order to manage and maintain important affiliations, minimize conflict, or ease implementation of policy (Clarkson, 1995; Roberts & Mahoney, 2004; Savage, Nix, Whitehead & Blair, 1991; Welp, de la Vega-Leinert, Stoll-Kleemann, & Jaeger, 2006). We focused on stakeholder groups for another reason. In our examination of Furniture Bank's stakeholders, we adopted the idea of crowdsourcing (Brabham, 2008; Howe, 2006; Surowiecki, 2004), where problem solving is facilitated by a diverse range of "laypersons."[1] However, instead of targeting the broader public (or the "crowd"), we aimed for stakeholder groups, a process known as stakeholder-sourcing (Lim, Quercia, & Finkelstein, 2010). To set the context for the research, we now turn to furniture banks in general, and then we introduce Furniture Bank in Toronto.

Furniture Banks

According to the Furniture Bank Association of North America, there are nearly 100 furniture banks in North America today, the first of which appeared in the early 1980s (FBANA, 2014a). Generally, the mission of furniture banks is to provide free, gently used furniture to families and individuals experiencing severe life crises "such as mothers and children escaping domestic violence, victims of natural disasters, formerly homeless people moving back into housing, people living with physical or mental disabilities and working families living below the poverty line" (FBANA, 2014b). The organizations vary in structure, but most connect donors and social service agencies.

Furniture Bank, Toronto

Furniture Bank in Toronto began in the late 1990s and was founded by Sister Anne Schenck, who also sits on the board of directors. Its mission, like other furniture banks, is to transfer gently used furniture and household goods donated to them by individuals or corporations to those in need. Overall, in 2011, Furniture Bank worked with over sixty community partner agencies to provide services to 2,572 families. Women and children from shelters comprised 26 per cent of their clients, the formerly homeless 42 per cent, new Canadians 28 per cent, and other clients 4 per cent.

The following passage put together from the organization's funding proposals describes how it has grown throughout the years (Riva & Kislenko, 2012):

> Furniture Bank began in 1998 with the understanding that a sense of pride, self-esteem, comfort, and security – in short, a sense of home – are critical ingredients for people to transition out of lives of passivity and hopelessness and into ones of vigour, purpose, and direction.
>
> At every step of the way in those early days, countless individuals and organizations found their way to our humble project and helped us get off the ground. A warehouse and delivery trucks. Pro bono legal services and boots-on-the-ground volunteers. Guidance on securing some much needed start-up funds from the City of Toronto. We moved into our second home with facilities on Madison and Peel Avenues, which housed our work for a decade. A dedicated truck of our own became a reality in 2002.
>
> Like many organizations in their infancy, we went through some classic growing pains and faced typical organizational obstacles in our first few years. But as we proved the model – and the need – more support solidified and momentum began to build. Starting in 2005 the City of Toronto had officially taken us on as a partner in their ambitious Streets to Homes program, which helped raise our profile with more strategic partners in the charitable and social service sector.
>
> By 2008, we had completed a strategic review and built additional critical relationships, as well as professionalized our operations management, logistics, and staff structure. We had found a new property to house our work, and were in the early stages of building a system to track our business data and kick start a robust fundraising engine. Since 2008, we have added an average of one truck to our fleet and three members to our staff every single year. Furniture Bank has become increasingly complex.
>
> Our Furniture Link operation has also had its own growth story. Originally conceived in 2004 as a furniture re-finishing business, it charged inconsistently for furniture delivery – and never for pick-up. But by 2007 Furniture Link had learned enough about the market to abandon re-finishing and move to a business model based on charging for donation pick-ups as well as delivery. It became fully structured and operational in 2008, founded on our existing truck fleet and our core expertise in moving logistics.

Since the launch of Furniture Link in 2004, the social [purpose] enterprise has steadily made up a larger share of Furniture Bank's revenues – doubling from the initial year to 2012. In that same timeframe, total revenues have grown tenfold. To us this is proof of our dedication to reinventing the revenue model for charities. Even as we are able to grow our pool of grants and small-donor contributions, we are even more adept at ensuring that our social [purpose] enterprise growth outpaces all other inputs.

Beyond the numbers, we do all of this – pursuing the charity mission as well as building the enterprise engine – because of the impact we see in the lives of real people. Since our humble beginning we have helped furnish 20,000 households – and in so doing, we've touched the lives of nearly 50,000 individual women, men, and the children for whom they seek to piece together a better home.

Along the way, we have also brought over 100 people from vulnerable and marginalized backgrounds and communities into our operation. These "participants" have found a place on our staff team, acquired vocational training, grown with us, and then left to continue their path with a better toolkit in hand.

In 2012, we formalized our employment program under Furniture Link to focus on providing skills training and employment opportunities to youth at risk and newcomers to Canada.

Clients are referred to Furniture Bank by one of over sixty community agency partners, and include those leaving shelters or abusive situations, and newcomers to Canada. In other words, clients do not approach the organization directly, but go through a screening process first. There is no cost to the clients for the furniture and household items; however, there is a charge for delivery provided by Furniture Link.

As the social purpose enterprise arm of Furniture Bank, Furniture Link prepares participants for employment in logistics, call centre operations, and warehousing. Since its inception, it has provided training for ninety-three participants. It currently employs over twenty people, and operates five trucks, six days a week, making about 7,000 pickups and deliveries in a year. In the past it has also provided skills development in furniture repair and woodworking.

Employing the definitions established in Chapter 1, Furniture Bank can be considered a hybrid model combining features of both a social enterprise and a social purpose enterprise. Like many *social purpose enterprises*, Furniture Bank runs a formalized training and employment program for individuals who have experienced barriers to employment.

However, like a *social enterprise*, it generates a considerable portion (65 per cent) of its total financial revenue through furniture pickup and delivery fees, including fees earned through a service agreement with the City of Toronto that covers the delivery charge for a portion of its clients (Figure 11.1). Although the revenue is generated through the enterprise, the income would not have been earned if not for the central social mission of Furniture Bank – the transfer of free furniture and household goods to individuals and families in need. As such, the income generation of Furniture Link is not only inherently tied to the social mission of Furniture Bank– it is also conditional on it. Contrary to the description of the typical social purpose enterprise in Chapter 1, Furniture Link contributes substantial financial support to the parent organization and is a central component of Furniture Bank's business model.

Furniture Bank relies heavily on donations of furniture and household items from individuals and corporations. In 2011, donors provided furniture and household items valued at almost $1.3 million. Items are described as "gently used" and are carefully checked by employees for contamination before being accepted and placed in the warehouse. Furniture Bank employees are trained to recognize the signs of bed bugs, and the premises are inspected regularly by a professional pest control company. Those who wish to donate furniture can either drop it off at Furniture Bank warehouse or arrange for pickup and delivery by Furniture Link. A call centre with three employees operates within Furniture Bank to do the scheduling. Donors receive in-kind receipts for tax purposes. Valuations are done in-house according to size and category of item.

Furniture Bank also operates several volunteer programs. Volunteers are an integral part of the organization and perform a great variety of tasks, from serving on the board of directors and being involved in governing the organization to:

- working with clients to help families walk through the showroom;
- sorting in the warehouse to replenish everyday essentials for clients;
- helping with administration including scheduling and file organization;
- supporting fundraising by sharing their research and writing skills;
- becoming a Chair Affair volunteer to support Furniture Bank's signature annual event (Furniture Bank, n.d.)

Figure 11.1. Furniture Bank, Monetary Resources (2011)

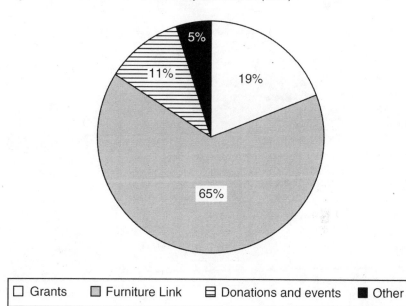

The organization has a very engaged and business-minded board, which includes lawyers, accountants, operations and logistics professionals, and experts in program development, waste reduction, and marketing. Corporate volunteers also play an integral role in the client experience at Furniture Bank. Under the corporate volunteer program, businesses can arrange volunteer days at Furniture Bank, where their employees provide hands-on support to individuals and families selecting furniture and other household items in the showroom.

In 2011, there were almost five hundred volunteers, not including the board, who donated 11,200 hours of service to the organization. If a value is placed on their services based on an average hourly rate of $15.00, these contributions can be estimated at $168,000. Together with donations of furniture and household items, these non-financial resources are equal to the financial resources received by the organization for the year (Figure 11.2).

Figure 11.2. Furniture Bank, All Resources (2011)

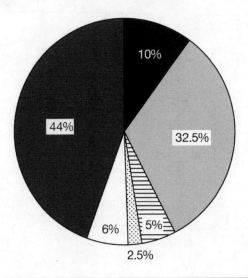

| ■ Grants | ▨ Furniture Link | ⊟ Donations and events |
| ▨ Other | ☐ Volunteer contributions | ■ Donated items |

Methodology

This case study was conducted as community-university research. Community-university research is a unique branch of research in which community and academic partners collaborate in all aspects of the study.

In light of our theoretical framework we examined stakeholders' perspectives on the following questions:

R1. What is the impact of Furniture Bank?
R2. What are the opportunities for Furniture Bank to increase its impact?
R3. How would the community be different if Furniture Bank did not exist?

To collect data, we conducted focus groups, performed online and in-person surveys, and analysed organization documents. To foster a richness of information, the method of purposive sampling was chosen for primary data gathering (Palys, 2008), taking into account that different stakeholder groups (as well as individuals within groups) would have varying perspectives on the impacts of Furniture Bank that reflect their history and relationship with the organization. The stakeholder groups were selected based on whether they affected or were affected by the organization (Freeman, 1984) and if they were close enough to the organization in order to be able to judge its impact. The stakeholder groups included in this study were furniture and household items recipients, community agency partners, Furniture Bank staff (employees and volunteers), donors (financial and non-financial), and corporate volunteers.

Written client profiles (n = 14) and client comments (September to November 2012) collected by Furniture Bank were also analysed as part of collecting data on the impact on stakeholders. Other organization documents that were analysed included financial statements, annual reports, volunteer reports, and media articles. The organization's website (www.furniturebank.org) was also reviewed.

Focus groups were conducted with management staff, front-line staff, and volunteers, with a total of thirteen participants. As "collective conversations or group interviews" (Kamberelis & Dimitriadis, 2011, p. 545), the focus groups were meant to explore the participants' perceptions on the type of social, economic, and environmental impact they believed Furniture Bank was making in the greater community. Participants were also questioned on what they believed the greatest opportunities and constraints were for increasing Furniture Bank's impact, and how they imagined the community would be different if Furniture Bank did not exist. The focus groups lasted between one and two hours, and the proceedings were recorded and later transcribed.

The focus groups gave us direction for the next stage of the research, which was to administer online surveys with the key stakeholder groups impacted by the organization. The stakeholder groups surveyed were the executive directors (n = 15) and caseworkers (n = 36) of Furniture Bank's community agency partners; employees (n = 7); client-service volunteers (n = 10); board members (n = 7); donors (n = 158); and corporate volunteers (n = 20). The total number of respondents for these surveys was 253, an overall response rate of 20 per cent.

Although our overall response rate of 20 per cent is relatively low, online surveys are known to have a typically lower response rates compared to other survey modes (Fan & Yan, 2010). We acknowledge that the size of the sample limits our ability to generalize findings to the larger population of Furniture Bank's stakeholders. However, our analyses were based less on quantitative explorations (e.g., average responses from stakeholder groups) and more on the qualitative responses gathered from the survey. We were primarily concerned with the diverse ways in which participants understood Furniture Bank's impact, and we were able to explore this with the wealth of responses that were given.

In addition, a written questionnaire was completed by participants (n = 17) from three corporate volunteer groups on their last day of volunteering at Furniture Bank. The questionnaire asked participants to describe how they had felt before, during, and after their visit to Furniture Bank and to describe the impact that volunteering at Furniture Bank had on them. We were interested in the personal experiences of corporate volunteers after spending a day at Furniture Bank.

Findings

This section presents the findings from furniture recipients, community agency partners, Furniture Bank staff (employees and volunteers), donors, and corporate volunteers.

Furniture Recipients

Furniture Bank has collected client stories over a number of years, and these stories were analysed for signs of how the experience with the organization impacted furniture recipients. Secondary data were used, given the special considerations involved in researching a vulnerable population who are often reluctant to participate in studies with researchers from outside their communities. All client profiles illustrated situations of economic hardships, and many described immigrants and refugees who had fled war, violence, and persecution. Often clients and their families lived in fear and isolation. Unemployment and underemployment were continued barriers to economic stability. Some struggled with illness, drug and alcohol addiction, and previous experience with the justice system. From the profiles, clients were under much stress on their arrivals to Furniture Bank, despite their recent transition into permanent housing.

For obvious reasons, furniture and household goods bring tangible comfort to people in an otherwise unfurnished home. For one client who was undergoing chemotherapy, which caused "extreme back pain ... that prevented her from lying down," having proper furniture meant having the basic comforts needed "to rest and recuperate with dignity."

Less obvious is the way a donated item, however insignificant in and of itself, can influence individuals to seek opportunities for themselves:

> A key item Erhuvwu requested was an ironing board, so she could present herself in a professional manner as she worked towards career goals in customer service. The efforts paid off and Erhuvwu soon found herself upgrading her education at an adult learning centre.

Beyond the daily benefits from the functional aspect of furniture and household items, it is the perceived community support that can restore a client's hope for the future, and the generosity of that support which inspired some to return to Furniture Bank as volunteers themselves. Through volunteering, they helped to extend the organization's reach to many others who were not unlike themselves, and at the same time they developed skills in customer, financial, and administrative services that support Furniture Bank's client services and the business office.

Further document analysis was conducted with client comments gathered by Furniture Bank. Clients provided feedback to Furniture Bank about their visit at the end of their appointment. The large majority of clients were very satisfied with their experience. Overall, the comments support the primary theme that emerged through the client stories: with the security of a furnished home, a new beginning is possible.

Community Agency Partners

To understand Furniture Bank's impact through its community agency partners, fifteen executive directors and thirty-six caseworkers were surveyed about their interactions with Furniture Bank on behalf of their agencies, as well as their perceptions of their clients' experience with Furniture Bank. According to the accounts of the executive directors, their agencies' relationships with Furniture Bank developed out of necessity: 63 per cent indicated that to their knowledge, Furniture Bank is the only organization that facilitates access to free furniture. "There is no other service like the Toronto Furniture Bank and without it our client group and others would be without a *home*," one executive director commented. When asked about how their particular agency's partnership with Furniture Bank contributed to their overall ability to deliver services to clients, 87 per cent of executive directors rated the partnership extremely valuable or very valuable, with the remaining 13 per cent rating it valuable.

The clients' positive experience was consistent with survey findings from caseworkers at Furniture Bank's referring agency partners: 91 per cent of respondents indicated that they believed their clients were satisfied to very satisfied with the furniture they receive, and 83 per cent believed their clients were "satisfied" to "very satisfied" with the household items as well.

Not all of the items that clients were looking for were available in the showroom during their visits. Caseworkers noted:

> The quality (of furniture) varies greatly depending on what has been donated – which I think is unavoidable. Some people receive matching couch sets and are overjoyed and other folks are not as lucky and feel sad about the mismatched furniture that is available to them.
>
> A client attended with need for beds and when they went for their appointment, none were available.

Overall feedback, however, was very positive, as one caseworker indicated: "Many clients have come back after a few years to tell us that they will always be grateful for everything they received from [Furniture Bank]." Another concurred, "Furniture Bank has been an excellent resource to our agency and the clients we serve."

Furniture Bank Staff

The focus groups and surveys with staff (employees and volunteers) emphasized the impact that Furniture Bank was having in the greater community. As one respondent described, the impact on clients reverberates far beyond the satisfaction of their material needs: "it gives them a little bit of grounding for stability."

Instances were noted where the impact of the clients' experience at Furniture Bank inspired them to return and give back to the organization that supported them in the past: "We see those same core individuals come back and volunteer for us. So I think that's a huge impact that we create to those folks."

Several staff noted that they knew different volunteers at Furniture Bank, who because of their volunteering were able to get references that led to getting jobs. For newcomers, volunteering at Furniture Bank can be an important part of their settlement process. According to one employee:

> It gives them an experience to mix and mingle with others, share their stories, where they're from, to improve their English speaking, and their interpersonal skills in general ... They can say somebody gave them a chance here to get started, and to learn a little bit about the city of Toronto while they're making a positive impact, helping people they don't know.

A persistent theme with the focus group respondents was the personal reward they found in working with clients, volunteers, and donors:

> I'm personally humbled and touched by some of the comments that are made from donors when they come in to drop things off: "We just moved to a small place. And you know you guys do great work. Keep on doing the good work." And they walk out. They don't even want a tax receipt. And that to me is where our strength lies, in building that type of goodwill, where they're so happy to bring stuff because they know it's going to the clients.

Collaboration with other community partner agencies was noted as a dimension of community building. As one respondent concurred, "I would say the agencies ... maybe they couldn't do what they do as well without this separate organization that helps their clients in ways that they don't." To staff, the impact of these collaborations improved efficiency in service delivery overall, as the partners can concentrate on their own programs (be it counselling or skills training, et cetera), while Furniture Bank takes care of the furnishing of their clients' homes.

Participants of the Leg Up (Furniture Link) program were also impacted. Training and employment at Furniture Link has resulted in both financial and social benefits for participants such as income, increased human capital, improved health through supplementary health coverage, and community integration. By supporting people's transition from the streets into homes, it was noted that Furniture Bank also impacts government spending by potentially reducing other service needs of the clients (e.g., ambulance, hospital, and police services).

The environmental impact of Furniture Bank was also emphasized. The organization diverts reusable furniture from the landfill by promoting and facilitating the opportunity for people to be environmentally responsible, while also giving donors the opportunity to improve some-one else's well-being: "I see that as a really big win, and not just from what we divert from landfill but by making the greater population be responsible ... And that's one of the big impacts that I see."

Both employees and volunteers felt that raising awareness was an important pursuit:

> Last year we did a couple of programs, morning televisions and CBC pro-grams. The following 3 weeks we had a flurry of increased donations. So when we do get the word out to the community, we've seen an immediate response. And my feeling is that we don't do enough of that.

For employees, other opportunities lay in improving Furniture Bank's ability to serve those in need by either increasing service volume (e.g., increasing hours of operation, formalizing the employment/train-ing program within Furniture Link for higher intake, and improving logistics for increased efficiency) or adding new programs and services (e.g., expanding client eligibility criteria and expanding the employ-ment and skills-training program to other target participants such as unemployed youth and newcomers).

While management staff highlighted the opportunities that corporate partnerships could bring – from high-volume furniture donations from hotels and other businesses to the opportunity to bridge into full-time employment for participants of the Furniture Link training program – front-line staff supported greater community outreach and personalized the individual donor experience by creating "connections between do-nors and clients in any way [they could], with letters and feedback."

Client services volunteers noted there could be better communica-tion between the organization and clients (or their referring agency) about the process at Furniture Bank, so that clients are more prepared when certain high-demand items (e.g., beds) are sometimes not avail-able. Others mentioned ideas that could improve the efficiency of the process for clients to pick out and receive furniture and household items. Board members emphasized establishing furniture banks across Canada, facilitating peer-to-peer giving, and expanding Furniture Link both to increase skills-development opportunities and to secure a more robust funding base.

Municipal policies regarding the disposal of unwanted items were a prominent discussion point. Some staff viewed the City of Toronto's policy of free curbside garbage pickup as a hindrance on donors' social and environmental responsibilities to donate their old furniture (even at a cost). Other staff felt conflicted over the pickup fee for donors, although the income also contributed income for staff wages.

When asked to imagine the impact if Furniture Bank did not exist, the answers emphasized the loss of vital community service:

> That kid who doesn't have a table to eat at, is eating on the floor, doesn't have a table to do his homework, he's not sleeping well at night. It's going to impact his learning, and it's going to impact him in school.

Donors

Furniture and cash donors to Furniture Bank were asked about the impact of Furniture Bank through an online survey (n = 162). The majority (64 per cent) of respondents had supported Furniture Bank for less than one year, with 91 per cent having been a supporter for less than five years. In the past year, 23 per cent of respondents had made a cash donation, 80 per cent had made an in-kind donation of furnishings and household items, and of those, 15 per cent had made both. Of those who made an in-kind donation, 77 per cent indicated they used Furniture Link's commercial pickup service. Overall, donors were extremely impressed with Furniture Bank: 97 per cent had told family, close friends, acquaintances, community organizations, businesses, or other organizations about it. Almost 99 per cent rated Furniture Bank's services as very valuable or extremely valuable.

Donors were asked what they would have done had they not donated their furniture or household items to Furniture Bank, and 62 percent indicated they may have donated it to another charity, 31 per cent would have discarded as trash, 38 would have given items to family or friends, 26 per cent would have sold items privately (e.g., garage sale), and 14 per cent said they did not know. Options for removing large-scale furniture seem to be limited, as many charities are not equipped to receive or pick up items such as couches or dressers. As one donor remarked, "There really doesn't seem to be any other way to donate furniture, so we would have been at a loss. Household goods would have been donated to friends or to Goodwill."

As with corporate volunteers, donors believe the biggest opportunity for Furniture Bank to increase its impact in the community was to expand existing services (59 per cent). Half (50 percent) of donor responses called for increasing awareness. As one donor explained, "I believe

Furniture Bank is the 'best kept secret.' If more people knew about it, the domino effect for overall impact and positive societal impact would be huge." A number of donors recommended increased publicity: "Better advertising ... a lot of people I've introduced to this organization had no awareness of its existence," and "I didn't know FB existed and the majority of the people I talk to don't either." Another offered, "Make them a household name like the food bank."

Donors suggested skills training as a new service: "Creating a cabinet-making, upholstery school providing education, re-training and future employment for qualified individuals." Another proposed "broadening the geographic scope of the clients it serves" (expanding the existing program), seeking out corporate partnerships (expanding networks), and reducing or eliminating the pickup fees for donated furniture.

If Furniture Bank ceased to exist, 54 per cent of all donor respondents indicated that they believed that people would no longer have access to free or low-cost furniture and household items. Many donors commented that there would certainly be a harmful environmental impact, with "opportunities for disposal of unneeded household items would be reduced significantly."

Corporate Volunteers

The corporate volunteer program plays an important role not only for the client experience at Furniture Bank, but also in creating civic awareness and cultivating future volunteers and donors. Corporate volunteers were asked to document their experiences prior, during, and after their time at Furniture Bank. It was very evident that their time at Furniture Bank had a great impact.

Prior to the experience, volunteers were curious about what to expect in terms of the clients they would be assisting and the environment of the warehouse itself. However, they were excited for the volunteer opportunity and eager to get started. As one volunteer explained, "I was excited about the opportunity of helping people with such a personal and important decision." Another noted, "[I'm] a little nervous not knowing what to expect."

Once the volunteering began, participants' feelings of uncertainty gave way to a sense of "happiness" and feeling "gratified." As one participant wrote, "It is a very interesting experience. You realize the need of those less fortunate. I felt very happy while helping." Another volunteer stated: "[It was] a learning experience and extremely rewarding at seeing the joy reflected in the eyes of the receiver, and even more rewarding to hear how thankful they were for what they were receiving."

Volunteers were also privy to instances where clients were unable to entirely meet their needs at Furniture Bank:

> [I] helped 1 family of 4 and 1 single. The family came early and got to choose a lot of big useful items, and [the single person] came later so selection was not as good, but she was very happy with everything; sad that there were no mattresses.

Witnessing first-hand the gap between the limited availability of goods and the needs of the clients (which sometimes go unmet), seemed to inspire and motivate the volunteers to consider ways of doing more, as described further below.

AFTER VOLUNTEERING

The volunteer experience was unequivocally positive and allowed for participants to discern first-hand the ways in which their efforts made a difference to the lives of Furniture Bank clients. As one participant explained, "I realize that we can all do our part to volunteer. People from all walks of life, background, all need help." From another volunteer, "I feel glad and great that I was able to do this. It opens up awareness, how the smallest thing can go a long way." The overwhelming consensus among participants is that more could be done, not just as a volunteer but also a donor. Several participants indicated their intentions to return as volunteers to Furniture Bank. As one remarked: "Looking forward to (the) next visit in February."

Other typical experiences in the volunteer interviews included:

> I just realized that I have been very lucky since I moved to Canada. I have everything I need and I shouldn't keep what I don't use at home as there are a lot of people in need.
>
> The experience has helped in making [me] a better person by reminding me of how I should appreciate the simple things and be grateful for the luxuries I have.

Participants described being "enriched" by and "grateful" for the volunteer experience, feelings that can be considered personal returns. They were able to realize how their volunteer efforts tangibly contributed to an improvement in the lives of Furniture Bank clients: "Seeing how easily we can help make a difference for these folks ... This is something I can see myself doing into future," explained one participant.

The expressed desire to contribute more is not only for themselves but included the hope that others might do so as well:

> I've seen friends throwing away things that are in really good condition. I feel that I can't let them do that anymore. I'll see what I can bring and how I can help more.
>
> [I] will try to raise more awareness about [the organization's] needs, especially for mattresses.

Although participants' self-perceived impact is evident even after one day of volunteering, further research is needed to explore more long-term impacts, including changes in patterns of volunteering, donation, and other involvement with Furniture Bank or other social purpose enterprises.

Discussion

In this chapter, we sought to answer three questions:

R1. What is the impact of Furniture Bank?
R2. What are the opportunities for Furniture Bank to increase its impact?
R3. How would the community be different if Furniture Bank did not exist?

To address these questions, we adopted a stakeholder approach and used a variety of methods to gather data. Some data confirmed similarities across stakeholder groups; other data highlighted the unique perspective of a particular group.

Impact of Furniture Bank

As was presented in the findings section, each stakeholder group had its own perspective of Furniture Bank's impact, based on their interactions with the organization. These impacts are now considered along a continuum that ranges from those that relate to individuals (clients/customers) to those that affect society at large.

1. "HOMES" FOR FURNITURE RECIPIENTS

The underlying narrative of the client profiles (which was echoed within the survey and focus group findings) suggests that stabilizing people's housing needs allows for their advancement into other positive life directions, be it towards an education, a career, or family unification. The "furnished home" marks the beginning of a new phase in life after difficult periods, with children being able to refocus on school, newcomers finally settling into a secure home, and families regaining stability. For clients, the impact of having a properly furnished home may lead to improved self-esteem and self-confidence, as well as restored hope for the future.

2. NEWCOMER SETTLEMENT

For clients who are newcomers to Canada, acquiring furnishings for their new home is an essential step in their settlement process. For the volunteers at Furniture Bank (former clients or otherwise) who are newcomers as well, volunteering provides them the opportunity to integrate and find support while supporting others in the community.

3. EMPLOYMENT AND TRAINING

Aside from those Furniture Bank employs full-time, Furniture Link employs and trains individuals who have faced barriers to employment, including some who are part of the Ontario Disability Support Program.

4. COMMUNITY ENGAGEMENT

Furniture Bank fosters community participation in many ways: for the volunteers who contribute their time and energy and for donors who contribute furniture and household items. Community engagement is often multifaceted and may involve multiple motivations. Volunteers donate in-kind services and donors contribute in-kind goods, but both may have contributed for their own reasons. Volunteers gain experience and references that often lead to paid employment; in-kind donors dispose of unwanted furniture and receive a tax receipt in return. Furthermore, both volunteers and donors benefit emotionally from knowing their actions are helping others in need. As such, these stakeholders can be considered holding simultaneous roles as both donors and beneficiaries.

5. COMMUNITY SUPPORT NETWORK

Both executive directors and caseworkers at partnering community agencies noted the impact that Furniture Bank has on their organizations' ability to carry out their missions. Furniture Bank staff was also cognizant of the importance of good relationships with community agency partners, recognizing that Furniture Bank was part of a comprehensive service approach and that it was important that the organization did its best as part of that process.

6. COMMUNITY WELL-BEING

A number of stakeholder groups broadly noted that Furniture Bank's cumulative effect on individual and organizational level generates an impact at the community level. The redistribution of gently used furniture lessens economic disparities; workers with skills-training and employment experience make a more employable workforce; goodwill and greater social cohesion are fostered when people pitch in for the benefit of the community. For stakeholders, the increased social and environmental awareness through their involvement with Furniture Bank can lead to changes in behaviour that bring about a larger community impact (e.g., volunteers who are motivated to become donors and to raise awareness among friends and family).

7. REDUCED GOVERNMENT SPENDING

The spin-off effect from supporting people's transitions into stable homes is reduced public spending on services such as health and social services that would otherwise be needed to support people who are precariously housed.

8. ENVIRONMENT

The environmental impact is well recognized within the organization and among certain stakeholders in the community. It is a convincing motivation for donors, a point of pride for staff and volunteers, but less recognized (comparatively) among executive directors and caseworkers of community agency partners.

Opportunities to Increase Impact

When asked for input regarding the greatest opportunity for increasing the impact of Furniture Bank in the community, over three-quarters of the respondents answered (197 out of 253), providing 225 different comments. While overall the most frequently cited opportunity to increase impact was to expand existing services, other very innovative ideas were presented. The breadth and depth of comments give credence to the approach of facilitating stakeholder feedback, both for generating new knowledge and for determining the legitimacy of the organization.

One tension that had its base in the business model of the organization concerned the fees charged for pickup and delivery. This tension revolves around the financial and social "bottom lines" of the organization. In Furniture Bank's case, the trade-off is between charging for pickup and delivery services for the financial sustainability of the organization, and offering free pickups, which would increase furniture donations but drastically reduce the revenue flow to the organization. Caseworkers and volunteers mentioned the burden of delivery fees for some clients. Donors, on the other hand, felt that fees led to a decrease in potential donations. In this regard, it seemed they were viewing Furniture Link as a mainstream business, not as a social purpose enterprise, and certainly not understanding the business model of the organization. In the discussions with staff, the issue of fees was considered more as a necessary constraint rather than an opportunity for increasing impact by reducing or eliminating fees, as they understood the financial implications of that option (i.e., a social purpose enterprise cannot achieve or increase social impact if it does not have the financial means to continue operations). Beyond eliminating fees, no other suggestions were made to resolve this tension. However, an opportunity may exist to more clearly communicate the rationale behind Furniture Link and the fee structure, and how it ties into the sustainability of the organization.

One tension that was a function of external factors was the shortage of certain items, especially mattresses. This led to disappointment on the side of furniture recipients and their caseworkers, and also was mentioned as an issue for staff to focus on in order to increase impact.

For both of these types of issues, an opportunity exists for stakeholder-sourcing solutions. For instance, corporate volunteers, by the end of their placement at Furniture Bank, have a great desire to do more. Before the group leaves, they could be asked for their ideas on increasing impact, and more specifically, on issues that are of current concern.

The Community without Furniture Bank

It was clear from the responses that Furniture Bank plays an important and unique role in the community. This was well expressed by the community agency partners, who recognized that without Furniture Bank, the integration of their clients into their own households would be significantly compromised. Donors would also be affected but in a different way. They would lose an opportunity to donate furniture in a socially responsible way. Environmentally, there would also be an impact, as a portion of the furniture donated to Furniture Bank would end up in a landfill.

Implications for Practice

From an operational standpoint, engaging diverse stakeholders can foster accountability, legitimacy, and the generation of new ideas. After reviewing the initial results of this study, key personnel of Furniture Bank reflected on the implications for the organization. These four comments are a sample of the thinking within the organization:

> As an organization, we often focus on one side or the other: clients or donors. We more rarely look at staff, board, volunteers, caseworkers and agency executive directors. That is where some of the most interesting points have come up in doing such a stakeholder review. We know that we are an ecosystem, where the various stakeholders are intricately connected, but what we didn't realize until the study were the clear distinctions of perspective between and within each group.
>
> As an organization, this evaluation is forcing us to both ask some strategic questions and look at some quite specific areas where we have an opportunity to build bridges between different groups. It has also made us question our staffing model to ensure that there are wider doors opened between the various groups that make up our ecosystem.
>
> Donors are much more on the "business" side than we realized. We need to do a better job of linking people to our cause and our theory of change as an organization. Our volunteers have so much insight as some were donors at one point (or will be in the future) and some were clients not too long ago.
>
> Knowing that exposing a donor to more of our space means that they are both more likely to donate; to give financially as well as in-kind (and provide referrals as well) has made a huge impact in how we are now

organizing our drop-off donor experience, as well as our call centre scripts, encouraging more of an "opening" into who we are at the organization. On social media, we recently started to reveal more images and stories about who our staff are, as well as the environment of the space itself, which is rooted in the understanding that we have to constantly be connecting and keep the doors open between donors and staff and volunteers.

Stakeholder Theory Revisited: Implications for Further Research

By taking a stakeholder approach, this research highlighted three new dimensions that could be considered in a stakeholder theory for social enterprises/social purpose businesses: first, the prevalence of multiple, sometimes conflicting, roles held by the same stakeholder; second, the shift from the organization as the central focus of a stakeholder analysis to that of the organization as coordinator of stakeholder groups and as a component of an ecosystem addressing a particular issue; and third, expanding the intent of stakeholder analysis to "manage" stakeholders to include the potential of knowledge generation for problem solving.

Stakeholder research has emphasized relationships between an organization and its stakeholder groups, implying that stakeholder groups are distinct (Van Puyvelde, Caers, Du Bois & Jegers, 2012). Our study, instead, has shown that individuals can belong to more than one stakeholder group concurrently. For instance, those who have furniture picked up by the social purpose enterprise arm of the organization are both customers and donors. We argue that, at least in the analysis of non-profits and social enterprises, it is important to consider the possibility of dual or multiple stakeholder affiliations. This represents a different approach to the traditional categorization of stakeholder groups.

Moving the focus of a stakeholder analysis, from having the organization at its centre to the issue being addressed, would be an interesting exercise. What would a stakeholder map look like if the settlement of women and children from shelters, for example, were at the centre? This suggests to us that viewing a stakeholder in relation to the organization might be limiting in the case of social organizations. Rather, stakeholders could be viewed in relation to the aims or mission of the organization and the overall impact in the community.

Participating in this research provided a creative outlet for respondents. They managed to generate novel ideas that have great potential to increase the impact of the organization. This is a relevant contribution to the well-being of the community and suggests that stakeholder contributions go beyond contributing time, money, and in-kind items. Indeed, stakeholders' willingness to be part of the solutions to problems and their commitment to sharing ideas constitute important contributions that are seldom included in a stakeholder analysis. From a social accounting perspective, this intellectual capital is an important factor that should not be overlooked (Mook, 2013; Mook et al., 2007).

This brings to light another area for further research: what motivates people to contribute ideas in this way, especially in the context of a nonprofit organization where the benefits are not directed to "owners" but to the community at large? This line of research could build on studies that examine the motivations of people who participate in open-source projects, looking at internal factors such as intrinsic motivation and altruism and incentives related to personal benefits (von Krogh, Haefliger, Spaeth & Wallin, 2012).

Finally, another area for further research is the relationship between the social and financial bottom lines. Examining the increased complexity of multiple roles within stakeholder groups, and how this complexity impacts the different bottom lines, could help social enterprises understand what strategies need to be taken in trying to balance these two often-conflicting goals.

NOTES

1 The idea of soliciting stakeholder feedback in this way is similar to an approach to generating knowledge known as science-based stakeholder dialogues (Welp et al., 2006). This type of stakeholder dialogue is not aimed at managing relationships or mitigating conflicts; it is held in order to gather local knowledge and link different domains of discourse. Dissent and innovation are valued as they suggest areas for further inquiry.

REFERENCES

Brabham, D.C. (2008). Crowdsourcing as a model for problem solving: An introduction and cases. *Convergence: The International Journal of Research into New Media Technologies*, 14(1), 75–90.

Clarkson, M.E. (1995). A stakeholder framework for analyzing and evaluating corporate performance. *Academy of Management Review*, 20(1), 92–117.

Fan, W., & Yan, Z. (2010). Factors affecting response rates of the web survey: A systematic review. *Computers in Human Behavior*, 26(2), 132–139. http://dx.doi.org/10.1016/j.chb.2009.10.015

Freeman, R.E. (1984). *Strategic management: A stakeholder approach*. Boston, MA: Pitman Publishing Inc.

Furniture Bank. (n.d.). About us. Retrieved from http://www.furniturebank .org/www/about-us

Furniture Bank Association of North America (FBANA). (2014a). List of Furniture Banks. Retrieved from http://www.furniturebanks.org/list-of-furniture-banks/

Furniture Bank Association of North America. (FBANA) (2014b). FAQs – Frequently Asked Questions. Retrieved from http://www.furniturebanks .org/faqs/

Howe, J. (2006). The rise of crowdsourcing. *Wired 14*(6). Retrieved from http://www.wired.com/wired/archive/14.06/crowds.html

Kamberelis, G., & Dimitriadis, G.J. (2011). Focus groups: Contingent articulations of pedagogy, politics, and inquiry. In N. K. Denzin, & Y. S. Lincoln (Eds.), *The SAGE handbook of qualitative research* (4 ed., pp. 545–562). London, United Kingdom: SAGE.

Lim, S.L., Quercia, D., & Finkelstein, A. (2010). StakeNet: Using social networks to analyse the stakeholders of large-scale software projects. *Proceedings of the 32 International Conference on Software Engineering*, May 2–8, Cape Town, South Africa, 295–304. http://dx.doi.org/10.1145/1806799.1806844

Mook, L. (Ed.). (2013). *Accounting for social value*. Toronto, ON: University of Toronto Press.

Mook, L., Quarter, J., & Richmond, B.J. (2007). *What counts: Social accounting for nonprofits and co-operatives* (2nd ed.). London, United Kingdom: Sigel Press.

LeRoux, K. (2009). Managing stakeholder demands: Balancing responsiveness to clients and funding agents in nonprofit social service organizations. *Administration & Society*, 41(2), 158–184. http://dx.doi.org/10.1177/0095399709332298

Palys, T. (2008). Purposive sampling. In L.M. Given (Ed.), *The sage encyclopedia of qualitative research methods* (Vol. 2, pp. 697–698). Thousand Oaks, CA: Sage. http://dx.doi.org/10.4135/9781412963909.n349

Riva, G., & Kislenko, S. (2012). History of furniture bank. Internal documents.

Roberts, R.W., & Mahoney, L. (2004). Stakeholder conceptions of the corporation: Their meaning and influence in accounting research. *Business Ethics Quarterly*, 14(3), 399–431. http://dx.doi.org/10.5840/beq200414326

Savage, G.T., Nix, T.W., Whitehead, C.J., & Blair, J.D. (1991). Strategies for assessing and managing organizational stakeholders. *Executive*, 5(2), 61–75.

http://dx.doi.org/10.5465/AME.1991.4274682

Surowiecki, J. (2004). *The wisdom of crowds: Why the many are smarter than the few and how collective wisdom shapes business, economies, societies, and nations.* New York, NY: Doubleday.

Van Puyvelde, S., Caers, R., Du Bois, C., & Jegers, M. (2012). The governance of nonprofit organizations: Integrating agency theory with stakeholder and stewardship theories. *Nonprofit and Voluntary Sector Quarterly, 41*(3), 431–451. http://dx.doi.org/10.1177/0899764011409757

von Krogh, G., Haefliger, S., Spaeth, S., & Wallin, M.W. (2012). Carrots and rainbows: Motivation and social practice in open source software development. *Management Information Systems Quarterly, 36*(2), 649–676.

Welp, M., de la Vega-Leinert, A., Stoll-Kleemann, S., & Jaeger, C.C. (2006). Science-based stakeholder dialogues: Theories and tools. *Global Environmental Change, 16*(2), 170–181. http://dx.doi.org/10.1016/j.gloenvcha.2005.12.002

12 The Complex Relation between a Social Enterprise and Its Parent Non-profit: The Case of Northwood Translation Bureau

JENNIFER HANN AND DANIEL SCHUGURENSKY

Introduction

The Northwood Translation Bureau (NTB) is a social purpose enterprise that has operated in Toronto since 2006 under the umbrella of Northwood Neighbourhood Services (NNS), a non-profit settlement agency founded in 1982. This chapter presents our research on the economic and social impacts of the Northwood Translation Bureau, and it is based on in-depth interviews with twenty-one translators.[1] The chapter is organized in three sections. The first presents the institutional setting, the historical context in which the study was undertaken, and the profile of the research participants. The second discusses the impact of NTB and some concerns raised by participants. The last section provides a summary and outlines some preliminary conclusions.

Setting and Participants

Northwood Neighbourhood Services

Since its creation three decades ago, Northwood Neighbourhood Services (NNS) has been providing settlement and support services to communities in northwest Toronto. NNS is part of Toronto Neighbourhood Centres, a network of about thirty Toronto non-profit multiservice organizations that are dedicated "to enabl[ing] diverse communities to work together to promote justice and a healthy life for all" in local neighbourhoods. This network of neighbourhood centres pays particular attention to the well-being of the most vulnerable communities, particularly immigrant communities. The neighbourhood centres are conceived as inclusive spaces for mutual support that act as hubs for social participation. NNS is located on the border of Weston–Mt. Dennis. This is one of Toronto's thirteen districts identified as "Priority Neighbourhoods" in a United Way study on poverty that considered variables such as income, educational attainment, English proficiency, and access to key services.[2] In 2005, 24.5 per cent of area residents were identified as low income after tax, six points above the 19.4 per cent average of Toronto residents.

The mission of NNS is to build a healthier community by empowering "individuals, families and groups to achieve and maintain a state of physical, mental and social well-being." To fulfill this mission, NNS provides many programs and services organized in eleven departments: settlement services, sponsorship agreement holder (family reunification campaign), child/parent programs, seniors' recreational programs, English conversation circles, dress for success, income tax training and clinic, violence against women programs, youth recreational programs, a "green" program, and social enterprise.

Settlement services are an integral part of NNS, providing assistance to more than 7,000 people every year. The emphasis on settlement services is not coincidental. Canada receives 250,000 immigrants every year from over two hundred countries, and has the highest per-capita immigration rate in the world (Citizenship and Immigration Canada, 2011). The province of Ontario receives approximately 55 per cent of those immigrants. In the last few decades, this influx of immigrants has changed the face of Canada. Today, approximately 20 per cent of all Canadian residents are foreign born. In Toronto, the largest Canadian city, approximately 50 per cent of the population was born abroad, making it one of the most diverse metropolitan areas in the world. New immigrants to Canada are more likely to have a university degree than Canadian-born people. For instance, in 2006, the proportion of the Canadian-born adult population with university degrees was 19 per cent, but among recent immigrants it was 51 per cent. According to the tenets of human capital theory, immigrants' educational advantage should translate into an occupational and income advantage. However, recent immigrants earn much less than their Canadian-born counterparts and often experience great difficulties breaking into the Canadian labour market (Frenette & Morissette, 2005; Reitz, 2007; Statistics Canada, 2008; Slade, 2012).

Indeed, over the past twenty-five years, the economic and social integration of new immigrants to Canada has markedly worsened.

Interestingly, at the same time that the Canadian immigration selection process emphasizes the recruitment of high-calibre newcomers through a point system, the earning levels of those immigrants have dropped significantly relative to Canadian-born workers. In 2000, for instance, 27.5 per cent of recent immigrants with university degrees were below the low-income cut-off – seven times that of their Canadian-born counterparts (Picot & Sweetman, 2005). Recent research findings show that in the last decades, the earnings gap between Canadian-born workers and immigrant workers has widened, and that the amount of time needed for the earnings of those two groups to converge has lengthened (Beach, Worswick, & Green 2011). As Frenette and Morissette (2005) observed, the greater relative earnings growth experienced by recent immigrant cohorts has only partially offset the drastic deterioration in their relative earnings at entry.

These patterns of economic inequalities are often aggravated by dynamics of racial discrimination. For instance, in a study about barriers to the labour market experienced by Ghanaian and Somali youth in Toronto, Gariba (2010) found widespread perceptions of employment discrimination among participants. Likewise, a study on highly educated immigrants from sub-Saharan Africa found that three-quarters of research participants had experienced downward occupational mobility, with the majority employed in low-skilled, low-wage, insecure forms of survival employment (Creese & Wiebe, 2012). Another study found considerable employer discrimination against applicants with ethnic names or work experience from other countries (Oreopoulos, 2009). In short, even as Canada attracts a high proportion of well-trained immigrant professionals, structural barriers in the labour market deny those immigrants access to jobs commensurate with their training and expertise (Danso, 2007).

It is in this context that the settlement services offered by NNS try to help refugees and new immigrants to integrate as quickly and easily as possible into all areas of Canadian society, and to realize their potential by achieving their personal dreams and aspirations. The NNS settlement services range from individual and group counselling to assistance with employment, immigration, housing and school issues, and translation. They also include information sessions held in several community locations on topics such as health, nutrition, finances, employment, education, civic participation, and equity. To ensure that these services are aligned with local realities, NNS employees and volunteers are familiar with the culture and language of immigrant communities in the area.

Northwood Translation Bureau

Of the eleven departments of the Northwood Neighbourhood Services, "Social Enterprise" is particularly relevant to the subject matter of this book. It all started in 2006, when Jamila Aman, NNS executive director, attended a Maytree Foundation's training session at York University. One of the five modules of the program – social enterprise – resonated as a viable project for NNS. Shortly thereafter, the NNS management team met and generated sixty social enterprise ideas. These ideas were subsequently filtered to determine their alignment with NNS' mission, start-up costs, risk factors and organizational readiness. The top three ideas – a summer camp for children, a refugee sponsorship program, and a translation service – soon became a reality, and are still operating as viable social enterprise ventures. Our NNS partners repeatedly recognized the contribution of the Maytree Foundation for funding the executive directors' training, and noted that without it, these social enterprises would not exist today.

The Northwood Translation Bureau, or NTB, was established in 2006. There were two main reasons for its creation. The first was a growing need for translation, notarization, and interpretation, both within NNS and at several of Northwood's partner organizations. The second was the need to create jobs for foreign-trained professionals while they wait for credential evaluation and certification and until they find jobs in their respective fields.

NTB translators are immigrant professionals who collectively provide services in more than ninety languages. These languages include Albanian, Amharic, Arabic, Armenian, Bosnian, Bulgarian, Cantonese, Chinese, Croatian, Czech, Farsi, Filipino, French, German, Greek, Gujarati, Hindi, Hungarian, Italian, Japanese, Korean, Latvian, Lithuanian, Macedonian, Mandarin, Marathi, Persian, Polish, Portuguese, Punjabi, Romanian, Russian, Serbian, Somali, Spanish, Swahili, Tigre, Tagalog, and Tigrinya.

The services offered by NTB include the translation of immigration and financial papers; legal contracts and documents; manuals and technical documentation; medical, biomedical, and pharmaceutical papers; and personal documents such as birth and marriage certificates, as well as wills, divorce papers, and educational documents. Interpreters are available to escort clients to interviews, assessments, and other meetings, and to help them with interpretation at the courts. NTB translators are capable of doing both consecutive and simultaneous translations.

NTB has over one hundred people active on its current roster of translators and interpreters. The roster fluctuates every year, as some translators relocate to other areas or manage to secure full-time employment and new translators join the bureau.

On average, 60 per cent of the revenues generated through NTB are used to compensate the translators. The remaining 40 per cent is channeled to unfunded NNS programs and services. One such program is the English conversation circle, which is intended for newcomers who do not fit into the LINC or ESL structure[3] but who would like to practise their English listening and speaking skills. Another is the sponsorship program, which assists more than forty refugees to sponsor their family members each year. The revenues from the translation bureau help to cover the salary of a sponsorship worker. In addition, NNS uses funds generated by the translation bureau to pay for refreshments for community meetings and subway tokens for low-income clients who otherwise would not be able to attend meetings or participate in various programs and services. The fees charged by the translation bureau are slightly below the prices charged by most other translation companies. On top of that, the Bureau offers translation services at a reduced rate for newcomers, for persons covered by Ontario Works,[4] and for NNS clients. Moreover, in the case of NNS clients, it is common for counsellors, volunteers, and translators to offer free translations as needed.

The use of social purpose enterprises to generate revenues for non-profit organizations is arguably a recent phenomenon, at least in the case of settlement agencies based in Toronto. Indeed, a study on the funding sources of settlement services in the Toronto area that included 166 agencies (among them NNS) identified two main sources of funding: government and foundations. The first included federal, provincial, and municipal initiatives and programs, and the second included agencies such as the United Way, Trillium, and Maytree (Lim et al., 2005). Interestingly, this study did not identify social purpose enterprises such as NTB as being sources of revenue for settlement agencies.[5] Therefore, the social purpose enterprise constitutes a new and creative response of settlement agencies to unprecedented funding pressures.

The Context and the Participants

To undertake the study on NTB, we started a partnership with NNS in 2010. At the end of that year, a few days before Christmas, the federal

government announced $53 million in budget cuts to immigrant ser-
vice agencies, with more than $43 million absorbed by settlement agen-
cies in Ontario. In the Toronto area alone, the cuts affected more than
ten agencies that provided settlement support services to newcomers,
including NNS, which was forced to cut its previous translation bureau
manager (Keung, 2010). The sudden loss of a manager in charge of supervising the operation resulted in NTB revenues dropping from about
$40,000 in 2010 to less than $20,000 in 2011. Our interviews were done
in 2011, in the aftermath of this funding cut.

We interviewed twenty-one translators on NTB's roster about their
experiences of immigrating and adjusting to life in Canada, as well as
being translators at Northwood. The translators were contacted and recruited by Azaria Wolday, the current manager of NTB, and our partner
in this study. All interviews were held on site at NNS. To protect the
anonymity of the translators and the confidentiality of the information
provided by participants, Northwood staff did not play any further role
in the data collection and analysis. Only the researchers have had access to the interview recordings and transcripts, and identifying details
have been altered or removed to further protect the anonymity of the
translators we interviewed. The twenty-one NTB translators whom we
interviewed came to Canada from sixteen different countries.[6] As a
collective, they were able to translate and interpret in twenty-three
languages: Albanian, Amharic, Arabic, Assyrian, Cantonese, Croatian,
Farsi, French, German, Hindu, Italian, Mandarin, Polish, Portuguese,
Punjabi, Russian, Somali, Spanish, Swahili, Tigrinya, Ukrainian, Urdu,
and Vietnamese. Thirteen of the twenty-one translators who participated in the study were women and eight were men. The participants
ranged in age from twenty-seven to fifty-four years old, and the average age was thirty-eight.

When we embarked on this study, we expected that most NTB translators were going to be recent immigrants who were having difficulties
in getting their professional credentials recognized in Canada. During
our interviews, we discovered that only three of the twenty-one translators had resided in Canada for less than five years. Nine translators
had lived in Canada for five to ten years, and the other nine had lived
in Canada for more than ten years. (Five of them had immigrated with
their families as children.) Eighteen of the twenty-one translators held
Canadian citizenship, and the other three were permanent residents.
In retrospect, it is not surprising that NTB translators we interviewed
were not newcomers. As discussed in the first section, the length of

time it takes for immigrants to catch up to the earnings of Canadian-born workers has increased (Beach, Worswick, & Green, 2011); hence, even longer-term, highly educated immigrants are forced to supplement their income with side jobs.

As a group, the translators were highly educated: all but one (who had a high school degree) had completed some level of postsecondary education. Four had completed college, eleven held bachelor's degrees, and five had obtained master's degrees. They had training and professional experience in various fields, including administration, business, education, engineering, hospitality, human resources, and journalism. Eleven translators had undertaken additional education or retraining in Canada. The few translators currently working in a job related to their original field of study had resided in Canada for most of their lives and had obtained a university degree in Canada. Two-thirds of the translators were working in or had recently held jobs related to settlement, social, and community services; others were connected to the settlement sector through volunteering or through part-time translation work.

The Immigration Experience

Although the majority of the translators had resided in Canada for more than five years, the experience of immigration had made a strong impression on their lives. We asked the translators to describe the most significant changes they had experienced as a result of immigration. The two most significant changes involved the difficulty they had experienced in securing employment due to the demand for "Canadian experience" and the related loss of social status. The search for work absorbed most of their efforts. As one translator noted, "the economic needs put on hold any other educational or social goals." Another observed that "the first thing people think about when they come here is work; they don't care about education, they don't care about another life, it's job, job, job, job!" Some translators also reported challenges related to language and communication.

Although most translators brought significant international work experiences with them to Canada, many discovered that employers were reluctant to hire any applicants who could not demonstrate Canadian experience. Some interviewees recalled that this request was particularly frustrating: "The first thing they ask you is, do you have Canadian experience? And I say, 'I've been here for a month. When would I get

Canadian experience?' I don't like this kind of question." Many translators highlighted the importance of connections and networking in order to gain Canadian experience in the workplace ("it's who you know, not what you know"), but they noted that as new immigrants they did not have access to a network of contacts to assist them in their job searches.

Many translators were unprepared for the difficulties they would experience in getting their credentials recognized. Some felt that they had received misleading information about their employment prospects in Canada: "Because when you apply to come to Canada, you have to have a university diploma. And you come to Canada, and your experience – the experience you have from back home is *back home*." Several described the shock and disappointment they felt when they realized that their credentials, expertise, and skills were not recognized or valued in Canada: "Now I understand how it works and I'm trying to adjust myself with the system but to be frank I have to start again ... and that makes the labour market in Canada very, very, very difficult for me."

The loss of professional identity, social status, and respect was a painful and common experience: "I believe that all the newcomers have the same problem. They are very well educated from where they came from, doesn't matter which country; they are well educated, and they work here delivering pizza." The loss of their professional identity often challenged the translators' self-esteem: "It affects you, like, when I was back home, claiming myself as an educated person and I had respect there, and I was so proud, right? But, here, nobody knows me and I'm just ... an immigrant, right? So there is a big gap."

For many translators, the loss of social status, respect, and recognition for their skills and expertise led to feelings of unhappiness and depression: "Now, I feel minus fifty as an educated person. And I feel bad about that. Because what I studied is gone. It's been several years. I didn't study something else. So sometimes really I do feel depressed and sad." Some commented about the resentment that new immigrants feel towards a system that excludes them. Sometimes this is openly expressed, but most often it is experienced in silence: "You are filled with anger because you know it's not just me. I guess maybe all of them, most of them, they have it but some they say it, some they don't say it. They just keep it inside, but when you talk with people, they feel like this."

Some of the translators who migrated from non-English-speaking countries remembered the difficulties that they experienced communicating in English when they first arrived in Canada. One woman recounted that at that time she did not possess the oral English language skills to book a doctor's appointment, and it was not easy to find assistance: "People did not have time to help me." These types of experiences motivated her to improve her English through taking ESL classes and eventually to become a translator to help new immigrants. Another translator told us that he continued to experience some anxiety regarding his communication skills in English:

> Sometimes I have some certain difficulties when people speak very fast, or use some special words ... I still have some unpleasant experiences, because when people wrinkle their foreheads, it's a little embarrassing in that my pronunciation or my vocabulary or my listening and comprehension skills are not good enough, but I try to improve.

Exploring the Impact of the Northwood Translation Bureau

Our interviews helped us to understand the ways that NTB financially and socially impacted its translators. These impacts are organized into four categories: job prospects, income, self-esteem, and personal and professional development. In addition, we examined NTB's impact on Northwood Neighbourhood Services (NNS) and on the community at large.

Job Prospects

As noted above, one of the barriers faced by new immigrants to secure a paid job in Canada is the lack of Canadian work experience. In a catch-22 situation, immigrants cannot gain Canadian work experience precisely because they do not have Canadian work experience. Since employers normally deem international work experience irrelevant, immigrants are left with only two options to gain Canadian work experience. One is volunteer work, which is unpaid; therefore, only those immigrants with enough savings can afford to pursue this option. The other is to try to find a job (even part-time) with those few employers who hire immigrants without Canadian experience. The Northwood Translation Bureau is one of those few employers. Often, immigrants pursued the two avenues simultaneously, translating part-time with NTB in conjunction with volunteering at NNS or other organizations.

The interviewees reported that working at NTB allowed them to obtain Canadian experience at a recognized organization, and helped them to build social capital in the new country: "It helped me a lot, this organization's name." They also noted that the close connection between NTB and NNS increased their job prospects. Many said that NNS staff provided assistance and encouragement in their job searches by sharing job postings and writing letters of reference: "If there's any opening, [NNS] emails me about that job and if I go there and I apply for the job, I can put [NNS] as a reference." The experience as interpreters and volunteers also improved their employability: "I feel more confident about applying for jobs, plus I did apply to become an interpreter, and I put that I did volunteer here as a reference, so it helped me this way."

One after another, our interviewees commented that their limited networks put them at a disadvantage when trying to find a job, but pointed out that their work at NTB helped to counteract this situation. In particular, they noted that the social aspect of translation work helped them to build new personal and institutional networks: "I got to know a lot of people, and I got to know different organizations and what they do. I met a lot of people, translators, mostly, and it expands your circle of friends and business contacts." For entrepreneurial translators, these contacts and connections could be used to create new business opportunities. In fact, one translator reported this new network was helpful in building a small business, and two others expressed interest in launching businesses that would offer services to newcomers.

While many interviewees were attracted to the idea of becoming professional translators, the time and cost involved in obtaining this credential were viewed as a significant barrier. For this reason, most were working or pursuing employment in social services, settlement services, and community services. For many of the translators, this type of work was a logical extension of their volunteer work and of the informal assistance they provided to others: "I did lots of volunteering things, I helped people register for housing, I did apply for welfare for people. I did all these things ... I said, well, if I'm doing this as volunteer, why can't I do it as a job?" In this context, their relationship with NNS through NTB was always perceived as helpful to them in terms of new job prospects.

For the translators who were pursuing careers in the settlement sector, translating was one entry point into the field: "This is the first time I actually went to a settlement agency. So I have more understanding like what are they doing as their job." Some mentioned that translating for newly arrived immigrants allowed them to practise and improve their counselling skills, and others noted that it allowed them to gain knowledge, skills, and expertise directly related to this type of work: "I think translation, interpretation and providing settlement services to immigrants are things that come parallel together," one translator reflected. The general consensus among the translators is that NTB gave them the opportunity to gain relevant work experience, assisted with making social connections, and thereby helped them to improve their job prospects.

Income

For most interviewees, the income from their translation was a welcome addition to their budget, but it was not substantial enough to pay their bills. Most of the translators described their work with NTB as "something that you do on your own time, at home, it's a good on-the-side job." At the same time, for some translators the on-call nature of the work was appealing in that they were able to accept assignments based on their interest and availability. None of the twenty-one translators felt that they could depend on their translation work at NTB as a sole or steady source of income because requests for translations were highly irregular. As one translator stated:

> It's not regular kind of [work] that I can count on and say okay, you'll get two translation assignments for every week, and if I get two translations each, say three or four pages a week, they are good, right? But now, I may not get assignments for months, right? It's not something you can count on right now as an income.

Although the income they earned from translating was small, it did allow translators to cover certain expenses. Some mentioned using this income to pay bills. Others use it to cover some travel expenses like gas or automobile insurance. Other expenditures mentioned by translators were on books, clothing, mortgage payments, and savings (including savings for their children's education). A few said that they found the income especially helpful when they were unemployed.

Some translators observed that translation income did not always compensate their efforts: "They don't pay based on how difficult is translation. There are levels of translating. Some documents are really, really hard, and you have to work on them." Likewise, another participant felt that the payment did not reflect the emotional effort involved in "catching the soul of that person" through interpretation. Other translators complained that the payments did not consider the travel expenses incurred in their assignments. Whereas some translators felt that the payment was fair relative to the market, others felt that it was slightly lower than the market rate. However, in spite of these issues, many translators emphasized that the work at NTB was personally gratifying and rewarding. One participant pointed out that "the benefits are financial and also moral." In conclusion, the income was not substantial, but it covered some expenses of low-income households, where any income opportunity is valued. As one interviewee told us, "It was better than just being at home."

Self-Esteem

The translators emphasized that their work at NTB increased their self-esteem. For some, simply being recognized and valued for their skills as translators made them feel confident: "I know that there are number of people that are willing to and wishing to do translation work ... I must be somewhat good to have this, so yeah it's a boost in self-esteem and confidence." For the majority, their increased self-esteem was directly related to helping others in need: "When you're helping the community, you feel good, so it does help your self-esteem. It does help. It gives you a purpose that you're doing more for others, so of course, the more we do, the better we feel." Others attributed gains in self-esteem to the feeling of pursuing a higher purpose ("moral satisfaction" and "meaning") and to the pride that arises from helping someone else:

> And I feel that whenever you help somebody, my self-esteem goes up. Like I feel proud, actually, I feel proud. I feel good when I assist somebody to achieve or to get what they deserve, and as we are working with more of like technically disadvantaged people, I mean, who cannot speak the language; assisting such people, gives me satisfaction.

Having the opportunity to translate with NTB made some feel more self-reliant about their abilities as translators: "It helped because you become more confident in your job." For new immigrants, this initial self-confidence gained at NTB was important because it helped them to overcome self-doubt and opened the door to accept new and more difficult challenges: "Working with NTB gave me the courage to do translations and to accept other assignments, and now I am interpreting at least two, three times per week. So I appreciate that because when you don't have courage no matter how educated you are, you cannot do anything."

Self-confidence gained at NTB was eventually transferred to other areas of life, not only job-related ones. Many translators described experiences translating and interpreting informally for their friends, families, and communities, and recalled impromptu interventions in daily situations: "On buses, when somebody just can't communicate, and you know that person speaks your language, you feel like helping that person because once yourself you were in that situation." This translator recognized the importance of early family socialization – "It's something that I have, my parents always instilled in me, you know, help others" – but attributed the confidence to actively engage in informal interpretations to their NTB experience. Another translator reported that she became more confident in other areas of her life, including her family life and her social life:

> My husband is funny because he says that now I am more independent, that I don't need him as much. You know, before I used to count on him doing this or doing that, but now I just do it on my own. And whenever we go out, he says I'm much more of a … not a cocky person, but your self-esteem just gives you the back-up to know that you have that experience and that you have to be treated well or you know to a certain point, not to be degraded by somebody else.

Personal and Professional Development

Most translators reported that their NTB experience contributed to their personal and professional development, and they identified different knowledge, skills, and dispositions gained through the translation process. Many noted that translating and interpreting increased their knowledge of specialized terminologies and vocabularies (e.g., legal and medical terminology) both in English and in their first languages. Other translators mentioned an improvement in their problem-solving skills, especially within the context of settlement, social, and community services. Experience led to a better understanding of new immigrants' problems and possible solutions: "If somebody has a problem I can use that experience for the next time. It is an asset." The experience as translators also helped them to become exposed to different professional fields and communities: "If you do translation you get to know lots of fields, you have to understand a lot of things from people, from the environment ... to get that knowledge, I have to go to different locations, to different organizations, and this way I learn." This also helped them to address new situations: "I gained experience dealing with any kind of situation, basically under pressure, problem solving. Being in a non-profit you have to deal with a lot of situations because there are people that come that are homeless, or that need help, or seniors."

Translators expressed how the information that they translated carried over into their personal lives: "I didn't know there were so many places that could help immigrants and that could be of great help to you, too. At Northwood I found that there are a lot of places where they give you a hand." Working with clients also helped participants to increase their empathy through relating their clients' experiences to their own. One translator stated: "When working with clients, it was almost like looking back into my past a little bit and see what they are going through."

Many translators referred to the impact of their translation on professional development. Working for NTB helped them to understand that their language skills were, in fact, highly valuable skills that could be used in various professional settings. Others noted that the experience also allowed them to learn more about the professional responsibilities and obligations of translators and interpreters – such matters as learning the do's and don'ts of the profession (not confusing their feelings with those of their client, how to proceed when clients needed help beyond the translation service, confidentiality issues, and ethical guidelines). They also developed a sense of personal and professional responsibility towards their clients, and learned how to mediate between social service providers and their clients.

Community

The community impact of NTB could be observed in two main areas. The first was the institutional arrangement by which 40 per cent of NTB's revenues are channeled to NNS. As mentioned, this provides a potentially significant funding stream for certain NNS community programs. The second was the personal commitment and practices of translators themselves. Several translators emphasized a strong personal commitment to providing vital information and settlement services within their communities by using the knowledge and expertise obtained through the translation process to assist others. As one translator told us,

> I'm not working for any organization to do settlement work, but all the time I do help people, unpaid. People in my neighbourhood, they know that I have been involved in this kind of work, so people come on, another friend or neighbour will say "oh, he knows the immigration process, he knows where we can find the OHIP card, where you can get the SIN card,[7] where you can find a school" and things like that, right? So I'm always wearing those shoes as a counsellor, even if I'm not paid or working with an organization.

Many translators said that they made their friends, neighbours, and communities more aware of the various programs, services, and resources available to them. For example: "There are many institutions out there readily available for them but there is a sense of fear, of the unknown, of not knowing how to access things that people that have been born here, that have been raised here, know that already exist." Another translator added: "If I hear something, a new service for a community, I tell my people, this thing is going to be in this community, you need to be engaged with it." NTB translators constantly build connections between their communities and NNS: "I always bring people here, refer people to here, make references and say, I'm bringing them here." Moreover, as a result of their experiences with NTB, some translators started to volunteer with NNS.

The translators believed that NTB plays an important role in fostering social inclusion – or, as one translator put it, the service "giv[es] people the feeling that they are not alone in this country, that we are with them; if you don't know this language, don't worry, we have people who can help you in your language. We just need to connect with them." Other translators talked about NTB's contributions to integrating marginalized communities, particularly families who do not speak any English and vulnerable populations like older immigrants and "people who are new to the country, who feel that have not really entered the process, who feel that they are not Canadian because they don't feel recognized."

Moreover, translating and interpreting allowed some to reconnect with their own language, culture and community, as recalled by one translator:

They asked me: "Are you going to come to us again?" We had so many topics in common, because we were born in the same country, and this means that we could understand each other without even words. Some glance, some proverb, some good word can build this bridge. It was very important. Just one short proverb, a line of a song, or something like that, you already feel the spark.

Concerns

One recurrent concern, expressed by translators working for other organizations, was frustration with intermediaries or brokers who subcontracted work and claimed a substantial portion of the revenue earned from the job. Another concern had to do with remuneration levels. Many translators felt underpaid for their services – both at NTB and elsewhere. One translator was blunt about this concern: "If you don't pay well, you don't get qualified translators; the amount you pay compromises the quality of the service that you give to your clients." This concern was heightened for specialized translations, in specific fields like engineering or medicine. In order to attract these highly qualified translators, NTB would need to provide both competitive salaries and appropriate compensation for travel expenses.

This situation poses an interesting dilemma for social purpose enterprises like NTB. If it wants to offer services to the public at subsidized prices and transfer some revenues to programs provided by the parent non-profit organization, it cannot afford to pay competitive salaries and working conditions, and will thus have difficulties attracting high-quality workers and guaranteeing a high quality service. If it pays competitive salaries and offers more desirable working conditions, the social purpose enterprise could attract high-quality translators, but it may lack the resources to fulfil its social purpose of subsidized prices unless it injects additional funds to the operation from other sources such as donations, government funds, or grants. This constitutes one of the main issues confronted by social purpose enterprises: how to reconcile economic and social goals.

A related concern was the different remuneration and working conditions enjoyed by translators depending on their language of specialization: essentially supply of translators and demand for the service. One translator said, "If you come from a language that has a lot of translators and interpreters it is difficult to earn a living as a translator." Translators with fewer competitors within their language group can charge higher fees. However, independent of the language, translation seems to be a potentially precarious career path. As one translator stated, "This is just to get by."

Summary and Conclusions

NTB as a Social Purpose Enterprise

Based on the framework presented in the introductory chapter, NTB can be considered a social purpose enterprise for seven reasons. First, NTB was not set up for owners to make a return on an investment, as in the private sector, but to pursue social objectives. Chapter 1 points out that in social purpose enterprises "commerce is subsumed within their social purposes: the betterment of a marginalized social group, which most often is the employees. Betterment includes helping the employees to develop their skills, which in turn enhances their earning capacity and other facets of their being." Earning money through the sale of translation services to improve the current and future well-being of translators is a key feature of NTB. However, we could add that NTB's social purpose also includes the betterment of the community – be it through the volunteer work of translators at NNS, through their direct assistance to community groups, or through the transfer of funds to NNS programs. Second, NTB sells services to consumers, but only on a small scale. It is a micro-operation that does not aim at controlling larger and larger portions of the market. NTB's main aim is offering a needed service to immigrant communities. Third, the NTB is a market-based entity founded and supported by a non-profit organization. NNS, the parent organization, has provided settlement and support services to communities in northwest Toronto since its creation in 1982.

Fourth, NTB generates economic and social benefits to a marginalized population, especially to new immigrants who face significant difficulties in finding employment because they lack Canadian work experience. Part of this benefit is a small supplement to translators' incomes, but perhaps more important (as noted below) is the improvement in self-esteem, the strengthening of social connections or social capital, and the increase in human capital such as skills and professional competencies. Fifth, NTB generates revenues from the sale of translation services, and NNS uses 40 per cent of revenue to fund community programs. Based on 2011 figures, this is a small amount, but in the past it has been larger. NTB operates as an income-generating unit within a non-profit organization. Sixth, both NNS and NTB benefit from the support of government, individual donors, volunteers, foundations and clients. The grants that NNS receives indirectly benefit the translation bureau because it includes the payment for a manager and promotion. Seventh, the NTB is a social purpose enterprise because it yields a return to society from this investment, not only by helping new immigrants to function more fully and independently in Canadian society but also by offering translation services to low-income groups, typically at a subsidized price and sometimes for free, and therefore contributing to the community programs offered by NNS.

Rethinking Benefits

NTB's beneficiaries are threefold: the translators themselves, the clients, and the community. The most significant and tangible outcomes are the economic, psychological, educational, and social benefits acquired by NTB translators, who improve their skills, sharpen their credentials, and accelerate their social and economic integration to the new society. By recognizing the international work experience of the new immigrants, NTB offers them a job opportunity that is normally denied to them in the Canadian labour market. In doing so, the translation bureau opens an initial door to new immigrants when most doors are closed, allowing them to add Canadian experience to their resumes and hence become more employable. There is a small monetary benefit, but the translation work is scarce and sporadic. Translators reported increased levels of self-esteem, which helped them to engage in different areas of Canadian society, both as volunteers and as paid workers. The NTB experience contributed to the translators' personal and professional development: they acquired new knowledge, skills, and dispositions (human capital) that could be applied to a variety of work and non-work related situations. Last but not least, translators reported a variety of social impacts, particularly regarding social and community networks. Besides the positive impact on translators, NTB allows new immigrants who need translation and interpretation access to good quality services at below-market rates, sometimes pro-bono. Furthermore, the transfer of 40 per cent of NTB revenues to NNS allowed the local community to benefit.

Even though NTB was conceived of as an income-generating social purpose enterprise, none of the translators viewed their NTB earnings as a primary source of income. They were aware and proud of the social impact of their work and valued the opportunity to use their translation/interpretation skills to serve others in need. Although some rudimentary training and referral to other certifying agencies is provided to NTB translators, this social purpose enterprise is unique in that it utilizes skills that participants already have (i.e., their ability to communicate in other languages and in English) and makes participants aware of the fact these skills are valuable and marketable. Therefore, the benefits of NTB may be viewed differently than were originally intended, but nevertheless are of great importance to the translators and their community.

A Final Comment

The case of NTB illustrates the impact of government funding cuts on organizations like NNS that run social purpose enterprises. As we already pointed out, NTB does not operate as a separate entity from NNS. It is very much embedded within it. When NNS suffered a significant government budget cut in 2010, it had to lay off five staff members, including one who was in charge of managing NTB. The absence of a manager halved revenues over the course of a single year. Currently, NNS is trying to secure funding to hire a full-time manager to oversee NTB. This may reverse the fortunes of NTB and increase the income from translation and the return to NNS.

If there were a large increase in NTB's economic fortunes, possibly this would create the need for conceiving of a different model than the four models set out in Chapter 1, which differentiated between social enterprises that fund the services of their parent organization (e.g., the ReStore and Habitat for Humanity) and those that are primarily dependent on their parent organization such as NTB at present. If NTB could become a major income earner, it could assume an equivalent economic status in its relationship with NNS – it could return to NNS as much as the organization subsidizes it. If that were the case, the NTB/NNS relationship would change and the organization could transform into a hybrid of a social enterprise and a social purpose enterprise. NTB is a long way from that goal, but it is something that could be achieved in the future.

NOTES

1   We want to express our gratitude to Azaria Wolday, our community partner, for helping us to recruit participants for this study and for answering our questions about NTB and NNS.

2 http://www.toronto.ca/demographics/pdf/priority2006/area_weston_
   full.pdf
3 LINC: Language Instruction for Newcomers to Canada; ESL: English as a
   Second Language.
4 Ontario Works is a program of the provincial Ministry of Community and
   Social Services that provides income and employment assistance for
   people who are in financial need and seeking a job. See http://www.mcss
   .gov.on.ca/en/mcss/programs/social/ow/index.aspx
5 This study was published in 2005, a year before NTB was created. This
   may explain the omission.
6 Albania, Bolivia, Chile, China, Ecuador, Eritrea, Guatemala, India, Iran,
   Italy, Lebanon, Pakistan, Russia, Somalia, Ukraine, and Vietnam.
7 OHIP stands for Ontario Health Insurance Plan. The SIN card is the social
   insurance number, and it is equivalent to the social security number in the
   United States.

REFERENCES

Beach, C., Worswick, C., & Green, A. (2011). *Toward improving Canada's skilled
   immigration policy: An evaluation approach*. Toronto, ON: C.D. Howe Institute.
Citizenship and Immigration Canada. (2011). Backgrounder: Stakeholder con-
   sultations on immigration levels and mix. Retrieved from http://www.cic
   .gc.ca/english/department/media/backgrounders/2011/2011-07-11.asp
Creese, G., & Wiebe, B. (2012). "Survival employment": Gender and
   deskilling among African immigrants in Canada. *International
   Migration (Geneva, Switzerland), 50*(5), 56–76. http://dx.doi.
   org/10.1111/j.1468-2435.2009.00531.x
Danso, R. (2007). Emancipating and empowering de-valued skilled immigrants:
   What hope does anti-oppressive social work practice offer? *British Journal of
   Social Work, 39*(3), 539–555. http://dx.doi.org/10.1093/bjsw/bcm126
De Maio, F., & Kemp, E. (2010). The deterioration of health status among
   immigrants to Canada. *Global Public Health, 5*(5), 462–478. http://dx.doi
   .org/10.1080/17441690902942480
Frenette, M., & Morissette, R. (2005). Will they ever converge? Earnings
   of immigrant and Canadian-born workers over the last two decades.
   International Migration Review, 39(1), 228–257. http://dx.doi.org/10.1111/
   j.1747-7379.2005.tb00261.x
Gariba, S.A. (2010). *Race, ethnicity, immigration and jobs: Labour market access
   among Ghanaian and Somali youth in the Greater Toronto Area* (Doctoral
   dissertation). University of Toronto, Toronto, ON.

Keung, N. (2010, December 23). Funding axed for Toronto immigrant agencies. *The Toronto Star*. Retrieved from http://www.thestar.com/news/gta/
  article/911205--funding-axed-for-toronto-immigrant-agencies

Lim, A., Lo, L., Siemiatycki, M., & Doucet, M. (2005). Newcomer services in
  the Greater Toronto Area: An exploration of the range and funding sources
  of settlement services. *Geography Publications and Research*. Paper 41.

Oreopoulos, P. (2009). *Why do skilled immigrants struggle in the labor market?*
  A field experiment with six thousand resumes (National Bureau of Economic
  Research Working Paper No. 15036).

Picot, G., & Sweetman, A. (2005). *The deteriorating economic welfare of immigrants*
  and possible causes. Ottawa, ON: Statistics Canada.

Reitz, J. (2007). Immigrant employment success in Canada, part II:
  Understanding the decline. *Journal of International Migration and Integration*,
  8(1), 37–62. http://dx.doi.org/10.1007/s12134-007-0002-3

Slade, B. (2012). "From high skill to high school": Illustrating the process
  of deskilling immigrants through reader's theatre and institutional eth-
  nography. *Qualitative Inquiry*, *18*(5), 401–413. http://dx.doi.org/10.1177/
  1077800412439526

Statistics Canada. (2008). *Educational portrait of Canada, Census 2006*. Ottawa,
  ON: Human Resources and Skills Development Canada.

SECTION D

Youth

This section has only one case, the River Restaurant (Chapter 13), an attempt at integrating marginalized youth into the mainstream workforce through employing them in a Toronto restaurant.

River Restaurant was started by **All-A-Board Youth Ventures,** a non-profit charitable organization that created small enterprises to give youth a year-long training experience.

This case is unique because the restaurant closed in 2011. The case raises an important issue: can social purpose enterprises in food service be successful with a workforce composed of marginalized youth? This issue is part of a debate about the best way to assist groups on the social margins: through enterprises that hire them exclusively or through workplace integration programs where they are a small minority.

13 Market-Based Solutions for At-Risk Youth: River Restaurant[1]

RAYMOND DART

They just wanted to live. They just wanted to pay their bills like normal people. They just wanted to have an apartment. And our [River Restaurant] family really was built around them, and I hear it all the time. The best part that I could ever take from River is that it really meant something to people. And that was more than how many customers we served, in my mind. It was more than how beautiful the restaurant looked on the inside, or how great the menu was on Saturday night. That is the piece I will always carry with me.

[Former River staff member]

This chapter analyses the River Restaurant, a social purpose enterprise in Toronto, which trained and supported at-risk youth. From Phnom Penh to Vancouver, restaurants that are social purpose enterprises – social purpose restaurants – are becoming increasingly common. Of course, there are different ways in which restaurant and food service organizations (including caterers, wholesalers, market gardeners, et cetera) can pursue social objectives. Farmgate enterprises, community-supported agriculture, "slow food," bioregional food, and so on, are just a few of the ways in which restaurants can connect with community development and environmental sustainability issues.

The research in this chapter is concerned with a subclass of social purpose restaurants that focus on training. Their social value comes from their setting as a vocational and life-skills training facility for social groups that are in some manner marginalized and often chronically unemployed. "Training restaurants" have a long association with chef and hospitality schools. Social purpose restaurants engaged in training, however, have some distinct characteristics: they tend to be located among "normal" restaurant and food service establishments, because they endeavour for their customer experience to be as normal as possible; they are funded at least partially from public sector agencies and philanthropic organizations; and most importantly, their staff trainees come from troubled and structurally disadvantaged backgrounds. Because of this, the training tends to include both industry-specific hospitality skills as well as broader life and job-readiness skills.

The Origin and Institutionalization of Social Purpose Restaurants

Although social purpose restaurants (SPRs) are a loosely associated movement, there is little sense of the history of this particular organization type. They were among the first kind of organizations associated with the modern "social entrepreneur" label. In Jed Emerson and Faye Twersky's germinal volume, *New Social Entrepreneurs* – which helped to launch and popularize social entrepreneurs and the social enterprise model – food service establishments that supported and trained "street-involved" (e.g., former homeless) individuals while simultaneously earning revenue for their host organizations were held up as exemplary. Rubicon Ventures is probably the best known and most widely referenced case study from *New Social Entrepreneurs* (Emerson and Twersky, 1996). Rubicon Ventures in San Francisco was built around a restaurant and catering business (as well as a grounds maintenance business) that employed homeless individuals in transition. Other SPRs referenced by Emerson and Twersky included the Expresso Thyself Café and the As You Like It Café, both components of larger social enterprise and non-profit service organization parents.

Rubicon itself is an interesting crucible of issues relating to SPRs. When *New Social Entrepreneurs* was published in 1996, Rubicon's food services division had gone through an initial phase when it was successful in producing food, training its in-transition client population, and generating commercial revenue from customers. However, concerns that Rubicon was still highly subsidized led to significant changes. The café facilities were closed, and the enterprise was reorganized as a high-end dessert catering and wholesaling business. Rubicon's social purpose restaurant (or café) seemingly occupied a relatively low-margin and low-volume market niche, and survival would require ongoing governmental or foundation support. With assistance from a number of sophisticated external players, Rubicon's food service division transitioned and eventually Rubicon Bakery came into existence (2004). This new organization was successful from both financial and training points of view. It was sold into private ownership in 2009, with the proviso that a portion of the profits would be directed to Rubicon Programs and that initiatives in supportive and transitional employment would somehow be continued. At this point (2012), Rubicon retains only one social enterprise program – in its grounds maintenance department.

The initial examples promoted by the Roberts Enterprise Development Fund (which supported Rubicon and also financed the Emerson and Twersky volume) were widely taken up by non-profit service organizations working with at-risk populations in the employment, training, and community economic development fields. There has been no systematic documentation of the SPR population, but there is a definite sense that the concept has been globalized and institutionalized.

SPRs, as part of socially responsible tourism and ecotourism (Chambers, 2009), are now commonplace in developing countries where rapid urbanization, high unemployment, and rural poverty are chronic challenges. In national capitals, such as Phnom Penh, Cambodia, and Hanoi, Vietnam, SPRs are favoured stops for western customers. In Phnom Penh, for example, Mith Samlanh (mithsamlahn.org) operates two restaurants and a café in the international districts of the city. These enterprises are staffed largely by former street children, who are given both employment and life-skills training as part of their experience. In Hanoi, a similar SPR called "Koto" (koto.com.au) – launched and managed by an Australian NGO, Know One Teach One –focuses primarily on helping unemployed and impoverished rural youth make the transition to independent and successful urban living through restaurant work.

The institutionalization of the SPR form is further evidenced by its relationships with celebrity chefs such as Jamie Oliver and even reality television shows. One of the world's well-known chefs, Oliver is famous also for his social advocacy around issues of food, health, and sustainability. Oliver led the creation of Fifteen (fifteen.net) – a restaurant in London that trains at-risk youth. Fifteen provides fifteen youth per year with opportunities to gain professional kitchen skills, to earn secondary or postsecondary course credits, to learn life skills, to earn a living wage, and to get work experience from an internationally famous employer. In addition, profits from Fifteen go to the Jamie Oliver Foundation. There are now two more Fifteen restaurants using the same organizational model: one in Devon in the United Kingdom and the other in Amsterdam.

The Social Purpose Restaurant Organizational Model

While there are diverse organizational models for social purpose enterprises, there are some commonalities among social purpose restaurants:

1. Raison d'être: SPRs are generally created to give disadvantaged and street-involved populations (usually youth) training in the hospitality and food services industry, job experience, life skills, a livable wage, and a healthy personal and social environment, in a real functioning restaurant or food services environment. SPRs are almost never restaurants first; they are mostly launched and supported by non-profit human services organizations that work with the marginalized target population.
2. Restaurants and catering businesses are appealing because of the relative ease of market entrance, a relatively modest learning and training curve for most nonspecialist positions, and a relatively buoyant future employment market because of contemporary trends around eating outside the home.
3. SPR staff includes the targeted group of at-risk youth, traditional restaurant employees such as professional chefs and managers, non-profit support workers who provide life-skills training, and broader organizational infrastructure workers. The proportion of at-risk youth is variable and often reflects how the SPR prioritizes its social objectives as compared to its financial priorities.
4. SPRs focus on a relatively small number of trainees. The training is in-depth, multifaceted, intensive (especially in terms of vocational restaurant skills and experience), and extensive (including broader job readiness, social skills, and life skills).
5. SPRs vary in the extent to which they use training at-risk youth as a value proposition or as an element of their branding. Most market on the basis of a hybrid value proposition – high-quality food and a legitimate good restaurant experience in a setting that also provides important social benefits to the community. SPRs in developing countries market their social purpose to a greater extent than most others.
6. The legal structure of SPRs is not well documented. Many are distinct legal entities, some are businesses, and some are non-profits. Most are directly controlled by a parent non-profit human services organization that initiated the SPR.

Overview of River Restaurant

The story of River Restaurant is rich, layered, and complicated. While it cannot be fully captured in anything as small as a chapter (even putting it "on paper" reduces some of the essential experiences of River), this section will provide an overview of the definitive characteristics of the organization and attempt to tell at least the major analytical and narrative threads of its story.

River Restaurant and its non-profit (and charitable) parent organization, All-A-Board Youth Ventures, began operation in 1998 after a relatively short gestational planning period in 1997. The restaurant operated continuously until August 2011 when it closed due to a number of factors that will be elaborated on later. During that period, a total of nearly 250 at-risk youth were trained in front-of-house (service) and back-of-house (cooking and prep) restaurant positions. As well, the youth completed structured individualized programs in life skills, job-readiness skills, and social skills. The numbers only tell a modest piece of the story: interview after interview with former River staff (i.e., youth trainees) tell of difficult lives profoundly affected, confidence developed, bad habits reduced, bad choices transformed, and more productive lives created or evolved. Many River staff members also talked proudly of new jobs or careers embarked on, or new educational opportunities explored. Based on the research, the compelling conclusion is that River Restaurant had a deep effect on a number of troubled lives.

River's operating model was quite simple: it operated as a normal restaurant on Roncesvalles Avenue in Toronto (a district with a large number of restaurants and cafés), with a relatively simple menu targeted at a mostly local neighbourhood clientele. Media publicity – drawn to the restaurant because of its special "social purpose" nature – brought a different customer demographic from farther away, but this group was never as large as neighbourhood customers. While the restaurant was regarded as having fairly good food, it was not a destination restaurant in the vast and impressive landscape that is the urban Toronto restaurant community.

To describe River in more detail first requires an understanding of the research process and how the information was collected. The case study of River began in the autumn of 2010, when River Restaurant was experiencing a significant downturn in business due to months of ongoing construction on Roncesvalles Avenue. For the research, my principal contact was Jennifer LaTrobe. She was the managing director of All-A-Board Youth Ventures (the non-profit parent of River) and had been with River since its early days. Jennifer was the person with the longest and most directly involved history with River, and she generously provided numerous opportunities for me to interview her in detail as well as to talk with her more informally. Jennifer also gave me access to a wide range of documents from All-A-Board Youth Ventures' and River's past and present, including annual reports, grant proposals, reports to funders, press releases, and so on. In addition, Jennifer facilitated my access to the active River staff and trainees and, more importantly, connected me to River's alumni network so that I could learn about "the River experience" during its heyday in the mid 2000s. In 2010–11 there were only one professional chef and three trainees at River Restaurant, but there was an elaborate network of alumni.

In this case study, I will attribute information from Jennifer LaTrobe to "JLT," since her voice is both unmistakable and essential to an understanding of River Restaurant. In contrast, I will refer to other members of the River community – staff, youth trainees, and funders from 1999 to 2011 – more generally to respect their confidentiality and anonymity and also because most of their stories and interactions with AAB/River were more transient. In total, between 2010 and 2012, I (with the help of Trent University graduate student research assistant) was able to perform more than twenty interviews with staff and trainees (including alumni) to help create a rounded, rich, diverse, and complex view of the River Restaurant story.

The Beginning of River Restaurant

The germ of the idea that led to River Restaurant came from Canada's west coast at almost exactly the same time as Emerson and Twersky published the story of the Rubicon Café in San Francisco in 1996. An insight came to a Vancouver couple with an unusual skill set and a background that blended corporate finance and community development. This couple had a strong interest in the problems of employment for disadvantaged urban youth. The couple moved from Vancouver to Toronto and one of them became a founding director of AAB/River.

As JLT described it, the founders wondered, "'Why doesn't someone just start a business that hires youth that can't get jobs?' It seems an obvious solution. [They were] kind of shocked that no one had done it, and in Vancouver there was at the time a Picasso Café that they looked at, but they didn't like the fact that it was featured as a [non-profit employment] program. It was kind of like, 'Can't we just do this without it featuring the [non-profit employment] program like that? Can't we just do this?'"

The early concept of River Restaurant came from the Picasso Café (described in Currie, Foley, Schwartz, & Taylor-Lewis, 2001) in Vancouver, but it had important differences that are hinted at in JLT's description. The River Restaurant concept was less like an employment program and more like a real restaurant. Organizationally, River was conceived of in business-like terms. Picasso had been designed initially along the lines of many government-funded community economic development initiatives – highly participatory, flexible, and youth driven. The River founders believed that was not realistic training for the job market.

One former staff person summarized this perspective as follows:

So in 1997, we hadn't opened the restaurant, yet. It was still a nascent idea. We opened it in June 1998 ... There was a bunch of people that then later we let go [of] that didn't quite fit the culture which emerged quite quickly ... the culture of, "We're running a business to be a business. We're not running a business to run a welfare situation." ... This wouldn't feel like work. This would feel like a program.

To fit and extend the concept of a business-like restaurant with what JLT described as a "working business culture" that would prepare youth for future work opportunities, the founding board members sought out a staff person who was not a non-profit sector youth worker or someone who was closely associated with at-risk youth agencies. Jennifer LaTrobe was hired, as she put it, "to be the oldie," and to offer solid organizational and professional skills to the River organization. In addition, Jennifer's background gave her strong skills in grant writing and fundraising, which were essential to River's emerging operating model. River commenced operations with its first youth trainees in June 1998.

Structure and Staffing

The perspective of most people, which was echoed in several reports published in the *Globe and Mail* and *Toronto Life*, was that River Restaurant looked and felt mostly like a normal restaurant. Its location on

Roncesvalles Avenue in Toronto – a historically Polish neighbourhood undergoing transformation and gentrification – meant that it was part of a small village of restaurants and cafés that served both a bustling local community and individuals visiting the café cluster from points afar. River's image and decor were described as "relatively middle of the road" in the sense that the restaurant wasn't trendy or expensive. There were only two differences from normal cafés, which were described to me in interviews.

The first was that it was sometimes apparent that floor staff (i.e., waiters) were inexperienced and uncertain of their role. One manager noted this comparatively chaotic and sometimes madcap aspect of River as follows: "I mean, generally, I get people with zero experience, and I mean zero experience. Sometimes it is their first job … It went right to the basics of how you greet someone, literally the words you actually say … The amount of trays that got dumped with stuff on them, and just that you can't bring food out to a table in your hand, you know, real basic things that you would think would just be a given; but no, no, they're not."

The second difference – and one that I personally observed in the final two years of the restaurant's operation – was the dated and worn appearance of the restaurant particularly in its later days. This highlighted the fact that River Restaurant was not as customer focused as typical restaurants, which strive to keep up their "look." As will be elaborated on later, customers were neither the first nor the second priority of River. The lack of upkeep also highlighted the funding and budgeting difficulties faced by an organization like River: it was readily able to get grants and donations to cover employment costs for trainees and supervisory staff, but as a social purpose enterprise, it was much less able to get capital for trendy (and expensive) decor.

Beyond its appearance, River's organizational model was relatively straightforward. River Restaurant was typically staffed by a professional chef and a professional restaurant manager. Both of these staff members needed to be a little atypical or special. Not only did they have to run a working restaurant, but they also had to be able to work with a very challenging youth trainee population.

A former chef described what drew him to work at River in broadly humanistic and non-restaurant terms:

I can talk to you about, you know, how I like what River does and that's part of the reason why I wanted to be here. I've spent many years working for people that are only concerned about the bottom line and nothing else. And I mean, obviously everyone cares and worries about money and things like that, but in this position here, I like the different pressures as opposed to the money-making pressure.

Note that the chef liked working at River because it was not primarily about money and the pressure of money making. This further sheds light on the interesting ways in which River was and was not "business-like."

A former professional floor manager and coordinator of waiters also referred to these competing priorities:

So the manager that hired me ended up quitting because she didn't know how to deal with the youth, how to motivate them, what to do if they didn't show up; all those sorts of things. And this is where my life changed, too, but I found I connected really well with them. So I was able to sort of build rapport and work with them instead of telling them what to do, you know. And then so I became the manager, as ridiculous as that sounds. So that was in the beginning, sort of right away realizing they had this brilliant idea and this restaurant, it's so key. You're teaching a marketable skill, you know, this is awesome except that now you're dealing with these people that have some pretty horrid stories and are pretty against authority and have never worked before and now you're here, you're doing it, and kind of realizing it was a lot harder than it looked like on paper.

Despite the commitment to running a normal restaurant, it is evident that a traditional business (and staffing) strategy would not have been viable at River.

The River Difference: Changes to the Youth Intern Approach

River's raison d'être was training and supporting at-risk Toronto youth. The approach taken by the board and managing staff of River was consonant with emerging ideas about social purpose enterprises and distinctive to the particular mix of people involved in its founding and evolution. River's difference was partly framed as a reaction against traditional, non-profit/governmental youth employment training. The founders of the organization and the developers of the model consistently described it as preferable to these alternatives because it was training relevant to the youths' post-River working options. As JLT described it, "No, restaurants don't have democratic meetings where they decide what they're going to serve. That doesn't happen ... so the culture got established very quickly that we were a 'business-business' and that to really train these youth in a business, you had to be a business."

River attempted to create organizational processes, expectations, and an environment close to what youth would experience in real jobs in that particular industry. Youth would learn what real work in a real business was like. It is important to note that River was not particularly business-like from a financial perspective: staff members weren't pushed to generate revenue or to reduce costs, and their interaction with River was not primarily a finance-for-work exchange. River was organized like a business in that it was highly organized and structured with straightforward expectations of staff and trainees, which included clear rules for working behaviour. As part of these human resource policies and processes, youth were given support to help them work within these expectations and also manage their broader life more successfully. River was therefore business-like in that it had real expectations of its youth trainees – it would even "let the trainees go" (i.e., terminate their job) if they were unable to work productively most of the time. They had a three-strikes policy, which was a good example of the way that River negotiated the challenging balance of trainee learning and necessary basic work expectations. From JLT:

> And if this [referring to a temper outburst] happens again, you know, we had a three strike policy with verbal warnings in there sprinkled about, but if you told them ... "the next time this happens, you know, it's your choice if you want to be here," and I always use that. It's your choice. You don't have to stay. We would love you to, but if you're not showing up to work, you're showing us that you don't want to be here and we can't keep you. We need the spot for someone else.

It is important to note that both River/AAB senior staff and trainees/ alumni, even those who were terminated, described these rules and structures in positive terms.

River's Model for At-Risk Youth

The number of trainees per year was highly variable. This variability came from several sources: the availability and type of governmental

funding for the trainees, the busyness of the restaurant, and the trainees' turnover and completion rates. Overall, River trained and supported on average fifteen to seventeen youth per year over its lifetime.

There were several important factors that affected the number of
youth trained. One was the length of the placements at River, and this
feature was exogenous to River/AAB itself. Depending on the provincial or federal government funding program available for youth trainees (which paid the trainees' salary as some kind of vocational training/
employment training program), the placement at River ranged from
four months to a year. Even a particular program would periodically
vary the time and conditions of its trainee salary and top-up arrangements. After the period of time prescribed by the grant or funding,
trainees were considered "trained" and ready to move on from River to
unsupported employment or to other life options such as additional
training or education.

Because of the volatile and challenging nature of the client/trainee
population, the River/AAB management staff (particularly JLT) put
considerable effort into recruiting and pre-screening the at-risk youth
who might eventually come into River Restaurant employ. River restaurant did not directly recruit youth trainees, though a few trainees
did find out about River from the networks of trainees, staff, and alumni. Instead, youth were recruited through a system of front-line social
service agencies that worked with at-risk and street youth. These agencies (including St. Stephen's House and other major youth-serving organizations) were a crucial bridge between River and its target client
population. Since River attempted to be a normally functioning restaurant, and because River/AAB had (at best) modest social service and
social support resources, it was important for the referral agencies to
recommend to River/AAB only those youth who were deemed ready
and able to take on a significant life change and new responsibilities.
This pre-screening was reinforced by River's own interview and hiring
process, in order to ensure that those who started at River were suitable
for the longer term. JLT described it as follows:

> Oh you can't keep hiring people you can't help. So the staff get better at
> hiring and firing. So [if] in the three-month probation things are going
> badly, not because of what their behaviour is in terms of job function, but
> in terms of those psychological states, those are the ones we had to wean
> out. We can't help mental illness problems. We know that. We've tried. We
> cannot help that group.

It is crucial to understand that because River Restaurant was a real restaurant setting, certain standards for customer experience needed to be upheld. Consequently, certain kinds of staff behaviours were unable to be tolerated on site. After the recruitment and pre-screening process, youth trainees were socialized into the River Restaurant working environment. This socialization included workplace training, actual work, and introductions to other trainees and to the permanent professional staff. Trainees were also given a variable amount of "life skills" training, ranging from discussions about partner violence to learning how to set up a bank account and manage their time effectively. When funds were available, a successful program (with $100 monthly cash bonuses) was initiated to help the youth trainees take on and achieve new and constructive behaviours. The combination of the pre-screening processes, the job environment, and the overall structure provided by the overall River/AAB produced what seem to be unambiguously successful youth-training results for the organization. Based on statistics prepared for a report to Human Resources Development Canada by River/AAB, over the ten-year period between 1998 and 2007, more than 90 per cent of youth trainees who started at River continued past their probation period into the full training period, and of those, slightly under 90 per cent were deemed "successful" by virtue of being either in full-time employment or in an education program within six months of graduating. Given the social and employment file of those who began at River, these seem to be fundamentally solid results.

While the statistics of graduation rates tell an important story, the recollections of River alumni are even more compelling. For many, their experience at River was clearly transformative. One alumna said that while "I wasn't coming from a white picket fence lifestyle, … it became like a little family there … it was probably the best job I have had in my life." Another said: "River definitely opened a door for me … Without them, I would probably be living in a cockroach-infested apartment with a guy who didn't respect me. I am thankful for River, every day." These are just a small number of illustrative quotes from former youth trainees, who overwhelmingly described their experience at River as positive and significant in both personal and vocational terms.

River's Financial and Economic Model

The financing and economics of River/AAB were fascinating and somewhat complex. As a social purpose enterprise, there are a number of expectations about the importance of generating commercial revenue (Madill, Broward, & Hebb, 2010) and redistributing profitability and profit into training (Boschee, 2006) that frame how we might look at an organization like River. This was reinforced by the dominant discourse at River among the non-trainee staff that described River in emphatically "business" terms. To reiterate JLT's words, "we're running a business to be a business; we're not running a business to run a welfare situation."

The financial model for River was by no means simple. River/AAB used multiple revenue streams to support the social enterprise's operation and mission, normally with an overall budget of around one million dollars per year. As a functioning restaurant, one revenue source was its commercial income from customers, whether these were individuals having dinner or catering clients who purchased food services in bulk. This income stream was subject to basic expenses (e.g., food ingredients and other "costs of goods sold") and also varied according to the busyness of the restaurant operation.

Another revenue source came from the social service agencies that funded the youth trainees. Street-involved and at-risk youth are priorities of the provincial and federal governments, which have numerous programs that incentivize the "street to apartment" and "welfare to work" transitions. Various agencies such as Human Resources Development Canada and Ontario Works provide grants to organizations like River to pay qualified at-risk youth as employees-in-training. These grants allowed River/AAB to pay trainees a full-time wage (their gratuities were over and above this amount) without needing to resort to their commercial revenue stream for this significant cost. The staff costs of this area would have been otherwise prohibitive, since trainees were not only inexperienced and therefore inefficient, but were also prone to numerous psychosocial and behavioural problems endemic to those who are street involved and chronically unemployed.

The final revenue stream that was important to River/AAB came from grants, donations, and philanthropy. The founding River/AAB group had backgrounds that gave the organization important advantages in this regard. A few founding board members came from "high finance backgrounds, bond trading and all that" and their networks included some of the wealthy Bay Street donor community. In addition, JLT's background in international development meant that right from the beginning (1997–8) River's staff included someone highly experienced at writing grants. She said, "Having spent half my life in business [consulting] and half my life in [international] development, it [River's need for grants] wasn't that hard to figure out." River/AAB's funding envelope contained grants from the Ontario Trillium Foundation, private foundations, and wealthy individuals.

The revenue mix at River was somewhat different than initially planned; the significance of this will be developed later in the chapter. JLT described how River's revenue mix was intended to follow a "one-third, one-third, one-third" blueprint: "one-third comes from the restaurant, one-third comes from foundations and people, and one-third comes from some form of funding from the government, whether it be Job Connect, Ontario Works, HRDC. We can't pick up the tab for the whole thing ... The restaurant can't possibly revenue that much money." While this model was a far cry from some exhortations that commercial revenue should be central to social enterprises –and although it fell short, too, of producing profit – it still was thought to represent a healthy balance at River/AAB.

The financial records at River, however, portray a financial mix at odds with the "one-third, one-third, one-third" model that the organization promoted and aspired to. Financial records taken from the core period of River's operation (2001–9) show that, on average, only 17.7 per cent per year of total revenue come from restaurant sales (see Table 13.1). Overall, various forms of government grants normally accounted for much more than the one-third of the organization's total revenue. (Note: due to the way that finances were reported to Canada Revenue Agency, it was less possible to separate out grant/donation funding types from each other than it was to separate out sales revenue from the basket of grants and donations.)

General Discussion: Major Themes and Issues at River Restaurant

River Restaurant was more a youth-training organization than a business

Despite the double bottom-line rhetoric of some in the social enterprise field, it is clear that River Restaurant existed first and foremost for its social mission of training and supporting street-involved and otherwise disadvantaged youth. In the organizational model of River Restaurant, the youth-training imperative and focus meant that the successful operation of a restaurant was primarily a means to an end. In contrast to a typical restaurant, customers were not a major focus – they were valued to the extent that their existence facilitated the valuable

Table 13.1 River Restaurant Revenue Breakdown: 2001 to 2009

Year	Total River/AAB Revenue	Total Restaurant Sales	% Restaurant Sales of Total River Budget
2009	$515,190	$88,981	17
2008	$532,489	$113,493	21
2007	$1,341,117	$147,169	11
2006	$1,016,560	$197,971	19
2005	$919,241	$169,956	18
2004	$920,177	$140,070	15
2003	$1,414,915	$332,096	23
2002	$1,084,871	$269,081	25
2001	$1,110,548	$117,095	11

training experience for the youth. Similarly, commercial revenue was not a major focus – it assisted in the overall financing but paled in comparison to government grants and fundraising income.

This suggests quite a specific kind of social enterprise, labelled in Chapter 1 of this collection as a social purpose enterprise. River Restaurant can best be understood as needing to be a working business primarily because that milieu was the best for accomplishing the organization's social objectives for at-risk youth.

There was both direct and indirect evidence for this major theme. The indirect pieces of evidence were actually the most compelling. When staff, managers, alumni, or community members talked about River, they rarely referred to the food, to the customers, or to the restaurant's commercial revenue. Instead, everyone talked about the youth trainees and the transformative experience that working at River facilitated for them. Overwhelmingly, those associated with River framed the restaurant in terms of the positive difference that it made in the lives of those who worked there.

Therefore, River emphasized something different than the double bottom line found in the literature on social enterprise (e.g., Boschee, 2001, Emerson & Twersky, 1996). Although River had a double bottom line, its dominant priority was the social mission and the well-being of the youth trainees. The evidence for excellence in achievement of this social mission is compelling. Data for this qualitative case study show a legacy of troubled lives turned around, of chronically unemployed youth transformed into much more satisfied, self-regulating, and vocationally skilled adults. River succeeded in what it was operationally intended to do.

River Restaurant was most effective with fairly functional at-risk youth

The contemporary "capacity-building" approach (e.g., Simmons, Reynolds, & Swinburn, 2011), characterized by the "hand up" rather than "hand out" discourse, is intuitively attractive for dealing with social groups that have endemic employment issues, and River's role in this regard needs to be understood in a specific and nuanced manner. River Restaurant did excellent work with *at-risk* and *street-involved* youth. However, these groups are not homogenous, and there is no evidence that River achieved (or aspired to achieve) miracles with some of the most difficult, substance-involved or psychiatric segments of these populations.

Of the youth trainees and alumni interviewed, most described having had clear at-risk and street-involved attributes when they began at River. A few, however, described their life more in in passive "couch potato" terms rather than describing substance abuse, being street-involved, or embodying any other connotations of "at risk." Despite this variation, all described their lives as troubled *but* moderately functional at the time of their contact with River. Those youth who trained at River were already among the more functional members of their group. Their specific social position, relative to the wider group of at-risk youth, can be comprehended by the particular institutional ecology of which River was a part.

River/AAB did not simply "find" at-risk youth for transformation into restaurant trainees. Rather, the youth needed to be part of the government-funded and sanctioned life stabilization and vocational training system that exists in most jurisdictions for youth in a wide variety of situations. Youth needed to be part of this institutional ecology to be eligible for the kinds of funding or subsidies received by River to finance their intern employment. At the same time, these youth were also in touch with (often numerous) members of the social services network in the urban area around River. This enabled a pre-screening of potential trainees, allowing River to recruit at-risk youth who were not so destabilized by their life experience that they didn't stand a good chance of success.

An organizational strategy such as this bears some resemblance to concerns of cherry picking and cream skimming (Van Thiel & Leeuw, 2002) in the social services sector, when only clientele with the most modest difficulties are even eligible for consideration. This imagery unfairly portrays River as focusing on the "low hanging fruit" of its clientele group. While some concerns are relevant, River's choice of clientele and its pre-screening were necessary and appropriate given the constraints of the social purpose enterprise model. Funding at River was insufficient for intensive social work or socio-psychiatric work. As JLT described it, "people talked about [cream skimming] clients. What an incredibly, stupidly negative spin to put on fit and function. Like, why would you hire people that you know are going to be over their head? You just can't help them. Why would you hire them? I mean, we would learn this the hard way."

Government funding was inordinately important

River was described by Jennifer LaTrobe and by those in the pantheon of Toronto's social enterprise community as a real and market-based business organization. The operational story of River, however, was much more orientated towards and reliant on public sector funding. In a sense, governmental funding was the "tail that wags the dog." It was much larger than the image and rhetoric of River acknowledged, and it was actually quite decisive in terms of the organization and operation of River.

One point that illustrates River's dependence on government grants was the high degree of isomorphism (DiMaggio & Powell, 1983) observed between the training model in use at River and the models of public sector funding available for youth trainees. The records of youth trainees at River show that their traineeships ranged from four months to a full year in duration. The high variability was not (ever) based on strategic choices made by the organization regarding the amount or duration of training required. Instead, training periods and training foci were built around the "program du jour," as Jennifer LaTrobe described them – whatever particular employment program the federal or provincial government happened to be funding that was most relevant to their youth clientele.

The public face and rhetorical description of River as a social enterprise, the "one-third, one-third, one-third" model frequently promoted in regard to its finances, the casting of it in business terms ... all of these aspects intersect in a complex way with the reality that River's largest source of funding was always the public sector. Financially, River's principal story was how it positioned itself in relation to governmental funding, and the secondary story was its relationship to important fundraising markets. Customers and restaurant operations consistently ranked third in terms of the financial reality of the organization.

While this aspect of River might be disquieting for someone who thinks about social enterprise and commercial revenue dependence in ideological terms (e.g., Boschee, 2001), the salience of government funding in River's operation is more aptly understood as a functional interdependence between River's successful youth training model and public sector funding priorities for at-risk youth. This "market" was the largest and most reliable one that River/AAB could access. Its internal marketing resources for commercial revenue were minimal. Most importantly, government funding was the most reliable and significant financial resource pool that was directly aligned with River's focus on being an at-risk youth training facility. JLT noted that at River, "it's easier for me to raise money than to get more customers."

It can't be a real business

There are several indications from the River Restaurant case study that the prospects for a commercial revenue-focused restaurant that also intensively trains at-risk youth are minimal and that such a restaurant might only succeed in very low-wage developing countries or in organizations which train very few youth relative to the total number of staff.

Jennifer LaTrobe was candid about this aspect of River. She emphasized more than once that River Restaurant "couldn't ever be a real business" in financial terms. For example, she wondered, "what kind of functional, serious business would get rid of its staff as soon as they are trained?" A typical restaurant business would thrive based on experienced staff – except in the case of a franchise restaurant, where highly prescribed behaviours and patterns are the operating norm. River's model precluded this level of standardization, and instead relied on the professional floor manager and chef for organizational continuity. The organization was consistently enlisting new trainees. As such, its operating efficiency and effectiveness would always be fundamentally limited. It is important to note that this made them more financially vulnerable in a consistently difficult business sector; as JLT noted, "it's a business species with a world famous failure rate" (for a broader perspective, see also Parsa, Self, Njite, and King, 2005).

River's operating model contrasted starkly with that of some other restaurants with social missions such as the previously mentioned Rubicon Café and Jamie Oliver's Fifteen, as well as the Potluck Café and Catering (potluckcatering.com) in Vancouver. These are examples of organizations that became viable and profitable business ventures by significantly reducing the number of youth trained in the organizations relative to their overall size and volume. River's model suggests that perhaps social purpose restaurants can choose either to be social mission intensive, focus on training, and expect less stellar financial results, or to be business intensive and train proportionately fewer youth relative to the size of the operation. Clearly, River's model was one in which the volume of youth training undertaken placed important constraints on its success from a financial, a customer-focused, and a food perspective. It could not operate like a "real" business in several important respects while training that many youth in an operation of its size.

River is similar to many other enterprises that are set up primarily to satisfy a social mission. In Chapter 1 of this collection, this type of organization is referred to as a social purpose enterprise. Like other social enterprises, River was supported by a parent non-profit organization and relied heavily on non-commercial revenues. Yet, in many ways it succeeded at its social mission of training at-risk youth both for finding work in the restaurant business and for coping with larger issues in life.

Afterword

River Restaurant ceased operation in August 2011, closing after slowly diminishing over a two-year period. The decline was a kind of spiral. The organization was cash poor because of road construction and because the only ready funding was for trainee salaries. Costs were cut; for example, advertising was stopped, and River significantly reduced its menu selection and inventory. The restaurant even shifted from cloth to paper napkins. These cuts further reduced the attractiveness of the restaurant for customers. Like other small businesses on Roncesvalles Avenue, River lost customers for more than two years while the roadscape and streetcar tracks were completely overhauled (2009–11). Numerous small businesses on Roncesvalles failed during that period, and likely River weathered it better than many perhaps because of the more modest role that restaurant revenue played for it.

In addition, a "fatigue factor" was reported. The interior of the restaurant became increasingly worn out and dated due to the sheer amount of work it took to fundraise for resources to keep up a professional-looking interior. (River had received significant funding from the Toronto Enterprise Funding in 2003 for renovating the restaurant, but many factors made revisiting this kind of initiative an unappealing and unworkable prospect.) Basic restaurant infrastructure expenses (e.g., a grease trap and other changes to satisfy fire code regulations) were similarly difficult for a non-profit social purpose enterprise to finance. Jennifer LaTrobe had done considerable work in attempting to recruit a celebrity chef at River, in order to improve the image and revenue of River like Jamie Oliver had done with Fifteen. However, the plan didn't work out, and this left River without what JLT regarded as a solid model for going forward. Jennifer LaTrobe noted that most restaurants last less than a decade, and that River Restaurant had likely done well by staying viable and training youth for as long as it did. For these multiple reasons, River Restaurant quietly closed and left as its main legacy the numbers of lives positively touched by its innovative and interesting model.

NOTES

1 Thanks to all of the members of the River Restaurant community that cooperated so helpfully with the data collection for this case study. Particular thanks to Jennifer LaTrobe, former managing director of River Restaurant, for her generosity and thoughtfulness

REFERENCES

Boschee, J. (2001). *The social enterprise sourcebook*. Minneapolis, MN: Northland Institute.

Boschee, J. (2006). *Migrating from innovation to entrepreneurship: How nonprofits are moving toward sustainability and self-sufficiency*. Minneapolis, MN: Encore! Press.

Chambers, E. (2009). From authenticity to significance: Tourism on the frontier of culture and place. *Futures, 41*(6), 353–359. http://dx.doi.org/10.1016/j.futures.2008.11.003

Currie, S., Foley, K., Schwartz, S., & Taylor-Lewis, M. (2001). *BladeRunners and Picasso Café: A case study evaluation of two work-based training programs for disadvantaged youth.* Vancouver, BC: Social Research and Demonstration Corporation.

DiMaggio, P., & Powell, W. (1983). The iron cage revisited: Institutional isomorphism and collective rationality in organizational fields. *American Sociological Review, 48*(2), 147–160. http://dx.doi.org/10.2307/2095101

Emerson, J., & Twersky, F. (1996). *New social entrepreneurs: The success, challenge and lessons of non-profit enterprise creation.* San Francisco, CA: The Roberts Foundation.

Madill, J., Brouard, F., & Hebb, T. (2010). Canadian social enterprises: An empirical exploration of social transformation, financial self-sufficiency, and innovation. *Journal of Nonprofit & Public Sector Marketing, 22*(2), 135–151. http://dx.doi.org/10.1080/10495141003674044

Parsa, H.G., Self, J., Njite, D., & King, T. (2005). Why restaurants fail. *Cornell Hotel and Restaurant Administration Quarterly, 46*(3), 304–322. http://dx.doi.org/10.1177/0010880405275598

Simmons, A., Reynolds, B., & Swinburn, B. (2011). Defining capacity building: Is it possible? *Preventive Medicine, 52*(3–4), 193–199.

van Thiel, S., & Leeuw, F. (2002). The performance paradox in the public sector. *Public Performance and Management Review, 25*(3), 267–281. http://dx.doi.org/10.2307/3381236

14 Social Purpose Enterprises: A Modified Social Welfare Framework

JACK QUARTER, SHERIDA RYAN, AND ANDREA CHAN

This book has presented findings on the impact of twelve distinct social purpose enterprises – or, in the case of microcredit initiatives, the organizations that created them. The research has focused primarily on the individuals working within these enterprises and whether their lives have improved. However, it has also examined the impact on other stakeholders such as the community and the sponsoring organizations. As noted in Chapter 1, even though there is a lot of enthusiasm for the social enterprise phenomenon, there are relatively few empirical studies that systematically investigate the experiences of participants in the type of enterprise discussed in this book – social purpose enterprises (or supported social enterprise). In that respect, this collection of case studies makes an important contribution. In this final chapter, we would like to briefly interpret and synthesize the findings from these case studies and discuss directions for future research.

Synthesizing and Interpreting the Findings

Social purpose enterprises can be viewed as by-products of at least two distinct social movements. First, they are heavily influenced by the humanistic movement, which has aimed to improve the quality of life of people on the social margins. This movement has many manifestations and has been labelled differently by various disciplines, as noted in Chapter 1. Within education, the label is "mainstreaming" (Schiller, O'Reilly, & Fiore, 2007); within psychiatry, the movement is referred to as "deinstitutionalization" or the "consumer-survivor" model (Stroman, 2003); and within housing, it is called "social housing" (Quarter, Mook, & Armstrong, 2009). Many examples could be given, but the general intent is to integrate groups on the social margins into society rather than to segregate them. Social purpose enterprises supplanted the sheltered workshop model partly in response to this broader humanistic movement.

Social purpose enterprises also have been heavily influenced by the neoliberal movement, which has envisioned a smaller government and a market-based solution for supporting marginalized social groups (Giroux, 2002; Hursh, & Henderson, 2011; Thorsen & Lie, 2006). Some would argue that the neoliberal movement is a more important influence than the humanistic movement, as government cutbacks have forced non-profit organizations to develop enterprises that are designed to generate revenue. In Chapter 1, we differentiated between social enterprises that become an effective revenue-earning arm of a non-profit organization (e.g., Habitat for Humanity's ReStore chain or the Salvation Army's thrift shops) and enterprises that are dependent on non-profit organizations for ongoing support. The organizations in this collection fall within the latter group, and to distinguish them from social enterprises that either operate independently or generate revenue for a non-profit organization, we have used the label "social purpose enterprise." Put differently, they are supported social enterprises.

Impact on the Individual

With the exception of the Good Food Market of FoodShare and Furniture Bank, the case studies focused on how these enterprises impacted the individuals who worked within the organization. Although each study characterized the benefits differently, in general the benefits can be categorized as either economic or personal – and the latter includes skills, or human capital, and social connections, or social capital. We shall review the evidence from each of those briefly in turn.

Economic Benefits

All the social purpose enterprises researched for this collection were set up to improve the economic plight of a particular socially marginalized group. These included people with severe disabilities (developmental and psychiatric), precariously housed women, youth with limited schooling, recent immigrants, racial minorities, and Aboriginal peoples. Put simply, these are groups of people who are not well integrated into the Canadian workforce, and who, in many cases, rely on pensions, employment benefits, social assistance, charity, and their families for support. There is some evidence from our case studies of economic improvement for these groups, but it is not compelling. The two case studies on microentrepreneurs (Alterna Savings and Miziwe Biik) showed some evidence of business gains. Of the people who participated in Alterna Savings' community loan program in 2012, 38 per cent reported an increase in their income ranging from $5,000 to $23,000. A 2009 study at Alterna showed that about two-thirds of the microentrepreneurs improved their income, but a follow-up of that group in 2012 showed that only about half had sustained their gains. Miziwe Biik's microcredit program is much smaller and focused on Aboriginal entrepreneurs. The results are mixed, with only four businesses still solvent out of nine that received microloans.

Some other cases involved business income, but participants worked part-time either by choice or by circumstance. The five social purpose enterprises that are part of Common Ground Co-operative have about sixty business partners who are part-time by choice, in order to supplement the pensions to which they are entitled because they have a developmental disability. Their average annual earnings in 2012 were $757. This was within the limit that their disability pension allowed them to earn, enabling them to retain coverage for their expensive medication. It is unclear what their earning potential would be without this limitation.

The precariously housed women working through Inspirations Studio also are self-employed, and for the most part their income is limited by circumstance. The women's earnings at Inspirations range from four hundred dollars per year to more than six thousand dollars per year, but many also sell their products outside of Inspirations, and their earnings in those markets (some of which may be *sous la table*) were not documented through the research.

In the case studies involving salaried employees, most participants were part-time, with one exception: The Learning Enrichment Foundation (LEF) childcare centres. LEF's childcare staff members predominantly worked full-time and earned an average salary, including benefits, of about $35,000, which is comparable to and perhaps exceeds that of childcare workers in general within the Greater Toronto Area. Childcare is a low-paid profession, often attracting women who are recent immigrants and visible minorities. LEF's childcare staff members reported a significant improvement in their economic well-being – indeed, many of them had been without jobs previously. Nonetheless, in an expensive city like Toronto, they would be considered to have incomes that fall below the norm.

Some of the other organizations within this study hire full-time workers, such as Recycle Action (RA), a social purpose enterprise that is part of Groupe Convex in southeastern Ontario and serves people who have developmental disabilities. However, the people with developmental disabilities predominantly work part-time for $11.50 per hour. This is true, as well, for couriers at A-Way Express Courier, who have psychiatric disabilities and rely on disability pensions. One of the points made in the A-Way case study is that "the pay from commission for the average courier could be below the minimum wage." The part-time translators at Northwood Translation Bureau also experienced meagre earnings. After rebating its parent organization, Northwood Neighbourhood Services, in 2011, there was only $12,000 to divide among twenty-one translators, who also had incurred expenses while undertaking the work.

The River Restaurant was one of the social purpose enterprises studied for this book that trained participants rather than employing them permanently. Before it closed in 2011, River trained youth to find employment in other restaurants. The goal was to be financially self-supporting, but in the last year for which figures were available, River earned only 17 per cent of its revenue from restaurant services. Ray Dart, who undertook that case study, questions whether a restaurant that makes trainees its primary workforce rather than a small subset of its employees can succeed:

> River's model suggests that perhaps social purpose restaurants can choose either to be social mission intensive, focus on training, and expect less stellar financial results, or to be business intensive and train proportionately fewer youth relative to the size of operation. River's model was clearly one where the volume of youth training undertaken placed important constraints on its success from a financial, a customer-focused, and a food perspective.

Academy of Computer & Employment Skills (A.C.E.S.) is another training organization. The research for this collection did not indicate whether the graduates of this social purpose enterprise successfully obtain employment and improve their economic circumstances. However, the data indicate clearly that English language proficiency is the primary characteristic that determines who is able to access the training program.

Two of the case studies were of organizations whose primary target is low-income communities – in other words, communities at large rather than the people working within the organization. The Good Food Market of FoodShare focuses on low-income communities that lack access to quality foods, and Furniture Bank[1] acts as a conduit between businesses and families who want to dispose of quality furnishings and the low-income families that are the beneficiaries of them. The results of these case studies will be discussed largely under community impact.

Personal Benefits

HUMAN CAPITAL

While there can be some doubt about the economic benefits of these social purpose enterprises, the personal benefits to the participants are comparatively easy to identify. Groupe Convex, which houses social purpose enterprises for people with developmental disabilities, highlights as one of its founding principles "opportunities to develop skills and knowledge." The River Restaurant's purpose was to train young people in "hospitality skills as well as broader life and job-readiness skills." The Learning Enrichment Foundation, which encompasses the childcare centres that were the focus of the case study, offers a certification program as well as training in language and many other skills that recent immigrants – its primary clientele – need for gainful employment. The Academy of Computer & Employment Skills (A.C.E.S.) "offers immigrant-oriented training programs in office administration, computerized accounting, medical reception, and supply chain administration." Microentrepreneurs seeking loans from Miziwe Biik are required to obtain basic training from the Aboriginal Business Resource Centre, and similarly, microentrepreneurs seeking loans from Alterna Savings are required to learn basic business planning skills in order to become eligible. The translators at the Northwood Translation Bureau earned a meagre income from their work, but they reported that their roles at the NTB helped them to build self-esteem and to acquire the necessary skills for personal and professional development. Perhaps most importantly, they obtained "Canadian experience" – which, as immigrants to this country, was an important prerequisite for entry into the workforce.

Similarly, the researchers for the case study of A-Way Express Courier conclude that "developing the human capital of its employees appears to be a major impact of A-Way." The A-Way couriers experienced the ravages of mental illness, which can lead to social isolation and disengagement from work settings. As a result, basic skills decline – and so skills development is of great importance. Moreover, as at the Northwood Translation Bureau, the human capital that A-Way couriers develop can be a stepping stone to careers both within and external to the organization, a point expressed by a manager at the organization:

> Oh yes in countless occasions we've been a stepping stone for [people] ... to get back into the workforce, it's definitely a job for people that are isolated or haven't worked in a while to get out and work and move onto better jobs, and also within A-Way there is lots of room to move up. For example, I started as a courier and I moved up to the Business and Projects Manager after going through several other positions. (Manager B)

The Inspirations Studio case study also discovered that the women who participated developed skills – and not simply artistic skills, but also business and interpersonal skills. Many described how the studio helped them to develop a sense of worth and enabled them to step away from the depression and isolation that they experienced in the shelter where they were housed. As one stated so eloquently, "It is a free space to learn to be creative."

SOCIAL CAPITAL

For people who operate within the social mainstream, networking may seem natural. However, for those on the social margins, networks – particularly networks that lead to employment – can atrophy (Cheng, 1995; Lin & Dumin, 1986). Therefore, making connections is an important benefit. The connections can be personal or professional, ongoing or transient. For people who are isolated, merely engaging others while offering their services can be a benefit.

In the Common Ground Co-operative case study, the partners refer to forms of social engagement such as talking with customers, participating in the Toronto Transit Commission Awareness program so that they become adept at getting back and forth to work, working together with other partners to make decisions about their business, and relating to their job coach. One staff member summed up the social benefit succinctly: "For some of these people it's the only contact they have with people." (Staff 1). At A-Way, the couriers expressed that in addition to getting out of the house to do their job, which involved interacting with others

both at the office and in their deliveries, they broadened their friendships and participated in more activities: "You are now in a community,
part of the larger community. And you learn to network. Like, they have
all kinds of things up there. From programs, peer support, sometimes
they have outings. It's more about being a member of society."

The trainees at the River Restaurant were probably less isolated than
the employees of A-Way and Common Ground. Nevertheless, the networks established by alumni were critical to their gaining access to the
food service industry. The Northwood Translation Bureau translators
reported how their work broadened their horizons and helped them to
build connections with different professional fields and communities:
"I have to go to different locations, to different organizations, and this
way I learn." They also described how they use their new connections
to help others become aware of available services and resources. One
way that they do this is through volunteering in Northwood Neighbourhood Services.

At LEF, the childcare workers as a group believed that their access to
services and their relationships with family and their community have
improved since joining the organization. Furthermore, those who volunteered or participated in community organizations (i.e., who undertook opportunities to build social capital) indicated higher measures of
well-being in multiple areas compared to those who did not.

Networks have not only proliferated among individuals, but also
among organizations. Inspirations Studio belongs to the Social Purpose Enterprise Network (SPEN); as well, the studio and its parent
organization, Sistering, have partnered with Parkdale Green Thumb,
Inner City Health Associates, and Community Care Access Centre.
These organizations help Inspirations and its potters to deliver their
services. Similarly, the microentrepreneurs at Miziwe Biik were assisted by representatives of the Toronto Aboriginal Business Association, and microentrepreneurs at Alterna are connected with "free
tele-classes, networking cafés (offering professional coaching in informal social gatherings), and business literacy workshops." In addition,
Recycle Action, an integral part of the Groupe Convex network, offers
various supports to the individual social purpose enterprises.

Impact on the Community

Community impact, in part, overlaps with the discussion of social capital, as a common dimension of both community and social capital is

social interaction. The FoodShare case study focused on how the Good Food Market impacts the community and brings together the neighbourhood. The market shoppers report healthier food choices. Shoppers also say that the market is an important event during which neighbours meet and socialize. As the case study authors discovered during their research, "an overwhelming 98 per cent say that the GFM has made their neighbourhood a better place to live."

Furniture Bank is designed to assist low-income families by helping them to obtain free, quality furnishings from businesses and wealthier households. Furniture Bank partners with a network of community agencies in Toronto to support those who are leaving abusive situations or shelters, as well as newcomers to Canada. To the larger community, it presents a socially and environmentally responsible way to dispose of reusable furniture and household items. Although the Inspirations Studio case study did not specifically assess community impact, Inspirations and its parent organization, Sistering, are making an obvious contribution through assisting precariously housed women to find gainful employment.

The Groupe Convex case study attempted to gauge Recycle Action's environmental impact and its social return on investment through estimating the value of reduced carbon emissions attributable to this social purpose enterprise. The Academy of Computer & Employment Skills (A.C.E.S.) training program draws its participants most heavily from faith-based communities, and presumably its training gives back to those communities. The Northwood Translation Bureau is embedded within a settlement centre, Northwood Neighbourhood Services, and the translators volunteer and participate actively within NNS. As noted, childcare workers at The Learning Enrichment Foundation (LEF) reported volunteering for LEF-organized events such as the Santa Claus parade and the organization's Christmas party. They also described becoming more involved in the broader community, including their church congregations.

The microlending programs also appear to have had a positive impact on the community. Alterna has situated its microloan program within its community development department, which was at first part of its marketing department, but is now separate, in recognition of its increasing significance. In the case study of Miziwe Biik, "Respondents report a deeper connection to the Aboriginal community and more pride in their Aboriginal roots, which they are anxious to pass on to the next generation. This program also has led to desperately needed bridging to the mainstream community, at the same time that it supports and develops critical social capital capacity within this marginalized community."

Impact on the Sponsoring Organization

Each of the social purpose enterprises in the study had a parent organization that founded and supported it. The relationship took different forms: some organizations were totally embedded within the sponsoring organization (Inspirations, Northwood, The Learning Enrichment Foundation, Good Food Market, Furniture Bank), and others were incorporated separately (A-Way, Common Ground's business partnerships). This reliance on external support is a defining characteristic of social purpose enterprises. The various types of support from the parent organizations are detailed in the chapters: managerial support; funding, which is often transferred from government and foundation programs; marketing assistance; procurement strategies; training programs. The list is extensive.

The social purpose enterprises also give back to the parent organization, though not equivalent to what they receive. Alterna and Miziwe Biik microentrepreneurs make payments on their loans, but this is not sufficient for the parent organization to break even financially. Similarly, only 40 per cent of revenues from the Northwood translators and 5 per cent from the associated businesses of Common Ground are returned to the parent organizations. Of the social purpose enterprises in this collection, those closest to breaking even in a traditional financial sense are the childcare centres at The Learning Enrichment Foundation, the Academy of Computer & Employment Skills (A.C.E.S.), Recycle Action, Furniture Bank, and A-Way. However, these organizations' revenues include funds from government programs and foundations.

The chapter by Jennifer Hann and Daniel Schugurensky on the Northwood Translation Bureau argues that it is possible to have enterprises that are both dependent on a non-profit parent for ongoing support and that also earn enough to cover the costs of the non-profit, thereby becoming an effective revenue arm of the organization. When a substantial portion of the organization's revenue are from government programs, knowing how to strike a balance between taking support from the parent organization and also giving back to it can be challenging. However, if that balance were to be achieved, a new organizational form would emerge that differed from either a social enterprise or a social purpose enterprise as defined in this collection. Of all the cases examined here, perhaps the best example of this hybrid form is the relationship between Furniture Bank and Furniture Link. The chapter by Andrea Chan, Laurie Mook, and Susanna Kislenko points out that Furniture Link – the enterprise supported in various ways by Furniture Bank – generates 65 per cent of the revenue for the parent organization. Perhaps Furniture Bank and Furniture Link could be seen as a hybrid of the two forms, social enterprise and social purpose enterprise.

Conclusions and Future Directions

The groups that are served by the organizations in this research collection are on the social margins and require various forms of support. The social purpose enterprises help them join the mainstream workforce through training (Academy of Computer & Employment Skills, River Restaurant); through employment (Learning Enrichment Foundation); through self-employment (Alterna and Miziwe Biik microloans program, Inspirations Studio); and through partial forms of employment that serve as income supplements (Groupe Convex, Common Ground Co-operative, A-Way, Northwood). Two social purpose enterprises in this collection – FoodShare's Good Food Markets and Furniture Bank – focused primarily on low-income groups in the community. Their goals weren't specifically employment – although both programs generate jobs, both paid and volunteer, through their services.

For most of these social purpose enterprises, the elephant in the room is funding from government programs. No one wants to talk about it because it is precarious; as well, within the context of neoliberalism, it is no longer seen as positive. These social purpose enterprises publicly emphasize generating revenue from the market because this fits with the dominant political discourse about smaller government. The case studies call into question, however, whether government's role can be reduced without harming these organizations. Government support comes in various forms: block grants to the parent organization (Sistering, Common Ground, Northwood, A-Way, Miziwe Biik, FoodShare, Furniture Bank); pensions for individuals with disabilities or on social assistance supports (Groupe Convex, Common Ground, A-Way, Inspirations, River Restaurant, Alterna, Furniture Bank); subsidies for services (The Learning Enrichment Foundation, Academy of Computer &

Employment Skills, Furniture Bank); and support for related training programs (Miziwe Biik and Alterna). Donors to these organizations also receive tax credits, which means a revenue loss for government. It would be challenging to disentangle all of the ways that government assists these organizations.

Perhaps we should directly critique the discourse around using social purpose enterprises to reduce dependency on government. Our research suggests that the overall yield of these organizations is positive. With one exception – River Restaurant – the social purpose enterprises appear to achieve their goals. The River Restaurant succeeded in training youth in need while it operated, but it was unable to sustain itself financially and folded. Put differently, there was insufficient revenue from the combination of government and other sources to sustain the business. Many small businesses cease operations, so River was not distinct in that regard. However, River was not just a conventional small business. Rather, it was a social purpose enterprise that had external support and was designed to train youth in the restaurant business. It was able to achieve its training mission while it operated, but lacked the revenue to continue operations. The case study of River raises an important issue: is it possible for a restaurant whose primary purpose is to train its workforce for employment in conventional businesses to sustain itself if all of its employees are trainees? Perhaps a hybrid arrangement that mixes a targeted group of trainees with a more skilled workforce would have a greater chance of success. This may involve diluting the organization's social purpose and drawing it closer to a conventional business model.

The other organizations in the study have sustained themselves: they have had sufficient revenue, both from external sources and from the market, to continue providing their services. Their beneficial impacts manifest themselves in many ways, as discussed above. Arguably, without government investment these benefits would not have been achieved. Therefore, the social purpose enterprises in this collection have a paradoxical role: they were created largely in response to the neoliberal push for smaller government and greater reliance on the market. They have played the role for which they were created by selling services and earning revenue in the market, but they would not be able to do this without government support. They need government support to reduce their dependency. However, even though this support benefits the participants in many ways, it is unclear whether it has helped the social purpose enterprises to reduce their dependency. A detailed social return on investment might provide harder evidence as to the government's return on its investment. One of the cases in this collection, Groupe Convex, undertook an SROI and detailed the yield.

The next stage of our research project addresses this question directly by assembling an SROI for all of the cases. SROI and other social accounting methods (Mook, Quarter, & Richmond, 2007) will allow the researchers to quantify social benefits and to look at the imputed market value of the social benefits in relation to the financial investment. Doing this will make it possible to assess whether the financial investment from governments and other funders of social purpose enterprises yields a positive social return.

An important form of investment in these social purpose enterprises is the ongoing support from the parent organization. As discussed above, some forms of support are very tangible; others are less so. An important aspect of any social return on investment should be to unpack these supports as forms of investment no different than the investments of government or donors. In this way, we can begin to understand the social return resulting from these investments, as well.

As noted, Groupe Convex used a social return on investment, and it could serve as a model for other cases. It showed that if a broad array of costs and benefits is included, Recycle Action yields a positive return on investment to government and to other organizations. However, in order to yield the positive return, the accounting has to include more than economic benefits – because the economic impact, narrowly defined, of these social purpose enterprises could be described as underwhelming. However, the research brings to light other important benefits: such as developing participants' skills, or their human capital, and developing their networking ability, or their social capital. There are also important psychological benefits in that participants feel more self-confident and have greater self-esteem, but this is difficult to quantify in a social accounting framework.

Here an important distinction should be made between the people who work within the organizations and are the subject of these case studies and people in the mainstream workforce. Organizations that serve marginalized populations will most probably require additional revenue sources as compared to other organizations. This could be considered part of their nature, as distinct from what becomes possible through the environment or nurture. This nature/nurture distinction has been applied to non-profit organizations by Hager and Brudney (2011), and it is relevant to the organizations in our research. Their nature differs from that of mainstream businesses; therefore greater nurture is required, a primary form being government programs.

This argument also calls for a new definition of success for social purpose enterprises. They are businesses – but they are businesses with a difference, and different standards should be applied when measuring their success. This bolsters the above proposal that a careful social return on investment using various models should be performed in order to understand whether the imputed market value of the benefits exceeds the financial investment. Our assessment from this initial research is that there are apparent benefits, but a careful analysis against the investment should be undertaken.

In the introduction to this chapter and in Chapter 1, we presented two driving forces behind the rise of social purpose enterprises: neoliberalism and the humanistic movement. These drivers are most associated with the term social enterprises, but we have created a subcategory in order to differentiate social enterprises (which live up to the neoliberal standard of a market player that reduces the role of government) from social purpose enterprises (which continue to rely heavily on government programs). Organizations of this sort are creations of Canada's social welfare system, but they are modifying it by attempting, as much as they can manage, to generate income from the market. They might be viewed as exemplars of a "modified social welfare" framework because they rely on government programs but pursue self-sufficiency to the extent that it can be achieved. Although organizations of this sort must play to the political forces of the day and emphasize their market role, they are more by-products of the humanistic movement that has sought the fuller development of people with disabilities and other groups on the social margins. That said, their market role is genuine, but the motivations differ. Rather than focusing on business development, however, the market role can be cast in terms of human and social development. Business development, of course, can contribute to human and social development – and for the social purpose enterprises in this collection, it appears that they have.

NOTES

1 Although Furniture Link, the furniture pickup and delivery service of Furniture Bank, has an employment and training program for individuals with limited employment opportunities, the employees of Furniture Link were not the focus of the case study.

REFERENCES

Cheng, T. (1995). The chances of recipients leaving AFDC: A longitudinal study. *Social Work Research, 19*, 67–76.

Giroux, H.A. (2002). Neoliberalism, corporate culture, and the promise of higher education: The university as a democratic public sphere. *Harvard Educational Review, 72*(4), 425–463.

Hager, M.A., & Brudney, J.L. (2011). Problems recruiting volunteers: Nature versus nurture. *Nonprofit Management & Leadership, 22*(2), 137–157. http://dx.doi.org/10.1002/nml.20046

Hursh, D.W., & Henderson, J.A. (2011). Contesting global neoliberalism and creating alternative futures. *Discourse: Studies in the Cultural Politics of Education, 32*(2), 171–185. http://dx.doi.org/10.1080/01596306.2011.562665

Lin, N., & Dumin, M. (1986). Access to occupations through social ties. *Social Networks, 8*(4), 365–385. http://dx.doi.org/10.1016/0378-8733(86)90003-1

Mook, L., Quarter, J., and Richmond, B.J. (2007). *What Counts: Social accounting for non-profits and cooperatives* (2nd ed.). London, United Kingdom: Sigel Press.

Quarter, J., Mook, L., & Armstrong, A. (2009) *Understanding the social economy: A Canadian perspective*. Toronto, ON: University of Toronto Press.

Schiller, E., O'Reilly, F., & Fiore, T. (2007). *Marking the progress of IDEA implementation: The Study of State and Local Implementation and Impact of the Individuals with Disabilities Education Act*. Bethesda, MD: Abt Associates.

Stroman, D. (2003). *The disability rights movement: From deinstitutionalization to self-determination*. Lanham, MD: University Press of America.

Thorsen, D., & Lie, A. (2006). What is neoliberalism? Department of Political Science. Norway: University of Oslo. Retrieved from http://folk.uio.no/daget/What%20is%20Neo-Liberalism%20FINAL.pdf

Contributors

Kunle Akingbola is an assistant professor in the Faculty of Business Administration, Lakehead University, and a research associate in the Social Economy Centre, University of Toronto.

Caroline Arcand is the executive director of Groupe Convex, which is a network of social enterprises employing mostly people with intellectual handicaps.

Ann Armstrong (Emeritus, Rotman School of Management, U of T) directed the Rotman School's Social Enterprise Initiative for several years and remains involved in Rotman's Internationally Educated Professionals program, as well as in executive and undergraduate teaching.

Chinyere Amadi is a researcher at the Carleton Centre for Community Innovation and a graduate student in the School of Public Policy and Administration at Carleton University.

Ida Berger is a professor of marketing at the Ted Rogers School of Management at Ryerson University.

Courtney Bishop is a behavioural consultant with Hamilton Brant Behaviour Services and a recent graduate from the Master of Arts in Applied Disability Studies through Brock University.

Jeanette Campbell is the former executive director, Common Ground Co-op, with 20 years experience in the non-profit sector and a main focus on employment supports for persons with developmental disabilities.

Andrea Chan is a PhD candidate at the Ontario Institute for Studies in Education of the University of Toronto.

Michael Classens is a PhD candidate in the Faculty of Environmental Studies, York University.

Honey Crossley is the executive director at Working Skills Centre, assisting immigrants to gain the competencies needed to participate fully in Canadian society.

Ray Dart is the director of the Business Administration program at Trent University, Peterborough, Ontario.

Jackson Foster is the Good Food Program manager at FoodShare.

Mary Foster is a professor of marketing at the Ted Rogers School of Management at Ryerson University.

Peter Frampton is the executive director of The Learning Enrichment Foundation and is on the board of the Canadian Community Economic Development Foundation (CEDNet)

Itay Greenspan is a lecturer at the Paul Baerwald School of Social Work and Social Welfare at the Hebrew University of Jerusalem.

Femida Handy is a professor at the University of Pennsylvania's School of Social Policy & Practice and the editor-in-chief of the *Nonprofit and Voluntary Sector Quarterly*.

Jennifer Hann (MA, University of Toronto) is the communications and research coordinator in the Office of the President at Centennial College.

Susan Henry is Manager, Corporate Social Responsibility, at Alterna Savings in Toronto, where she manages the Alterna Savings Community Micro-Finance Program.

Andrew Holeton is an activist in the Social Enterprise Toronto (SET) network and is employed by The Learning Enrichment Foundation, heading up its social enterprise development arm.

Jennifer Hope is the executive director of Common Ground Co-operative Inc. in Toronto, helping adults who have developmental disabilities to work in social enterprise businesses.

Robyn Hoogendam is the coordinator of research and community development at The Learning Enrichment Foundation.

Edward T. Jackson is Senior Research Fellow in the Carleton University Centre of Community Innovation and a faculty member in the School of Public Policy and Administration.

Susanna Kislenko, who holds a master's degree in international relations from McGill University, is executive director of the Furniture Bank.

Annie Lok is a research assistant at the Centre for Voluntary Sector Studies, Ryerson University, and is currently in Ryerson's Disability Studies program.

J.J. McMurtry is Graduate Program Director of the Social and Political Thought program and an associate professor in the Business and Society program at York University.

Agnes Meinhard is associate professor of Organizational Behaviour and Theory and founder and current director of the Centre for Voluntary Sector Studies, Ted Rogers School of Management, Ryerson University.

Laurie Mook is an assistant professor in the Nonprofit Leadership and Management program at the School of Community Resources and Development, and research associate at the Lodestar Center for Nonprofit Innovation and Philanthropy, both at Arizona State University.

Kristine Neglia is a member of the Curve Lake First Nation and a master's candidate at Athabasca University.

Frances Owen is a psychologist and associate professor of Child Youth Studies at the Centre for Applied Disability Studies at Brock University.

Pauline O'Connor is the research manager and a senior research associate at the Centre for Voluntary Sector Studies in the Ted Rogers School of Management at Ryerson University.

Emily Pohl-Weary is a Toronto author, arts educator, editor, and PhD candidate at the Ontario Institute for Studies in Education, University of Toronto.

Jack Quarter is a professor at the Ontario Institute for Studies in Education, University of Toronto, co-director of the Social Economy Centre, and the principal investigator of the SSHRC-funded CURA, Social Business for Marginalized Social Groups.

Anne Readhead (MA, Brock University) is a residential manager for Community Living Port Colborne Wainfleet.

Sherida Ryan is a lecturer at the Ontario Institute for Studies in Education, University of Toronto, and codirector of the Social Economy Centre. She is the manager of the SSHRC-funded CURA, Social Business for Marginalized Social Groups.

Daniel Schugurensky is a professor at Arizona State University, where he holds a joint appointment in the School of Public Affairs and the School of Social Transformation.

Ushnish Sengupta is a PhD candidate at the Ontario Institute for Studies in Education at the University of Toronto, researching non-profit organizations.

Jennifer Sumner is Director of the Certificate Program in Adult Education for Sustainability in the Adult Education and Community Development Program, Ontario Institute for Studies in Education, University of Toronto.

Marlene Walk is a PhD student in social welfare at the School of Social Policy and Practice, University of Pennsylvania.